WITHDRAWN

The Romances of William Morris

While much has been written about William Morris in the last thirty years, little attention has been paid to his romances, which have generally been dismissed as 'escapist' or at best smiled upon as self-indulgent fantasy. This book sets out to examine more carefully the premises of such dismissive terminology, looking at the ways in which our sense of the 'escapism' of Morris's knack for fairy-tale writing can be modified or expanded when seen in relation to the development of his imagination in other spheres, both political and creative. Dr Hodgson persuades us that the romances can be treated more seriously than has been customary, and that they reflect Morris's progressing attitudes towards society and towards the place in it of art and imagination. Morris himself wrote that 'what romance means is the capacity for a true conception of history, a power of making the past part of the present'. His adoption of the romance, with its very specific and highly formalized demands, and his use of medieval themes, enabled him to explore, sometimes with freshness and vivacity, issues of a sexual, religious, social or political nature which were crucially relevant both to his own age and to his projection of the future.

Dr Hodgson's argument will be of interest to Morris specialists, but also accessible to those not familiar with his romances, since she is careful to describe the stories before placing them in the context of his thought, against the background of other thinkers who influenced him, such as Marx, Carlyle and Ruskin. In addition, the book will be valuable for those whose concern is with Morris as an artist; and for readers with a general interest in Victorian literature and in the development of Socialism.

THE ROMANCES OF WILLIAM MORRIS

Amanda Hodgson

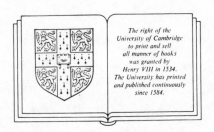

The right of the
University of Cambridge
to print and sell
all manner of books
was granted by
Henry VIII in 1534.
The University has printed
and published continuously
since 1584.

Cambridge University Press

CAMBRIDGE

LONDON   NEW YORK   NEW ROCHELLE

MELBOURNE   SYDNEY

Published by the Press Syndicate of the University of Cambridge
The Pitt Building, Trumpington Street, Cambridge CB2 1RP
32 East 57th Street, New York, NY 10022, USA
10 Stamford Road, Oakleigh, Melbourne 3166, Australia

First published 1987

Printed in Great Britain at
the University Press, Cambridge

British Library cataloguing in publication data
Hodgson, Amanda
The romances of William Morris.
1. Morris, William, *1834–1896* – Criticism
and interpretation
828'.809 PR5084

Library of Congress cataloguing in publication data
Hodgson, Amanda.
The romances of William Morris.
Bibliography
Includes index.
1. Morris, William, 1834–1896 – Criticism and
interpretation. 2. Middle Ages in literature.
3. Socialism in literature. 4. History in literature.
5. Romanticism – England. I. Title.
PR5084.H64 1987 823'.8 86–12915
ISBN 0 521 32075 5

To my parents

Contents

Preface

Into a by no means long life William Morris crammed an amount of work that astonished his contemporaries and continues to amaze modern critics. Artist, pattern designer, weaver, dyer, expert on medieval manuscripts, illuminator, printer, businessman, political agitator, book collector, translator – the list of his avocations seems almost infinitely extended. Among them that of poet and writer of fiction is usually given an honourable place; yet while there are studies of Morris's work as a designer and several commentaries on his political activity, there are few discussions which deal at any length with his literary qualities. His writing has tended to be used as a quarry for ideas relative to his other pursuits, rather than to serve as a topic worthy in its own right of serious consideration. This book is an attempt to correct this imbalance, making Morris's poetry and prose fiction the centre of critical attention.

Morris was not a designer and Socialist who happened to write in his spare time. When asked his profession in a court of law (in 1885) he described himself as 'an artist and a literary man'; he was equally committed to both occupations. It is certainly true, however, that as a writer he made no concessions to contemporary taste or critical opinion – he wrote in single-minded response to the kind of fiction he himself chiefly admired: namely, the romances of the Middle Ages. His refusal to adapt his style to prevailing criteria has caused his writings, especially his last prose fictions, to be labelled as eccentric and escapist, wish-fulfilling fantasies. Eccentric, idiosyncratic and fantastic these fictions are; they are also examples of a controlled symbolic imagination at work in a writer whose mastery of his chosen form – the romance – has been gained over years of experiment. This book aims to demonstrate the process by which this mastery was attained, and to suggest something of

Preface

the nature of Morris's romances, something of the satisfactions they offer to those who read them with due attention to their formal demands.

My obsession with Morris began many years ago and many people have helped me to transform it into the present work. I should like to thank Gillian Beer, of Girton College, Cambridge, for her generous advice and encouragement; Eric Mackerness, late of the University of Sheffield, for his patient supervision; the staff of the University Libraries of Cambridge, Sheffield and Nottingham, the British Library and Nottingham City Library; the William Morris Society; Lesley Bendall and Judy Zipser for their typing; and my friends, particularly Janet Jones and Sylvia Hardy, for their support and advice. My family, which has lived so good-humouredly with Morris, deserves my especial gratitude.

A.H.

Chronology

Chronology

Introduction: 'The embodiment of dreams'

I

She stood on the platform watching the receding train. A few bushes hid the curve of the line; the white vapour rose above them, evaporating in the pale evening. A moment more and the last carriage would pass out of sight. The white gates swung forward slowly and closed over the line.

An oblong box painted reddish brown and tied with a rough rope lay on the seat beside her. The movement of her back and shoulders showed that the bundle she carried was a heavy one, the sharp bulging of the grey linen cloth that the weight was dead. She wore a faded yellow dress and a black jacket too warm for the day. A girl of twenty, short, strongly built, with short, strong arms. Her neck was plump, and her hair of so ordinary a brown that it passed unnoticed. The nose was too thick, but the nostrils were well formed. The eyes were grey, luminous, and veiled with dark lashes. But it was only when she laughed that her face lost its habitual expression, which was somewhat sullen; then it flowed with bright humour. She laughed now, showing a white line of almond-shaped teeth.[1]

These are the first words of a novel published in 1894: George Moore's *Esther Waters*. In the same year a small, idiosyncratic printing press issued a prose fiction of which the first words are as follows:

Awhile ago there was a young man dwelling in a great and goodly city by the sea which had to name Langton on Holm. He was but of five and twenty winters, a fair-faced man, yellow-haired, tall and strong; rather wiser than foolisher than young men are mostly wont; a valiant youth, & a kind; not of many words but courteous of speech; no roisterer, nought masterful, but peaceable and knowing how to forbear: in a fray a perilous foe, & a trusty war-fellow.[2]

This is from William Morris's *The Wood Beyond the World*, published by his own Kelmscott Press. Despite their chronological proximity, these two volumes are notably dissimilar. To begin with, they differ in appearance. Moore's work is presented in the format of the conventional novel of his period: restrained, undecorated. Morris's book is flamboyantly unusual. Thickly black Gothic type, headed by an ornamental capital letter, is surrounded by a wide border of black and white, swirling acanthus leaves; facing the first page is a woodcut by Edward Burne-Jones, depicting an elongated maiden with flowing hair and dress, in a pastoral landscape. To give the final touch, the title of the chapter is printed in red and is finished with two red flowers instead of more conventional punctuation. This book may be less easily readable than the plainly presented *Esther Waters*; it is certainly distinctive.

To this difference between the appearance of the two books may be added other dissimilarities. *Esther Waters* is the story of an ordinary working-class girl, not remarkable for beauty or intelligence, and whose chief virtues are determination, a stubborn honesty and a capacity for hard work. The novel charts her struggles against poverty, illiteracy and the shame of bearing an illegitimate child. The novel has a social purpose, for Moore exposes through Esther's history the sordidness of lower-class London life, the dangers of gambling, the horrors of baby-farming. In the end Esther's fight for respectability and independence is to some extent successful: she has a secure home and has raised her son to decent manhood. But the novel ends with a note of foreboding underlying Esther's sense of achievement; happiness can only be precarious. This unromantic story is told in a suitably unadorned style. As may be seen from the extract, Moore concentrates on physical detail, on simple descriptions of the characters' appearance and the objects around them. Their speech, too, is rendered with an attempt at fidelity to the dialect of working people. In short, Moore's novel is an example of the kind of writing which his contemporaries called realistic. We respond to it, however regretfully, with recognition.

Morris's tale, on the other hand, is designed to take us as far as possible from the world we know. His too is a style which concentrates on detail, but the descriptions are of a fairy-tale setting: a magic wood in which a young hero has to evade the machinations of a witch and an evil dwarf, win the love of a virtuous maiden and ultimately achieve the position of king and begin to live a happy-ever-after life. The characters are idealized,

Introduction

closer to the types of legend than to the complex reality of
people as we perceive them outside fiction. And the language is
one that no one ever spoke, highly archaic in syntax and
vocabulary. The total effect is of elaborate artifice. Our response
must be to the book's strangeness, to the distance between our
everyday experience and that offered by the work of art. We are
dealing not with realism but with the formal conventions and
properties of romance.

There is no difficulty in assessing which of these two books
would have fulfilled more precisely the expectations of novel-
readers and critics at the time it was written. By the 1890s
realism had become the established dominant mode of prose
fiction. This had not happened without a struggle. In the 1850s
and 1860s there had been continual debate between critics who
favoured naturalism and those who believed that idealism was
required from literature. The argument tended to polarize
around the figures of the so-called 'realist' Thackeray and the
'idealist' Dickens – whose own spirited defence of the role of
fantasy and imaginative fiction did much to keep alive a belief in
the limitations of pure naturalism. Yet the tendency of the
major novelists was towards the realist approach. It can be
traced in the attempts, by Mrs Gaskell and the other 'social-
problem' novelists of the 1840s and 1850s, to tell the truth about
the horrors of the industrial society. It is clear also in the
theories of George Eliot, expressed so tellingly in her critical
writing and in her own fiction, about the novelist's duty to
provide accurate pictures of everyday life:

a photographic picture, if it be only of a kitten or a hay-stack, is a
pleasanter subject in the eyes of most people (were they brave enough
to admit it), than many a glaring piece of mythology.[3]

By the last quarter of the nineteenth century the battle for
realism seemed to many to have been won. The major writers of
the period were committed to it: the social realism of Gissing
and Moore, the psychological realism of Henry James and
Hardy's unflinching look at the ironies of human life set the
tone and guided critical and reading taste. Edmund Gosse, in a
National Review article on 'The Tyranny of the Novel', took up
again the photographic image employed forty years earlier by
George Eliot, in order to plead for even greater fidelity to reality:

3

Introduction

I am tired of the novelist's portrait of a gentleman, with gloves and hat, leaning against a pillar, upon a vague landscape background. I want the gentleman as he appears in a snap-shot photograph, with his every-day expression on his face, and the localities in which he spends his days accurately visible around him.[4]

Similarly, and more bluntly, D. F. Hannigan described 'The Decline of Romance':

We are sick of lying and cant and platitude. We want facts, not romantic dreams.[5]

Thus in its unequivocal denial of 'romantic dreams' *Esther Waters* was a novel finely in tune with fictional theory and practice in the 1890s.

Must one conclude, then, that in presenting the bemused public with *The Wood Beyond the World* Morris was being extravagantly eccentric? The series of prose fictions he produced during the last decade of his life, of which *The Wood Beyond the World* is an example, certainly appears aberrant when set against the work of James, Gissing, Moore and Hardy. Could Morris really have expected his romances to appeal to any larger readership than his immediate circle of friends?

It seems possible that he could. For while romance has been perceived as an outdated genre at least since Jonson called Shakespeare's *Pericles* a 'mouldy tale',[6] it has nevertheless proved a remarkably resilient form. Shakespeare gave the lie to Jonson with his great romance plays *The Winter's Tale* and *The Tempest*. And romance was by no means dead when Morris published *The Wood Beyond the World*; on the contrary, it was enjoying a resurgence. The critic Ian Maclaren perhaps spoke for many when he claimed to find the ultra-realism of modern writing offensive:

There are such things as drains, and sometimes they may have to be opened, but one would not for choice have one opened in his library.[7]

In the 1880s and 1890s writers such as Stevenson and Rider Haggard were proving that there was a market for a kind of fiction that did not require from its readers unremitting concentration on the unpleasant facts of nineteenth-century life. Not only were they writing successful romances, they joined other commentators in seeking a critical justification for the style they favoured. Their articles amount to something of a revolt against the prevailing critical doctrines which advocated realism.

Stevenson, as befitted a major practitioner in the genre, was one of the most dedicated justifiers of romance. His article 'A Gossip on Romance' in the first volume of *Longman's Magazine* (1882–3) claims that at the deepest level fiction performs a therapeutic service for the reader. Through intense imaginative response he is almost literally taken out of himself; in identification with the hero he is enabled to project and confront those things which in rational moments he represses and avoids. Through fiction it is even possible to face one's own death and learn to cope with the knowledge of mortality:

Fiction is to the grown man what play is to the child.[8]

The kind of fiction through which this pyschological treatment may be effected is called romance. This is perhaps the best reasoned and most interesting of the articles in defence of romance; but several others followed it. Again in *Longman's Magazine*, Stevenson wrote a response to Henry James's theories of fiction in which he denied that the art of the novel was to provide 'a transcript of life'.[9] The quality central to art was its 'significant simplicity';[10] the power of the artist lay in his ability to turn the tumultuous, illogical elaboration of life into a controlled, finite and rational artefact. The whole point about art, claimed Stevenson, was its difference from life. In 1887 the *Contemporary Review* published two apologies for romance by other well-known artists in the form. First came Rider Haggard, author of *She* (1887), with an article 'About Fiction' in which he declared, like Stevenson, that men wished to be 'taken out of themselves'[11] by art. For Haggard, however, this ecstasy is necessary so that we may attain a vision of perfection and ideal beauty. This can only be achieved in fiction by a form unencumbered by the ugliness of reality. He rejects as inadequate current modes of fiction, including both the American school concerned with minute dissection of feeling and motive, and Zola-esque naturalism. What is required is pure imagination:

Here we may weave our humble tale, and point our harmless moral without being mercilessly bound down to the prose of a somewhat dreary age.[12]

Introduction

The anthropologist and writer of fairy-tales Andrew Lang took a rather different view, feeling that there was room in modern fiction for both realism and romance. Yet at the end of his essay, with characteristic vividness of imagery, he took his stand as a champion of romance:

The dubitations of a Bostonian spinster may be made as interesting, by one genius, as a fight between a crocodile and a catawumpus, by another genius ... But if there is to be no *modus vivendi*, if the battle between the crocodile of Realism and the catawumpus of Romance is to be fought out to the bitter end – why, in that Ragnarôk, I am on the side of the catawumpus.[13]

Also on the side of the catawumpus was Oscar Wilde, who claimed that life imitates art and not the other way around.[14] But the most passionate manifesto came from Hall Caine. Like the other defenders of romance, he believed that mere faithful copying was not to be described as art:

Merely to 'reproduce nature and character' is not Art at all; it is Photography.[15]

The world needs not a recital of facts but expressions of feeling: it needs 'to be lifted up, to be inspired, to be thrilled, to be shown what brave things human nature is capable of at its best'.[16]

Advocates of romance, admittedly in varying degrees, tended to claim as forcibly as the realistic novelists that the form they employed could be useful. Few openly suggested that romance had necessarily to do with escapism. Indeed, some of them appeared to believe that romance had a highly exalted role to play in keeping alive man's belief in, and furthering his search for, moral and aesthetic values. For Stevenson, romance even contributed to the psychological health of those who read it. These ideas signify the pride taken in the genre by the romance writers. They were not ashamed of what they wrote and, though realizing that romance might be in need of defence, they offered no cringing apology. They believed that romance was actually a vital part of the literary scene, even in the late nineteenth century. Is it possible that Morris also trusted in the potential relevance of his fairy-stories and that he was not merely obeying a personal whim?

Introduction

Before attempting to answer that question, it is necessary to define more clearly the nature of the romance genre. So far I have spoken about it in a rather general way, using the term to designate all those fictions which are variously unrealistic. It might be argued at this point that all art is more or less unrealistic and therefore all fictions are romances; indeed several nineteenth-century critics use 'romance' as a synonym for 'novel'. Certainly any definition of romance will inevitably include aspects of fiction which appear in many or most 'realistic' novels. And as Gillian Beer points out in her monograph *The Romance* (1970), romances themselves differ so greatly that an all-inclusive definition is hard to achieve. I propose to adopt her solution to the problem and to cite not a restrictive or prescriptive formula but a 'cluster of properties' whose presence in a work may show it to be a romance:

> the themes of love and adventure, a certain withdrawal from their own societies on the part of both reader and romance hero, profuse sensuous detail, simplified characters (often with a suggestion of allegorical significance), a serene intermingling of the unexpected and the everyday, a complex and prolonged succession of incidents usually without a single climax, a happy ending, amplitude of proportions, a strongly enforced code of conduct to which all the characters must comply.[17]

One of these properties alone may not be enough to lead us to call a work a romance. Clearly a novel apparently highly realistic in setting and character may deal with love or adventure and have a happy ending (though the more artificially contrived the dénouement the closer, I would suggest, the work approaches to the conditions of romance). When several of these qualities appear in the same work, however, one may be justified in saying that the author has to some extent employed romance techniques. And if several such qualities appear, and do so without an admixture of non-romance elements – if all the characters are simplified and the happy ending is not undercut by irony or mockery or cynicism – then the work as a whole may be described as a romance. To it we will bring the expectations characteristically aroused by the genre and much of our interest as critics will centre on the methods by which the author responds to and controls these expectations.

Gillian Beer's list of 'properties' draws our attention to two major areas of concern. One is related to the formal aspects of romance, the other to the thematic concepts which are most appropriately expressed through this formal structure. Perhaps the most obvious thing about a romance is the distance placed between the reader and the events and people in the fiction. In romance we are transported to a world remote from our own in time or place or both. This remoteness may be achieved chronologically by suggesting that the action takes place in the past or the future; and spatially by decribing it as occurring in another country, or on another planet. Moreover, as Gillian Beer points out, the romance hero is himself alienated from his own society. He may be an explorer or a time-traveller. Sometimes his alienation is social rather than physical: Cinderella is a typical romance heroine in this respect. Not only are we distanced from the setting in which romance events take place, we also experience a certain detachment from the characters. We are presented with no psychologically interesting cases, no 'rounded' portraits of people with whom we may perhaps feel sympathy. Romance does not take us inside the head of its hero. Instead we receive only an uncompromisingly external delineation which is most likely to represent a familiar type – a one-sided embodiment of a particular personality trait, or even an allegorical figure. When reading romance there are certain questions we do not ask. It would be ridiculous to enquire into the motivations of the Ugly Sisters, to wonder what influences moulded them into the people they are, or to hope for any amendment in their behaviour. Their words and actions do not express complex inner debates and they cannot change: they are as they are because the story requires it. Simplification is essential to romance characterization, and is connected with a comforting congruence between external appearance and moral quality. The golden hair of the heroine is a sign of moral perfection; and even if evil characters assume for a while the outward semblance of good, their 'real' nature will ultimately be revealed and they will relapse into physical as well as moral ugliness. (Duessa in *The Faerie Queene* is a good example of this; and it occurs in reverse in the common story of the loathly lady.) It follows from these aspects of romance characterization that our response to the hero, for example, is not centrally concerned with who he is or why he acts as he does. We are more interested in watching his actions and perceiving the narrative pattern in which they have a place.

This is not to say that our emotions must be put to one side when we are reading romance. Shakespeare knew how affecting could be the reunion, after a play full of separation and disaster, of romance characters whose long search for each other is finally successful. In *Pericles* he could rely on his audience's appetite for two such scenes in close succession – despite the fact that Marina and Thaisa are merely fairy-tale figures and the hero himself scarcely more interesting in any psychological sense. The emotions, however, which are aroused by romance are constantly channelled and tempered by the highly artificial and controlled nature of the form. What we chiefly experience when Pericles is reunited with Thaisa is the relief which comes when formal perfection, long expected, is finally asserted – when a discord is resolved, when the last piece is put into the pattern, when stasis and completion are attained. Romance must have a happy ending – not for sentimental reasons but because the conventions of the form demand it. Fiction of this kind operates by rules which are part of the knowledge shared by reader and writer before the story begins. The motifs and narrative patterns of romance are familiar to us from childhood. If there are three brothers in a tale, we know that the youngest and weakest will turn out to be the hero. If the hero fights a dragon, we should be astounded were the dragon to win. If a riddle is asked, there will always be an answer and someone, or something, will eventually discover it. Romance does not leave loose ends: though the strands of the story may become almost hopelessly involved before they are disentangled, in the end ambiguities will be clarified, disguises removed, rightful positions attained and our expectations satisfied.

To speak of 'rightful positions' is appropriate, for with the extreme formality of the genre goes a thematic concern with right and wrong, good and evil. In romance, unquestionably, pure good and irremediable evil exist and are implacably opposed. Romance asserts that truth is recognizable, that honest actions bear fruit and that the world can be portrayed as a place of moral order rather than anarchy. Just as we would be startled if the hero did not kill the dragon, we would be horrified if he did not receive the hand of the princess as his reward. Justice and the keeping of promises are deeply embedded in the romance – even bad characters are constrained by the necessity to do exactly as they said they would. Thus the pattern of romance gratifies both our aesthetic desire for completeness and resolution and our moral wish that good should be more powerful than evil. The two are inextricably interlinked; so that to break the formal requirements of the genre is to question the moral certainties on which it is founded.

It will be clear that romance, perhaps more than any other genre, operates through the reader's awareness of its conventions. The delight in reading romance is to hold in tension our certainty of an eventual resolution with the temporary doubts and surprises caused by the twists of the narrative. While we are disturbed by the hero's apparent reverses, we are sustained by the knowledge that the pressure towards the happy ending will ultimately prove irresistible. And thus the most important quality of romance is perhaps the centrality of the narrative line. Our attention is focused on the sequence of events, for it is through them that the thrust towards that final achieved pattern will be channelled. The quest is a favourite romance motif, for its portrayal of a gradual approach to a desired and certain goal reflects the experience of each romance reader as we follow the tantalizing story to its satisfying conclusion. Romances are stories which move in a linear pattern towards a fixed and gratifying end.

III

The basic components of romance form are threefold: distance in setting, flatness of character and a happy ending. This study, then, will attempt to suggest some reasons why Morris should have written in a style so flagrantly at odds with the realistic fictional criteria of his period – and to examine the ways in which his views and beliefs found natural and potent expression in this antiquated form. At the beginning of his literary career it would seem that he turned to romance because it was the kind of writing he himself liked to read. For Morris, like many of his contemporaries, was obsessed with the medieval past. In the Socialist periodical *Justice*, in 1894, he tried to explain what had motivated the political struggle in which for a decade he had expended so much of his considerable energy. He attributed it thus:

the leading passion of my life has been and is hatred of modern civilization.[18]

This statement may be applied to much more in Morris's life than his political activity. From a very early age he reacted with distaste to many aspects of his society, particularly aesthetic ones; and this reaction took the form of a devotion to the past. The art of the Middle Ages, especially, provided him with a point of reference from which to condemn the decayed sensibilities of his contemporaries. His love of the medieval world began when he was a boy. We are told that he had read all of Scott's novels by the age of seven and that one of his favourite pastimes was to ride in Epping Forest dressed in a toy suit of armour. His devotion to medieval architecture may have dated from a visit to Canterbury Cathedral at the age of eight; it was reinforced by his studies while at Marlborough and by ecstatic response, during Oxford vacations, to the great cathedrals of northern France: Amiens, Beauvais, Chartres and Rouen. In his lecture 'The Aims of Art' (1886) Morris recalls after thirty years how he was affected by his first sight of the city of Rouen:

no words can tell you how its mingled beauty, history, and romance took hold on me; I can only say that, looking back on my past life, I find it was the greatest pleasure I have ever had. (XXIII. 85)

If we may judge by the evidence of his life's work as poet and story-teller, his discovery of medieval literature must have provided a similar revelation. His formal studies at Oxford made much less impact on him than his reading of Malory (in Southey's 1817 edition), Chaucer and medieval romances. By the time he left Oxford, Morris had laid the foundations of his eventual prodigious knowledge of medieval art and literature. It was to be his lifelong task to adapt medieval forms and practice to his needs as nineteenth-century designer, author and social critic.

Morris was very far from being unique in his predilection for medievalism. Many of his contemporaries turned from what they saw as the ugliness and injustice of their own society to a consoling, compensatory vision of the past. For large numbers of Victorians the medieval world came to represent a golden age of chivalry, courage and heroism. Alice Chandler has demonstrated how the Middle Ages 'were idealized as a period of faith, order, joy, munificence, and creativity'.[19] At the centre of such idealization stood the figure of the medieval knight. Tennyson's Sir Galahad is a clear example of the type:

> My good blade carves the casques of men,
>> My tough lance thrusteth sure,
> My strength is as the strength of ten,
>> Because my heart is pure.
>> . . .
> Then move the trees, the copses nod,
>> Wings flutter, voices hover clear:
> 'O just and faithful knight of God!
>> Ride on! the prize is near.'
> So pass I hostel, hall, and grange;
>> By bridge and ford, by park and pale,
> All-armed I ride, whate'er betide,
>> Until I find the holy Grail.[20]

This noble gentleman became a very important symbol to Morris and his Oxford friends. At one time they were seriously considering the foundation of a lay monastery into which, with Galahad as patron saint (and Morris as financial backer), they could retire from the unsatisfactory nineteenth-century world. At this early stage in his career Morris's passion for medievalism seems to have been connected with a desire to evade the social problems and artistic failures of his society. In a letter written to his friend Cormell Price in 1856 he takes an unequivocally apolitical and anti-reforming position:

I can't enter into politico-social subjects with any interest, for on the whole I see that things are in a muddle, and I have no power or vocation to set them right in ever so little a degree.[21]

Morris's acquiescence in the monastery plan relates to this sense of detachment; though he perceives (like Dickens's Stephen Blackpool) the 'muddle' of contemporary life, he feels he can have no active role in attempts to change and reorder it. To those who responded in this way the medieval ideal embodied in Sir Galahad was one of transcendent, otherworldly purity. Galahad's pursuit of the Grail imaged a search for personal holiness; it had little to do with active commitment to any struggle against social evil.

Canon Dixon, however, remembered Morris calling Tennyson's Sir Galahad 'rather a mild youth'.[22] For some nineteenth-century writers the image of the medieval knight was designed to inspire men to struggle for moral excellence, rather than to suggest withdrawal from a contaminating world. While he was at Oxford Morris read Charlotte Yonge's *The Heir of Redclyffe* (1853), a best-selling fictionalization of the idea that modern Englishmen should emulate the chivalric battles against evil performed by medieval knights. He also knew the work of Kenelm Digby, whose *The Broad Stone of Honour* (1822) influentially insisted that the values of medieval courtly society should be revived. Above all, Morris was deeply affected by the teaching of the great sages of his period, Carlyle and Ruskin, who required from the past not only a contrast with the present but a spur to action. Carlyle's Abbot Samson, for instance, in *Past and Present* (1843), is an object-lesson to modern Captains of Industry and the aristocracy, who have forgotten their obligations to the people they rule. Carlyle is not content merely to make comparisons; he continually exhorts his readers to go out and improve the state of contemporary society. Morris acknowledged Carlyle as one of his masters, and the effect of Carlyle's thundering prose must have gone far to neutralize the wish to retire into monastic seclusion.

Morris's attitude to the past, then, was influenced by two opposing views about the value of history. As an artist, he was therefore involved in a dilemma concerning artistic re-creation of the past. In the prose fiction published in the *Oxford and Cambridge Magazine* (1856) and the poems which formed *The Defence of Guenevere* (1858) there is a crucial tension between the concept of art as escapist and the belief in art as an incentive to practical commitment. It is by examining this tension that Morris's early use of the romance form can most usefully be clarified.

IV

Morris's ambivalence about the value of re-creating the past is all the more striking because of the context in which it is

Introduction

revealed. His earliest published work appeared in the *Oxford and Cambridge Magazine*,[23] a short-lived and idealistic journal produced by a group of his friends at Oxford and several Cambridge acquaintances. The editorial policy was eclectic, able to embrace both articles of high-toned religious feeling and pleas for tolerance for the free-thinker. Yet the magazine does have a clearly definable ethos. It expresses with great moral earnestness the feelings of young men who believe that their education has laid on them the responsibility to help those less fortunate. They wish to live lives of selfless dedication to the improvement of their society. This idea is expressed in such articles as 'The Work of Young Men in the Present Age' (probably by William Fulford) and Bernard Cracroft's series 'On Popular Lectures', which encouraged University men to offer their knowledge to the lower classes. In fictional terms, the same theme runs through Fulford's long story 'Cavalay: a Chapter of a Life', in which the youthful hero finds his destiny by learning the importance of duty and sacrifice.[24] Many of the writers are concerned that modern scientific and social innovations seem to be destroying some of the old values, without providing in their place the moral regeneration which England needs. In one of his articles on Carlyle, Vernon Lushington takes on something of his subject's prophetic tone of voice as he denounces the spirit of the age:

Educated in atheism and materialism, we believe in things only, care for things only, treating as quite subordinate the bodies and souls of men, even our own. Thus blindly do we exist and work, seeking for gold, not human affection, clamouring for measures and not men, finding in railways and steam-engines the progress of the species.[25]

Burne-Jones voiced similar doubts about the beneficial nature of modern developments:

the Present with all its achievements, its men turned to machines, and its machine-turned men – with all its powers of motion and creation, this newspaper present that sings its own praises till hoarse in the throat – blushes before the long-forgotten, unknown Past.[26]

Feeling as they did that established standards had been eroded, the contributors to the magazine were above all deeply concerned with the relationship of the present to the past, and with the role of history.

Introduction

In the April issue of the *Oxford and Cambridge Magazine* appeared an article about Oxford by Vernon Lushington's brother Godfrey. The essay begins with the statement that 'the past, it is written, ever explains to us the present'.[27] This was a belief which lay very close to the hearts of the magazine's contributors. Some felt that although manners and the social environment had changed through the ages, men had remained essentially the same. Human nature did not alter. Fulford made this claim explicitly in his discussion of Shakespeare's *Troilus and Cressida*, when he declared that 'man's spiritual nature ... is the same in all times and in all nations'.[28] We should, therefore, study the actions of men of the past, in order correctly to interpret our own feelings and motivation. Wilfred Heeley, on the other hand, felt that the relationship of modern to former ages was one of contrast rather than similarity. In his article on 'Sir Philip Sidney', which opens the first issue of the magazine, he explains why his contemporaries need to analyse the characters of their ancestors:

not that we may satisfy a flippant curiousity, but that we may gauge ourselves by them, that we may know why we are what we are, why they were other than we.[29]

Yet despite these differences of opinion about the way history teaches us about ourselves, the contributors to the magazine were united in the belief that the present could only be understood by reference to the past. In several long articles, Vernon Lushington discusses Carlyle's theories about the uses of history, and explains how:

he has planted all his judgements of modern English facts on their history ... And he uses history for a larger purpose than this immediate one; he reads in it, and in turn sets forth by it the Nature of Man, his noble powers and destinies, and the duties which at all times man owes to his fellow-men.[30]

It seems, Lushington continues, as if modern changes in values and standards have led to a rejection of the teachings of the past. Old and New are at war. It is imperative that the dichotomy between past and present be removed:

The wise befriend both Old and New, and endeavour to make them one ... the wise aim at *uniting* men in a quiet steady progress.[31]

Only thus will England develop as she should. Most of Lushington's colleagues held similar convictions.

If a knowledge of the past was so important for the progress of England, it was clearly vital that the ideas about the past entertained by intelligent and creative men should be true ones. The magazine's contributors constantly refer to the need for accurate descriptions of historical events and characters. Heeley's article on Sidney is the nearest approach to a manifesto in the magazine; in this essay Heeley rejects all historical analysis which is based on prejudice, romantic or imaginative distortions, or preconceptions. He wishes to see his ancestors as they really were:

We will have nothing more to do with phantoms, incoherent and inconceivable, however logical; we want to see men as they were and are; not with motives, but with impulses; not equations, with so many virtues minus so many vices, but men, with infinite possibilities of good and evil.[32]

His own portrait of Sidney will attempt to 'set Sir Philip Sidney before you as he looked and spoke, and wrote, and was'.[33] This phrase, or a variant of it, is repeated throughout the magazine. Heeley, reviewing the latest instalments of Macaulay's *History of England* (1849–61), complains that the historian has allowed his political prejudices and desire for stylistic effect to overcome his objectivity; he 'has failed in putting before us things and people as they were'.[34] Fulford reviews *Recollection of the Table-Talk of Samuel Rogers* (1856) by Alexander Dyce, starting from the premiss that all men wish, when reading about their predecessors, 'to learn truly what the men themselves really were'.[35] Vernon Lushington praises Carlyle as one of the few historians able to write about real men in all their diversity.

This concern for accuracy in recalling the past is manifested in the magazine's poetry and fiction as well as in the factual articles. Fulford's poem 'Childhood' is about the need for an individual to remember and assimilate his own youth. Several of the short stories discuss the effects of memory on behaviour, and of time on memory. In a tale called 'A Story of the North', the narrator begins by regretting that the great men of the past have largely been forgotten. After looking at a page of an illuminated book, he attempts to create 'a vision of the past',[36] and tries to present a picture of one of the unsung heroes of ancient times. At the end of his story, however, he has to admit defeat:

the lives of men in that far-off time came to me only in pictures: I could not hear them speak as they really spoke, could not know them as they were.[37]

He has not, after all, been able to endow the past with reality. Yet the tale ends with the promise of another attempt; the author feels that his efforts to re-create the past have been expended in a worthy cause.

In the June issue of the *Oxford and Cambridge Magazine*, Heeley reviewed the first volume of the *History of England* (1856–70) by Froude. In the course of his remarks, the critic summed up the benefits he and his colleagues sought from a study of the past:

We can never reproduce the Past; yet may we hope to make its good our own, if we believe that, through all change of circumstance, universal principles of right and truth lie at the base of every success, and form the real greatness of every noble deed and character.[38]

Morris's Oxford friends believed that an accurate and objective reconstruction of the past had an important effect on modern life and attitudes. It led, by contrast or analogy, to a restoration in modern society of unchanging moral values which had tended to become submerged in the race for material innovations. The authors of the *Oxford and Cambridge Magazine* believed passionately in progress; but they were convinced that true progress could only be achieved by a linking of the insights of the past with the energy and idealism of the present. As we have seen, Morris was conditioned by much of his reading to hold similar views. Moreover, his intense emotional attachment to the medieval age led him naturally to use settings and themes from this period in his own fiction. Yet his work constantly fails to endorse the ideas about the past which were held by his colleagues. Not only is he aware of the difficulties of accurately re-creating the past; he is sceptical about the value of any attempt to do so.

Morris knew himself for a romance writer from a very early stage in his career. He wrote to Cormell Price:

My work is the embodiment of dreams in one form or another.[39]

Introduction

His early fiction and poetry seeks to create a sensually powerful romance world and largely succeeds in the 'embodiment', the making fictionally tangible, of fantasy. Yet unlike Stevenson and Haggard and his friends of the *Oxford and Cambridge Magazine*, he seems unconvinced about the usefulness of the dreams he is presenting with such vivid force. If Morris's early work is romance, it is of an interestingly flawed and tentative nature.

CHAPTER I

'That old beautiful land': the early romances

Morris's emotional allegiance, as we have seen, was to the medieval past; his literary taste was for romance. So it must have been natural for him to use medieval settings for his own early fiction. 'Frank's Sealed Letter' is the only one of his stories to be placed in the nineteenth century;[1] after this experiment, Morris seems to have concluded that his métier was after all an evocation of the past rather than a description of the contemporary scene. From the beginning he had the gift of bringing before his readers with extraordinary vividness the details of medieval life. His descriptions of artefacts have a glittering clarity which testifies to his love and knowledge of medieval design:

behold therein lay armour – mail for the whole body, made of very small rings wrought most wonderfully, for every ring was fashioned like a serpent, and though they were so small yet could you see their scales and their eyes, and of some even the forked tongue was on it, and lay on the rivet, and the rings were gilded here and there into patterns and flowers so that the gleam of it was most glorious. (1. 294)

He is equally precise when dealing with the violent aspects of medieval existence:

Then one thrust me through the breast with a spear, and another with his sword, which was three inches broad, gave me a stroke across the thighs that bit to the bone; and as I fell forward one cleft me to the teeth with his axe. (1. 308)

Morris apparently shared the view of his colleagues that the artist's task was to bring to life scenes from the past and to present them to his readers with the utmost effectiveness. Clearly he had a considerable talent for achieving this objective.

He was not content, however, merely to tell romance stories. Morris's statements about the nature of artistic creation, his theory for instance that poetry should come as easily to the poet as a craft comes to a skilled craftsman, have done him a disservice among critics. The tendency has been to see him not as a conscious literary artist but as an unreflective spinner-out of tales. If questioned, Morris would undoubtedly have opted for the second of these two descriptions. Yet the disingenuous way in which he talked about his literary work belies the evidence of the stories themselves. Even in his early tales, for example, he is not content to employ simple narrative forms. On the contrary, the narrative line is often highly complicated; and this fact is one justification for the assertion that the stories are highly self-conscious examinations of the nature of the conventions they are themselves adopting. Not only are Morris's stories set in the past; their major theme is the nature and influence of the past and the difficulties encountered by those who wish to preserve it and transform it into art.

I

The first story that Morris wrote for the *Oxford and Cambridge Magazine* was probably 'A Dream', which appeared in March 1856.[2] It is a ghost story, told around a fire with outside the standard accompaniment of a winter gale. Lawrence and Ella, a noble knight and the beautiful lady who loves him, are separated in their youth. Ella's foolish desire to see Lawrence prove his love for her leads her to dare him to enter a mysterious cavern. Its evil reputation is confirmed when he fails to return. She has promised, however, to follow him if he is lost, and has prayed for a more than naturally long life to enable her to complete her quest. The story tells how Hugh the doctor sees in the bodies of a patient and his nurse the momentary reincarnation of the long-separated lovers. Many years later they are seen again by another witness in the persons of a queen and her knight. And more than a hundred years later still they meet for the last time. Lawrence and Ella become not figures in a story but visible and palpable to the story-tellers:

They stood opposite to each other for a little, he and the lady ... at last he made one step, and took off his gleaming helmet, laid it down softly, then spread abroad his arms, and she came to him, and they were clasped together, her head lying over his shoulder; and the four men gazed, quite awe-struck. (1. 174)

As they are reunited the bells ring in the New Year, and 'there beneath the eyes of those four men the lovers slowly faded away into a heap of snow-white ashes' (1. 174).

To their own amazement and horror, the story-tellers have conjured up their characters in a more than metaphorical sense. The story is about the power of fiction to blur the normal distinctions between fantasy and reality, past and present. Lawrence and Ella have twice before been glimpsed moving from the timeless world of their quest, in which they are disembodied, into the world of temporality and appearance. It can be no coincidence that their final incarnation takes place immediately after – presumably as a result of – the telling of their story. The power of the story, however, has a double effect. Not only do Lawrence and Ella exist beyond time; those who see them are themselves released from the normal temporal constraints. Perhaps the most chilling moments in the tale are those in which two of the group round the fire realize that the other two are narrating not old legends but events that they actually witnessed – more than a hundred years before. Hugh the doctor, who saw the first reincarnation, is referred to later in the story as dead; but he is currently present to tell his tale. And the other narrator, Giles, has been preserved to add his part of the story; like Lawrence and Ella he has an unnaturally long life. In his case, however, this is not the result of his own choice but imposed upon him so that he can act as a witness. Indeed, when he first saw the ghosts the experience changed his normal relationship with his environment, distancing him from it:

we three moved on together, and soon I saw that my nature was changed, and that I was invisible for the time; for, though the sun was high, I cast no shadow, neither did any man that we passed notice us. (1. 170)

Telling the story can draw characters from the past into the present; those who are involved in some way in the story are also (perhaps involuntarily) freed from the usual constraints on human existence and personality.

In this tale the usual distinctions between past and present cease to operate. Characters who began as fictional figures end as tangible in the present experience of the story-tellers. As a result, other distinctions are also abandoned. We have seen how

Lawrence and Ella merge with the personalities of those through whom they are momentarily visible. When they achieve their final meeting they have only their own personae; yet there is still ambiguity. They are both the same in appearance as they were when they first parted; but while in one sense time has stood still, in another they have been cruelly marked by the long quest:

her beauty ... seemed to grow every minute; though she was plainly not young, oh no, but rather very, very old, who could say how old? (1. 173)

The figures of Giles and Hugh are similarly ambiguous. They appear to be ordinary living men, yet one is a spirit and the other has had his life unnaturally extended. The two men to whom the story is related are forced by these complexities to reconsider their responses to appearances and, especially, to the past. Appearance is deceptive and identity difficult to establish. The past, no longer safely distant, may become disturbingly close. For the reader, there is an added dimension created by Morris's descriptions of his characters. Throughout the story it is the ghosts, Lawrence and Ella, who are presented in his vivid, colourful, precise style; all other figures are shadowy. The fictional personae are more powerfully present to us than those who tell their story. Is Morris suggesting not only that the past can be made, through story-telling, part of the present but also that it can appear paradoxically more vital, more 'real' than our everyday experience?

'A Dream' is a study of the operation of fiction, especially of fiction set in the past. Not a very extended or developed examination, certainly. But questions seem to be raised which have to do with the 'embodiment of dreams' and what happens to those who assist in such embodiment. This theme is further considered through yet another complication connected with the structure of the narrative. Giles and Hugh, mysterious narrators, are themselves figures in someone else's story. An authorial voice describes the whole tale as a dream which is now being retold by the dreamer. He brings his vision into the present consciousness of his readers as Hugh and Giles summon up the actual bodies of the characters in their story by the power of their narrative. The tale ends with a quotation from Tennyson's 'A Dream of Fair Women':

The early romances

No memory labours longer from the deep
  Gold mines of thought to lift the hidden ore
That glimpses, moving up, than I from sleep
  To gather and tell o'er
Each little sound and sight.   (I. 175)

Here are linked together Giles's and Hugh's memories and the dreamer's fantasy; both have been laboriously gathered and presented to their audience. Both have the power to transport the listener beyond the present and the ordinary, to remove the limitations imposed by our usual factual apprehension of the world. Perhaps in both cases this power may operate in ways which disturb us, since it removes some of the assumptions about the nature of time and the singleness of the individual personality which help us to deal rationally with our experience.

Many of the other stories Morris wrote for the *Oxford and Cambridge Magazine* have as a major preoccupation the normal distinctions between past and present, dream and reality, and what happens if they are removed. Many have as a characteristic effect the disorientation, the deliberate confusion, of the reader. In the first story to be published, 'The Story of the Unknown Church' (January 1856), the opening sentence is startling since it requires us to listen to the first-person narration of a dead man:

I was the master-mason of a church that was built more than six hundred years ago. (I. 149)

Gradually he recalls his church, and fixes his memory on one particular day:

I do not remember very much about the land where my church was; I have quite forgotten the name of it, but I know it was very beautiful, and even now, while I am thinking of it, comes a flood of old memories, and I almost see it again ... that old beautiful land! Only dimly do I see it in spring and summer and winter, but I see it in autumn-tide clearly now; yes, clearer, clearer, oh! so bright and glorious! (I. 149)

Already the reader is asked to juggle with two different times: the undefined and unlocated present in which the dead narrator is speaking, and the long past but increasingly specific moment which he has recalled. Almost immediately we are reminded of an even more distant past, as the narrator tells us that the church was being built to replace an older one, destroyed by fire, which was erected a hundred years before he was born. The story, like 'A Dream', is concerned with the relationships between the past, and day-dream, and the present. Again a character moves from memory and fantasy into reality. Walter the master-mason, while carving, slips into a day-dream about his friend Amyot who is away fighting in the crusades. He is roused from the dream by a voice calling his name – it is Amyot, unexpectedly returned. Immediately the narration slides away once more from the straightforward chronological time-sequence to tell in flashback how Amyot left for the Holy Wars. And the next section of the story jumps forward, leaving a chronological hiatus, to narrate Amyot's death – which was itself prefigured in Walter's dream.

Thus the story's concern with the way memory and fantasy affect our perception of events is mirrored by the use of ellipsis and prolepsis which distort the time-sequence of the fabula, the story-as-it-might-have-happened. Similar confusions may be found in the prose itself, especially in Morris's use of tenses which exhibits a disturbing fluidity. One sentence which occurs at the end of the memory of Amyot's departure is an example of his style:

we had said that we should always be together; but he went away, and now he is come back again. (1. 156)

The sentence begins in the distant past before Amyot left, but as the pluperfect indicates that period is recorded from the point of view of a later time. There follows a projection of the future made in that earliest time. Then comes a simple past tense, denoting the act which negated the possibility of the hoped-for future. And immediately, with only the slightest possible mark of punctuation, we are transported to a present ('now') in which Amyot's return is already in the past. This rapid movement from tense to tense may leave the reader breathless and perhaps understandably confused about the precise status of that 'now' of which the narrator is speaking. Extreme accuracy in the use of tenses has led to confusion rather than clarity. And if the reader is made uneasy by the way the prose seems to slide away from his mental grasp, Walter too feels disturbed when 'one ... whom [he] had seen in [his] dreams just before' (1. 155) appears to him in the flesh. Indeed he feels 'almost beside [himself]' (1. 155). He

briefly experiences a loss of identity similar to that of Giles and
Hugh in 'A Dream'. For him too, the return in the present of one
who had been within the boundaries of dream or memory has a
disturbing, disorientating effect.

Clearly the strange shifts of time, the narrative confusions,
are not caused by ineptitude on the part of a young author.
Morris is in complete control of other elements of his story; for
instance, the locations in Walter's dream are reflections, and
distortions, of the scenery around the church, and fully convincing as examples of the way dream-experience builds on and
transforms reality. Morris was preoccupied by the idea of time
and deliberately used his story to raise questions about its
nature and operation. This is attested by his insistent harping on
the word. In the penultimate paragraph alone we read 'I was a
long time carving it ... a very short time ... thinking of the time
... as I had time' (I. 158). The tale, like 'A Dream', suggests that
normal distinctions between past and present, dream and
reality, may not be as rigid as we would perhaps like to imagine.

In 'A Dream' and 'The Story of the Unknown Church' the
merging of past and present seems to necessitate frightening
realignments of perception on the part of those who are
involved. Two other stories are concerned with the suggestion
that the past and fantasy may actually be useful (though still
sometimes disturbing) to those who can relate them to their
own present experiences. 'Frank's Sealed Letter' is set, unusually for Morris, in a contemporary world. Its subject is memory.
The narrator, Hugh, tells us of his love for his childhood
sweetheart, Mabel, and describes his proposal to her, which she
contemptuously rejects. In the next scene, Hugh opens a letter
formerly sent to him by his dying friend Frank, which he was to
read only if Mabel refused him. The letter counsels Hugh not to
attempt to forget Mabel and his love for her, but to accept the
suffering his memories will cause and believe that they will
make him love other people more. Hugh, however, does not
follow this advice. He does his best to forget Mabel, works hard,
and becomes famous for his wisdom and loved for his
philanthropy. Yet he finds that he forgets Frank as well as Mabel
in his busy life. Eventually, years later, his control suddenly
breaks; memories of his childhood with Mabel come flooding
back, and he loses all will to work. He retires from the world,

and ends by contemplating suicide. At this point comes another of Morris's surprise realignments of his narrative. Hugh wakes up from a day-dream to find that he has only just read Frank's letter. All the years of struggle, success and ultimate failure have been imaginary. He now has to choose between accepting Frank's advice or following the path of his dream. He decides to take the former course, and the story ends as he prays that his memory will remain always green.[3]

Again Morris has played tricks with the chronology of his story. The present we had accepted, from which Hugh is narrating the tale, turns out to be false; what we thought had happened was only a dream, and what seemed past is still in the future. The actual present is a moment in what we had thought of as the past. Thus, as in the previous stories, we are made aware of the fluidity of time. Hugh's experience takes us further. We are led to consider whether the past can affect our present actions. Hugh attempts (in his dream) to forget his childhood and youth. When he suddenly remembers them again, his whole life collapses. He decides, therefore, to take the opposite course; he will live with memory, and suffer gladly the pain it causes him. Has he done the right thing? It is hard to judge; but certainly his dream of a possible future has led him to certain decisions about how he wishes to live in the present. He believes that memory of the past will also be valuable, since his identity, his self-image, is necessarily bound up with his past.

In 'Lindenborg Pool' the narrator not only finds himself recalling his own past, but also experiences something like a racial memory of an event which is the substance of an old legend. He finds his personality merging with that of the hero of the folk-tale; and his own actions of ten years previously appear strangely linked with those of his legendary predecessor. The outline of the story is taken from a collection of Scandinavian tales by Benjamin Thorpe, called *Northern Mythology* (1851–2). One of them explains the origin of an unfathomable lake. Formerly a castle stood where the lake now lies. On the eve of a holy day, when their masters were absent, the servants of the castle got drunk and played a trick on the local priest. They dressed up a pig in a night-cap, put it in a bed, and asked the priest to come to give it absolution as if it were a dying man. He did so, but just as he was about to administer the sacrament he realized the deception, and went away in anger, with the revellers laughing behind him. As he left the castle the clock struck twelve; the castle collapsed, and sank into an abyss from which a lake arose. Floating on the water was a stool, on which lay the breviary which the priest in his haste had left behind.[4]

In Morris's version, the story begins with a nineteenth-century man going on a midnight expedition to fathom Lindenborg Pool. The only thing we learn about him is that exactly ten years ago he committed a murder. As he contemplates the pool, he suddenly finds himself transported to a wood through which he appears to be riding. In a way which we may be coming to see as typical of Morris's early prose, his identity gradually merges with that of another man in another time and place:

Ah! what was that which touched my shoulder? Yes, I see, only a dead leaf. Yes, to be here on this eighth of May too of all nights in the year, the night of that awful day when ten years ago I slew him, not undeservedly, God knows, yet how dreadful it was! Another leaf! and another! Strange, those trees have been dead this hundred years, I should think. How sharp the wind is too, just as if I were moving along & meeting it; – why, I am moving! what then, I am not there after all; where am I then? (I. 246–7)

At first this disorientation is horrifying:

I shall go mad – I am mad, I am gone to the Devil – I have lost my identity; who knows in what place, in what age of the world I am living now? (I. 247)

But gradually he discovers that instead of losing his identity he now has two personae: his original one, and that of a thirteenth-century priest – the very priest who is riding to shrive the pig in the castle. The rest of the story is told through the priest's perceptions, but he also retains his nineteenth-century persona and sees such things as his drunken companion with a double perspective:

I watched him in my proper nineteenth-century character, with insatiable curiosity and intense amusement; but as a quiet priest of a long-past age, with contempt and disgust enough, not unmixed with fear and anxiety. (I. 247)

During the rest of the tale he continues to think with 'all thought strangely double' (I. 248). The baron whom he believes he is going to shrive has the same face as the enemy whom he killed ten years ago – in his other persona. When he reaches the castle, confusions continue. The people are moving about in 'a bewildering dance-like motion, mazy and intricate' (1.251); curtains swing to and fro, giving momentary glimpses of endless corridors. The people are not what they seem, for to the priest's horror some of them are women dressed as men. The dance tunes seem like ones he has heard before, in the nineteenth century. Finally he is totally bemused:

Still more and more people talking and singing & laughing and twirling about, till my brain went round and round, and I scarce knew what I did. (1.251)

Morris shows remarkable skill in evoking the blurred and shifting scene; the series of participles conveys the bewilderment of the narrator when faced with the phantasmagoric, subtly evil vision of the revellers. In the end he confronts a further confusion, of man with beast, as the pig breaks out of the bed and wounds him in the hand with its tusk. The priest breaks out too, using a sword to clear his way through the drink-maddened dancers and smashing the castle gate with super-human strength. Then he watches the castle sink and the pool appearing in its place. Here the story abruptly ends. Although we are reminded of the narrator's nineteenth-century persona by the final sentence ('And this is how I tried to fathom the Lindenborg Pool' (1.253)) we do not discover whether or not he completely returns from the thirteenth century.

By now we are familiar with confusions of this nature. There is a further one, however, in 'Lindenborg Pool': that of the narrator with the author. Morris frequently uses first-person narration in his early work, but usually distances himself as author from the speaker by such devices as the dream; or at least makes it clear, as in 'Frank's Sealed Letter', that the narrator has a character and name all his own. In 'Lindenborg Pool', on the contrary, the narrator speaks of himself as both 'I, the priest' and, immediately afterwards, 'I, the author' (1.250). At the beginning of the story, Morris (unusually) tells us how he came to write it. After reading Thorpe's account, on a stormy May evening, he felt he had to make his own version:

whether I would or no, my thoughts ran in this way, as here follows. So I felt obliged to write, and wrote accordingly, and by the time I had done, the grey light filled all my room. (1. 245)

He indicates that the story aroused something in his own subconscious, which he had to exorcise by writing. In the same way the narrator may be hoping to exorcise his guilt as a murderer by shriving the man who reminds him of his victim. Yet the man is no man; and the pig takes his revenge by wounding the priest as he escapes. Morris links himself as author with the narrator all the more firmly by carrying over into his fiction the date (May) and the weather of the evening on which he was writing. Thus there are three united characters at the centre of the story, and we do not know which of them is 'real' and to which the guilt of murder should be attributed. At the end we are not sure whether the nineteenth-century murderer has assuaged his conscience in the figure of the thirteenth-century priest, nor how far the feelings of either are reflections of feelings entertained by Morris the author. That there are connections seems the only certain fact. In some way priest and murderer are the same, though six hundred years separate them, and both spring directly from the author's subconscious.

It must by now be clear that for Morris these early stories were the product of his passion for the past in a deeper sense than as mere enthusiastic replicas of medieval legend. They are carefully wrought examinations of the relationship of history, and of fiction, to contemporary experience. In the stories we have so far examined, the past is summoned up and made manifest in the present – sometimes by means of telling, or reading, a story and often in conjunction with a dream or day-dream. This process has an effect on the dreamer, or reader, or story-teller which usually involves some confusion, disorientation or distortion of perception; the accepted limitations of time, place and personality may be transcended. And this experience is often sinister; though it may also (ambiguously) appear beneficial to those who learn from it. So the frightening loss of identity of the 'Lindenborg Pool' narrator perhaps leads to his assuaging the guilt of the murder; Hugh in 'Frank's Sealed Letter' believes that his experience of a fantasy past has taught him the value of memory so that he can order his future life in a productive way. Yet the blurring of past into present and fiction into reality may not always be helpful; and neither is it always voluntary. The listeners in 'A Dream', and those who see the reincarnations of the ghosts, do not choose to be present and to suffer the consequences. The author in 'Lindenborg Pool' wrote from a sense of compulsion. Sometimes the power of the past is forced upon us. All these stories seem to exist in an atmosphere of danger; to summon the past is to tamper with the usual limitations on human experience in a way which may have disturbing results.

Like his colleagues on the *Oxford and Cambridge Magazine*, Morris believed that it is important for men to understand the past, both their own and that of their race. In his review of Browning's *Men and Women* (1855) he praises the poet for his success in giving life to historical characters, adopting the magazine's usual terminology:

What a joy it is to have these men brought up before us, made alive again, though they have passed away from the earth so long ago. (I. 330–1)

But Morris had a greater awareness than his colleagues of the potential dangers of such vivification. In some of the *Oxford and Cambridge Magazine* stories he examines the role of the artist who attempts to make the past live in the present. For him, as well as for those who listen to his stories, there may be serious problems.

II

In discussing Morris's early stories I have found myself continually linking historical with fictional processes. It is indeed hard to distinguish the two in Morris's tales; they seem to have a necessary, though varying, relationship. In 'A Dream' the ghost story appears at first to be fiction but is later perceived to be the history of events actually experienced, in part, by the narrators. In 'Frank's Sealed Letter' the day-dream is stimulated by written communication and though it appears to tell of the past turns out to be fiction. In 'Lindenborg Pool' the reading of a legend prompts the author to write a fiction combining the ancient and a more recent past. These images indicate that Morris was considering the relationship of past and present not only in a general way but also with reference to his role as story-teller. In 'The Story of the Unknown Church' there is a vivid reminder of the way the artist attempts to unite past and present through his creative power. The master-mason is first seen carving on his church porch a figure of Abraham. His artist's fancy sees Abraham not with the appearance of a Jewish patriarch but as a knight, a contemporary of the artist:

riding far ahead of any of his company, with his mail-hood off his head, and lying in grim folds down his back, with the strong west wind blowing his wild black hair far out behind him, with the wind rippling the long scarlet pennon of his lance. (I.153)

From this vision his imagination slides into the day-dream which has such a disturbing relevance to the fate of Amyot his friend. Connections, as usual in Morris, are implicit; but it seems that the artist's imagination naturally abolishes distinctions between chronologically separate periods.

Yet the artist has to create an identifiable image, to fix upon a specific representation of his imaginative conception. And here we are approaching a second subject with which Morris was obsessed. We have seen how his belief in the close relationship of past and present expressed itself in images of whirling and blurring, of ambivalence between dream, fiction, fantasy and reality, of a merging of separate identities into composite personae. In contrast, his images which refer to the role of the artist – he whose task it is to present these strange confusions of experience – are regularly images of stasis, fixity, hardness, rigidity. His artists, characteristically, work in stone, the least flexible of media. The paradox obvious in the conjunction of these two kinds of image reflects the central tension in Morris's artistic theory at this period of his life. Time is fluid, past and present may merge. But if the artist tries to recall the past, to make it part of the present, does he only succeed in destroying its vitality? In capturing the essence of the past, does he render it powerless by fixing it in one particular mould? Or, perhaps worse, does his representation inevitably fail in its attempt to capture and embody living men and women and their volatile, evanescent experience?

The early romances

Like Browning in *Men and Women*, Morris uses images of fixity and stasis to suggest a fatal withdrawal from life. That which does not change is dead; to seek permanence is to cut oneself off from renewal and vitality. In 'Lindenborg Pool' the phantasmagoria of the castle is contrasted to an equally evil denial of life and growth in the sterile water-plants around the pool:

none ever flowering as other things flowered, never dying and being renewed, but always the same stiff array of unbroken reeds and segs. (1. 245)

In his story 'Svend and his Brethren' there is a telling antithesis between those who seek change and commit themselves to a quest for a better life, and those who refuse the opportunity. The sons of the king, after his death, plan to sail away from the land of their birth to found a new community in the west, the land of promise. Siur the smith has made them helmets whose crest is the phoenix:

all flaming with new power, dying because its old body is not strong enough for its new-found power. (1. 241)

In vivid contrast to this image of life springing unconquerable from death, those who refuse to go with the young princes are condemned to an horrific existence in suspended animation. When found many years later they look at first sight like statues, but it soon becomes clear that they are living men:

about the quays and about the streets lay many people dead, or stood, but quite without motion, and they were all white or about the colour of new-hewn freestone; yet were they not statues but real men, for they had, some of them, ghastly wounds which showed their entrails, and the structure of their flesh and veins and bones. (1. 244)

They clung to present evil and refused future good; their reward is this terrifying death-in-life instead of the new vitality springing with the phoenix from death. Nothing could more clearly indicate Morris's belief in the dangers of permanence.

In 'Svend and his Brethren' the artist succeeds in creating works of art which are valuable and productive. The helmets with their phoenix crests will protect the young princes in their future struggle for a new and better life. Yet Siur is also involved in an artistic commemoration of the past; and this creation is connected with more images of statues and of death-in-life. Siur has long been hopelessly in love with Cissela, the young princes' mother, who sacrificed herself in making a loveless marriage in order to bring peace between warring peoples. When she dies he carves a figure of her on her tomb. Her husband wishes to be represented in the vacant space beside her, but this Siur refuses to do. The king replies:

'Then perhaps I shall be my own statue,' and therewithal he sat down on the edge of the low marble tomb, and laid his right arm across her breast; he fixed his eyes on the eastern belt of windows, and sat quite motionless and silent; and he never knew that she loved him not. (1. 239)

By the time his sons leave on their quest he has frozen into immobility:

though his right arm still lay over her breast, his head had fallen forward, and rested now on the shoulder of the marble queen. There he lay, with strange confusion of his scarlet, gold-wrought robes; silent, motionless, and dead. (1. 240)

He has embraced death, in the form of a work of art. Unlike his sons, he has chosen stillness in contemplation of the past (and of fantasy, since he erroneously believes that Cissela loved him) rather than movement towards a future.

In 'Svend and his Brethren' we see an artist whose work is sometimes connected with vitality and change but is also linked with the past, stasis and death. In several other stories artists attempt to commemorate the past by carving tombs. The narrator of 'The Story of the Unknown Church' spends his life, after the deaths of Amyot and his own sister who loved Amyot and dies of grief, creating a tomb for the lovers. He portrays them 'lying with clasped hands like husband and wife' (1. 158) though they never were married. His carvings cause those who see them to weep as they recall the story. He dies when, after twenty years' work, he has carved the final flower on the tomb. In 'A Dream' the story-tellers (including, presumably, the spirits) have the ashes of Lawrence and Ella buried in a tomb which similarly has their figures carved upon it. This image of the carved tomb is recurrent in Morris's fiction; it may seem at first to express belief in the power of art to preserve the past. The dead are awarded a memorial, their appearance captured and fixed for all time. Is this not the ultimate success for the creative mind, that it can both summon up and preserve what is in the nature of things destroyed by time? Yet the imagery of tombs has a more ambiguous implication than this. The dead have indeed been commemorated; but in cold and motionless stone. If stasis carries in Morris's work the sense of dangerous sterility, as I have suggested, can the stone figures be simply accepted as valuable representations of the past? Or has vitality been destroyed by the very art which sought to preserve? Certainly the king in 'Svend and his Brethren' found only death by turning to the carved figure of his wife. Moreover the works of art in 'The Story of the Unknown Church' and 'A Dream' are falsificatory. Neither Lawrence and Ella nor Margaret and Amyot were actually married, though the carving presents them as if they had been. Is Morris suggesting that art may tell comforting lies rather than capture the truth?

There is a further problem for the artist. Walter the mason seems to be trying to create a lasting memorial to his sister and his friend. At the end of his story it appears that he has succeeded. Yet if we think back to the beginning of the work we remember that the church, and with it presumably the tomb, has long ago been completely destroyed. The permanence which the work of art seemed to offer has been proved illusory. Time can operate even on the artefact which was intended to defy its ravages. In 'A Dream' the lovers elude time for hundreds of years, but at the end, symbolized by the bells announcing the new year, it catches up with them and they crumble away. In Morris's stories the desire to escape from the restrictions of time is strong; but even art cannot offer a permanent refuge.

In 'Gertha's Lovers' another attempt is made to perpetuate the memory of two lovers. Olaf the king has died in battle, and his queen Gertha goes to the aspen grove where his body is lying and herself dies there. The people begin to build a church over the lovers' grave in their memory. For some reason it is never finished, but the partly completed building still stands:

to this day the mighty fragment, still unfinished, towering so high above the city roofs toward the sky, seems like a mountain cliff that went a-wandering once, and by earnest longing of the lowlanders was stayed among the poplar trees for ever. (I. 225)

This time there is no sense of impermanence, but the lasting memorial has been achieved only at the expense of completeness. Margaret and Amyot's tomb was finished down to the 'last lily' (I. 158) but did not survive. Not only, therefore, may art falsify the past. There is also a sense in which it can provide only a partial representation – and a suggestion that attempts at completion are liable to end in failure. It is the unfinished church which endures.

In 'The Story of the Unknown Church', at the end of a rapturous description of the flowers in the cloisters and churchyard, come two images which encapsulate Morris's interest in the possibility of art defying the processes of time. The first is an image from nature: the deadly nightshade plant which in the autumn produces all at the same time berries, flowers and leaves. The second image is also of a merging of what might be thought to be chronologically separated: a stone cross in the churchyard has carved on the one side Our Lord's birth, on the other his crucifixion. Morris provides no comment on the meaning of these images. Their juxtaposition seems to me to present a distinction between art and nature that was to become central to Morris's thought. The plant, combining as it so strangely does flowers and fruit, suggests a kind of permanence; of course each individual plant will die, but the species continues as each seed grows to fruition. The artefact combines birth and death, using symbols which suggest the possible redemption and immortality of man. Yet it, like the rest of the church, is ultimately destroyed by time. Perhaps the hope of eternal life it offers may be as illusory as its own permanence? Certainly in this story the cycle of nature's renewal has overcome man's efforts at building a lasting edifice:

No one knows now even where it stood, only in this very autumn-tide, if you knew the place, you would see the heaps made by the earth-covered ruins heaving the yellow corn into glorious waves. (I. 149)

In later work, especially in *The Earthly Paradise*, Morris returned obsessively to the question of whether man's attempts to cheat the operation of time, even through art, were not mocked by nature's insistent process of growth, decay, death and rebirth. In his early stories he is already adumbrating this theme.

The early romances

The complex responses to the past expressed in Morris's fiction are linked to his confused views about the temptation to withdraw from active involvement in contemporary society, which I have already outlined. In some states of mind he saw the past as a guide for present conduct; in others he embraced it as an escapist haven. These contradictory feelings relate to his doubts about the position of the artist who finds his vocation in a re-creation of the past. Can he ever really give life to the legendary or imaginative figures of his stories? Or does the act of artistic creation destroy vitality by attempting to capture and fix? And even if he can give vital expression, in what sense may he be said to have embodied the past in any truthful, or lasting, manner? Largely through the images of carved tombs, Morris approaches these questions in his early fiction – and as we have seen, provides answers which are at best tentative.

III

Doubts relating to the problems which beset the kind of artist he knows himself to be might seem to offer very adequate thematic material for a young author. Yet Morris has a further topic, in developing which he is again at variance with his *Oxford and Cambridge Magazine* colleagues. Not only is he aware of the difficulties and dangers of recalling or trying to dwell in the past. He is also doubtful even about the existence of such values as his friends and mentors perceived in medieval society. His fellow authors accept that what was good in former ages remains good, and that a return to medieval ways of ordering society would be a change for the better. Morris wrote two stories, 'The Hollow Land' and 'Golden Wings', which deliberately undercut the beliefs and conventions of the Middle Ages and present them as inadequate standards by which to live. 'Golden Wings' is the simpler of the two stories, and may be considered first.

The story begins with a quotation from the romance of Sir Perceval, as given in *The Thornton Romances* (1844) edited by James Orchard Halliwell:

> Lef lythes to me,
> Two wordes or three,
> Of one that was faire and fre,
>   And felle in his fighte. (1. 291)[5]

The narrator's first words compare his situation with Perceval's:

I suppose my birth was somewhat after the birth of Sir Perceval of Galles, for I never saw my father, and my mother brought me up quaintly. (1. 291)

Sir Perceval is that common figure in medieval romance, a child brought up in ignorance of courtly society.[6] Perceval's father is killed in a tournament, and his mother takes her son to live in a lonely forest, determined that he shall not die in the same way. Yet, as the author of the romance says, nature cannot be denied its course, and as soon as the boy sees knights in armour for the first time he captures and tames a horse, and to his mother's horror rides away to find the court. The romance tells of his adventures, his uncanny and indeed magical powers of self-defence, his marriage and his reception into Arthur's courtly society. He successfully upholds knightly values to the end, for he is eventually killed fighting in the Holy Land.

Morris's hero, Lionel, seems set to follow a similar pattern. Although brought up in poverty and obscurity, he is told by his mother that he is a king's son. When he has (almost accidentally) killed one of his enemies, his mother gives him a glorious mail-coat, helmet, shield and sword. Their beauty awakens in him a passionate desire for knightly power and fame. He sets out to win honour. But despite his glittering armour, he signally fails to achieve such success and recognition as are attained by Perceval in *The Thornton Romances*. His first exploit is to fight in a tournament, and as we might have expected he begins by overthrowing all his opponents. However, at the end of the day he is himself ignominiously beaten, and carried off the field for dead. After this failure, he is only too eager to go to the aid of an old man whose son has been killed by the wicked Red Knight. He rides away full of confidence:

it never once seemed possible to me that I should be worsted. (1. 300)

His attempt is a disaster. The Red Knight first casually kills the old man, and is about to do the same for Lionel when rescue arrives in the shape of Sir Guy le Bon Amant. To add to Lionel's humiliation, Sir Guy was the victor in the tournament, and is also betrothed to Alys, the king's daughter, with whom Lionel has fallen hopelessly in love.

The early romances

Lionel has failed in war, but at this point in the story it seems that he is after all to be lucky in love. Lady Alys is to marry Sir Guy because he has saved her life and fought on behalf of her honour, as Lancelot so frequently did for Guenevere. Unfortunately, in another departure from the conventions of romance, she loves not Sir Guy but the unsuccessful Lionel. By this time Lionel has become almost incapable of independent action, since everything he has chosen to do has turned out for the worst. Alys takes the initiative; the lovers elope, are married, and are besieged in their castle by the king and Sir Guy. Lionel and Alys become quite withdrawn from their society, living for each other and looking forward to a beautiful but illusory future. At the end of the story the besiegers break into the castle, and Lionel (in another of Morris's sudden twists of the expected plot) is brutally killed before Alys's eyes.

This story seems to be a rejection of the conventional motifs of chivalry. Starting from a typical romance beginning, Morris shows what might really happen to an ordinary man who was unable to cope with adverse circumstances. Even in his elopement and marriage Lionel is entirely passive, doing as Alys and her friends tell him. His one moment of assertive strength is during the siege, when a soldier on the opposing side calls Alys a whore. Lionel seizes and violently kills him in a sudden access of power. Even this gesture is futile, for he is surrounded and nearly killed, and has to be rescued, with considerable difficulty, by a friend. Lionel's heraldic device is a pair of golden wings on a blue ground. This is an emblem of his aspirations, none of which are fulfilled. When he realizes that the castle can hold out no longer, he flings his shield and helm over the battlements, takes off his armour and breaks his sword, destroying the beautiful trappings of chivalry which first inspired him. Yet not even love, his one remaining desire, is left to him. We never discover who his father was and which kingdom he should have inherited, qualifying himself to marry the princess. The story of Lionel is at all points the antithesis of a medieval romance.

At the beginning of the story the image of the tomb returns. Lionel tells us that near his home a battle was once fought; the graves of the slain are deep pits close to the church. The cause of the battle was a quarrel about a woman, and she is buried in the church. She lies:

in a most fair tomb; her image was of latoun gilt, and with a colour on it; her hands and face were of silver, and her hair, gilded and most curiously wrought, flowed down from her head over the marble. (1. 291)

The contrast between this gorgeous image, which after all is only a statue, and the unmarked graves of those who died for the sake of the woman, emphasizes the futility of all such battles. Lionel is later to die himself in a similar cause. Morris wishes to demonstrate that the realities behind medieval romance were harsh and brutal. Although he enjoys the outward show of medievalism, as his vivid descriptions of the tomb and Lionel's armour make clear, he knows that the past is no place to which to retreat. Within the story itself escape is impossible, as Lionel and Alys discover. 'Golden Wings' makes us question the value of setting up the past as an ideal by reminding us that the conventional ways of evoking the past are distortions and evasions of the truth. Perceval is acceptable in romance, but in reality Lionel's disastrous fate is much more likely.

'The Hollow Land' is the longest and most complex of the *Oxford and Cambridge Magazine* stories, and deals once more with the difference between the trappings of chivalry and true honour. Again the narrator is the central character, and again the setting is an unspecified medieval period. Florian the narrator is the younger son of the Lord of the House of the Lilies, and the plot turns on a feud between this House and that of Red Harald. The feud arises when Harald's mother Swanhilda is going in state to marry King Urrayne, with Florian's elder brother Arnald as one of her pages. As the procession is leaving the town Arnald stumbles, and the canopy he is helping to carry catches on Swanhilda's head-dress. In a fury she strikes him over the mouth with her sceptre. Arnald and Florian swear revenge for this public dishonour. Years later, when Swanhilda has killed Urrayne and reigns in his stead, Florian and Arnald find an opportunity to avenge themselves. Going by night to the town where she lives, they capture and execute her. When Harald tries to bring judgement on the House of the Lilies for the murder, the members of the House defy him, and begin a kind of guerrilla war on his lands and cattle from their mountain stronghold.

To Florian, and at first to the reader, the expedition to kill Swanhilda is an exciting and heroic adventure. He and Arnald believe they are perfectly within their rights to take revenge both for the insult offered to their family many years ago and for the queen's murder of her husband. Florian tells her that he is taking her 'to judgment' (1.261), and a mock trial is staged with Arnald as judge and executioner, taking his warrant for the action from his men who are standing round:

'Fifteen years ago, when I was just winning my spurs, you struck me, disgracing me before all the people: you cursed me, and meant that curse well enough. Men of the House of the Lilies, what sentence for that?' 'Death!' they said. 'Listen! Afterwards you slew my cousin your husband, treacherously, in the most cursed way ... Men of the House of the Lilies, what sentence for that?' 'Death!' they said. (1.262)

Much play is made by Arnald of the fact that Swanhilda will die like a queen (he will himself behead her) and will receive honourable burial. Yet throughout this section of the story there are hints that the men of the House of the Lilies have been led by their code of honour into grave errors about their rights to avenge themselves. When Swanhilda asks Arnald for his 'warrant from God' (1.262) for his action, he can only hold up his sword; this 'might is right' attitude may seem to us inadequate justification for murder. The killing takes place on Christmas Eve, and one of Morris's most beautiful lyrics is placed before the capture of Swanhilda, reminding us of the contrast between Christian ideals and the vengeance being carried out:

> Queen Mary's crown was gold,
> King Joseph's crown was red,
> But Jesus' crown was diamond
> That lit up all the bed
> *Mariae Virginis* (1.259)

To emphasize this contrast, the murderers are helped by the prior of a monastery outside Swanhilda's town, who bears a grudge against her. He covers the soldiers' armour with white albs, so that they shall not be seen against the snow. When some of the queen's guard try to resist the onslaught, Florian discovers an unholy joy in fighting. One of the guard strikes him in the ribs with the flat of his sword, and he responds with a berserk anger:

I was quite wild with rage; I turned, almost fell upon him, caught him by the neck with both hands and threw him under the horse-hoofs, sighing with fury. (1.260)

This horrible overreaction to a very mild attack shows the inadequacy of the murderers' motives. Our belief that they were right to take justice into their own hands is further shaken when we see them the next day defying the forces of justice. All the dependants of the House have been gathered to hear Mass in St Mary's Church. As the choir sings the Kyrie this plea for God's mercy is interrupted by news that Red Harald and the king are approaching the church. Instantly the Abbot and priests turn themselves into soldiers; like Florian and his men on the previous evening, they are wearing armour under their vestments. The king asks Arnald to submit the case to 'the judgment of God' (1. 266). Arnald can understand no judgement but that of force, and offers to settle the quarrel by single combat with the old king. When this is refused he contemptuously leads his men out of the city to their refuge in the hills, despising the king's forces for not daring to stop them.

This first section of the story, showing a refusal to accept any law but that of might, has made us sceptical about the value of the code of honour to which the House of the Lilies adheres. In Chapter Two we see some of the members of the House beginning to question their right to execute judgement. Finding themselves at last trapped by Red Harald and his followers, all but Florian are totally demoralized. Hugh, an old retainer, is blunt about his feelings:

thirty years ago I thought this: that the House of the Lilies would deserve anything in the way of bad fortune that God would send them. (1. 268–9)

Arnald cries 'O unhappy, unhappy, from that day forward!' (1. 268). At last even Florian admits to a doubt:

Had our House been the devil's servants all along? I thought we were God's servants. (1. 269)

With his enemies in this state of depression, Red Harald easily takes his revenge, and Arnald and Florian are killed. Might has finally been proved not to be right after all.

The story might have ended with the disillusion and death of the hero, as does 'Golden Wings'. However, in this case Morris continues to follow Florian's fortunes in what might be described as Purgatory, where he learns the truth about judgement. First he finds himself in a beautiful land, perhaps Paradise or Eden, where he meets a maiden called Margaret. She is dressed in white and scarlet, the iconographical colours of Christ, and she explains to Florian that God was punishing Swanhilda and had no need of Florian's intervention. Unlike Florian she pities Swanhilda, and gives him a new perspective on his action:

Unjust? yes, truly unjust enough to take away life and all hope from her; you have done a base cowardly act, you & your brother here, disguise it as you may: you deserve all God's judgments. (1. 280)

There is no indication that Florian really understands what she is saying, and it is presumably because of this that he is taken from the Hollow Land and made to act out his sins again. Awaking in what seems to be the real world, he swims and is nearly drowned in a river, and then finds himself naked in the ruined hall of his father. A man is painting the walls of the hall in vivid yellow and red, and his subject is the story of Arnald, Florian, Red Harald and Swanhilda. The man tells Florian that he is painting God's judgements. Florian replies that if so he is using the wrong colours. They fight, and Florian seems to have killed his adversary. He finds bread and wine in the corner of the hall, and eats and drinks; then he paints his enemy's face red and yellow. Suddenly he is struck with pity, washes off the paint, and tends his victim until he recovers. The man then begins to teach Florian painting.

The passage across the river seems to be a re-enactment of birth and baptism. Florian is beginning his life again, and – as in life – he is confronted by Red Harald (we are told that this is the painter's name). The colours he is using to paint God's judge-ments, red and yellow, are in the early part of the story used to represent evil and violence. Red Harald's name and the scarlet clothes he wears are examples of this, and so is Arnald's red hair, which is contrasted with the saintly white locks of the old king. In the church Arnald sits under a gold-fringed canopy, and it was just such a canopy which he carried above Swanhilda at the beginning of the story. She wears a golden crown and carries a gilded sceptre, and when she strikes Arnald the red blood runs over his clothes. So when Harald in the Purgatorial vision claims that red and gold are the colours of Hell, we are prepared to accept them as images of the lust for power which causes evil on earth.[7] As he did in his previous life, Florian refuses to recognize the nature of evil, and acts out once more his conflict with Red Harald's family. This time he seems to have been successful, and celebrates his success by painting Harald in his own damning colours. Yet he has also consumed bread and wine, eucharistic symbol of the mercy of God, and now at last for the first time he can feel pity. He helps his enemy back to life, and has taken the first step in his regeneration.

He finds it extremely difficult to learn to paint:

Then I tried to learn painting till I thought I should die; but at last learned it through very much pain and grief. (I. 287)

As time goes on, Harald and Florian begin to understand the true nature of God's judgements; they are able to transmute the primary colours of red and yellow into their derivatives purple and green. Eventually they watch a pageant of the return of a dead king to his country. The main colours borne by the procession are scarlet and purple, combining the colours of Hell and those of the transformed or modified judgement. There are also maidens dressed in Christ's colours of red and white. The dead king, of whom we are told he 'counted but as one' (I. 288), would seem to represent Christ. His crest is two hands clasped together as if praying for forgiveness. When this procession has passed by, with its suggestion of a combination of justice and mercy attained through the death of Christ, Florian finds he can return to the Hollow Land and Margaret. She leads him to the gates of a glorious palace:

then we walked together toward the golden gates, and opened them; and no man gainsaid us. And before us lay a great space of flowers. (I. 290)

Here the story ends; Florian has expiated his sin and received the mercy of Heaven.

In one of his few attempts at mysticism, Morris has given us in 'The Hollow Land' a description of acceptance into the Kingdom of God. Yet even here he is unable to present us with unalloyed optimism. For one thing Red Harald, who might seem to have completed his own Purgatory, is unable to reach the Hollow Land with Florian. He is turned back by a weeping woman in red, who was also seen by Florian before he was expelled from the land. This figure seems to indicate that sin still has a hold on Harald. More importantly, the ecstatic ending of the story is at odds with the beginning, where the narrator speaks of having lost the Hollow Land. He describes it in terms which confirm its place as a symbol of goodness and peace:

Lives passed in turmoil, in making one another unhappy; in bitterest
misunderstanding of our brothers' hearts, making those sad whom God
has not made sad: alas, alas! what chance for any of us to find the
Hollow Land? what time even to look for it? Yet who has not dreamed
of it? Who ... has not felt the cool waves round his feet, the roses
crowning him, and through the leaves of beech and lime the many
whispering winds of the Hollow Land? (I. 254)

The sense of loss in this passage conflicts with the idea that
Florian is at the end of the story received into Heaven. Perhaps
he is speaking during the time between his rebirth and the
procession of the dead king. This seems unlikely, for there is no
indication that the chronological sequence of the story is interrupted or that Florian does anything while away from the Land
except learn his lesson about judgement. Perhaps Morris began
the story not knowing what the ending was to be, and found a
vein of unusual optimism after the first part was printed (the
tale was divided between two issues of the magazine). Whatever
the reason, the memory of this depressing opening casts a chill
over the happy ending of the tale. If Morris was truly suggesting
that even Heaven is a temporary state, he was making a daring
attack on theological teaching, and demonstrating with the
utmost clarity his inability to believe in ultimate happiness. He
was questioning not only conventional moral values but the
basic tenets of Christianity.[8]

IV

It would have been strange if Morris, steeped as he already was
in the art and literature of the Middle Ages, had not followed
what was a growing trend in mid-Victorian literature and drawn
on medieval life for inspiration in his own fiction. Not only was
he most emotionally at home when re-creating the past; he was
beginning to see how such medieval literary techniques as
colour-symbolism could be employed in nineteenth-century
writing. Like the medieval romance writers, Morris used the
actions and appearance of his characters, and the everyday
objects around them, for the symbolical expression of complex
psychological states or ideas. Thus in romance, if a knight fights
against a dragon, the event is not only a moment in the story,
but also refers to the combat with evil which is going on in the

man's own soul. A rose in a garden represents love; the wall around the garden reminds us that love is difficult to attain. In the same way Morris may describe an elaborate tomb, both delighting in the sensuous beauty of the object and using it as an image of the futility of artistic attempts to preserve the past. Morris's use of colour is likewise reminiscent of medieval literary style. Instead of telling us that Margaret in 'The Hollow Land' is an expression of the justice and mercy of Christ, he merely describes her as dressed in red and white. It is for the reader to make the necessary connections. In his work for the *Oxford and Cambridge Magazine* Morris gradually developed his powers of description and his use of a symbolic method which derived from medieval romance.

It is all the more striking that Morris was unable at this period to accept the romance form as a whole, with all its implications. For the most notable thing about Morris's stories is that not one of them (with the possible and ambiguous exception of 'The Hollow Land') is a formally perfect romance. Many of the romance patterns and motifs are there: typical and undeveloped characters, the quest as a structural imperative, acceptance of the supernatural, a degree of symbolism, the use of distant and strange settings and so on. But what is missing is the necessary romance happy ending. And here we see how Morris's complex feelings about his own artistic endeavours have a radical effect on his art form. The narrative disjunctions, the idiosyncrasies of syntax, the impression of confusion and disorientation so obvious in the early stories are symptoms of Morris's doubts about the potential and value of his art. Romance asserts the possibility of reconciliation and achievement, placing a final image of lasting harmony as a counterbalance to its depiction of struggle and evil. Yet even if one excepts 'The Hollow Land', the overwhelming impression made by Morris's early stories is that moments of happiness are at best transitory. Disillusion and death are more powerful forces. The tension between Morris's love of romance and his inability to believe in its most important implication gives the weird, flawed, passionate stories of his early period much of their effectiveness. He seems always to be straining after a resolution which he cannot allow himself to achieve. This is linked, as analysis of the stories shows, with Morris's belief that the past he loved so much was ineffectual when faced with the evils of the present. He can neither retreat into it nor use it as a weapon, as Carlyle and Ruskin exhorted him to do. He can only celebrate it, reminding us all the time that what he is describing is mere vanity and illusion. Like Lionel's jewelled armour, his literary creation cannot protect him from harsh realities.

In 1858 Morris published a volume of poetry called *The Defence of Guenevere and Other Poems*, which contained several poems originally written for the *Oxford and Cambridge Magazine*. The collection shares with Morris's early stories a sense of futility. Many of the poems are concerned with the unpleasant realities behind the romantic façade of medieval legend. Morris took his inspiration partly from the *Chronicle* of Froissart; it has been said that Morris was heavily influenced by Froissart's 'embittered and disillusioned attitude toward the viciousness and savagery of medieval warfare'.[9] Morris begins 'The Haystack in the Floods' with a vivid evocation of misery which is a long way from the heroism of fantasy:

> Along the dripping leafless woods,
> The stirrup touching either shoe,
> She rode astride as troopers do;
> With kirtle kilted to her knee,
> To which the mud splash'd wretchedly;
> And the wet dripp'd from every tree.   (1.124)

In this poem love is defeated by brutal death, and the heroine is doomed to be tried and drowned as a witch. Similarly in the dramatic poem 'Sir Peter Harpdon's End' the realities of treachery, bitterness and disillusion in the Hundred Years War are brought out with considerable force. The hero, affiliated to the now losing English side, has to watch the gradual erosion of his hopes for fame and victory and to suffer an ignominious death. In 'The Eve of Crecy' Morris describes a French knight's desire for success in battle and the love of his lady; nothing in the narrator's words detracts from the feeling of optimism, but the title grimly reminds us that the knight will in all probability be killed the next day. There are many examples in *The Defence of Guenevere* of Morris's refusal to be blinded by the surface glitter of romance, his determination to make his readers feel the true misery of life in the violent Middle Ages.

Linked with this idea is a feeling that aspirations are futile.

The early romances

Once Morris and his friends had seen Sir Galahad as their patron saint. Now Morris shows Sir Galahad regretting that he has given up the love of women for a sterile, comfortless chastity which will in the end achieve nothing. Galahad is comforted by a vision of Christ and his saints, but the final words of the poem 'Sir Galahad: a Christmas Mystery' emphasize how ineffectual is the painful struggle to attain an unreachable ideal:

> everywhere
> The knights come foil'd from the great quest, in vain;
> In vain they struggle for the vision fair.   (l. 30)

Although we remember that Sir Galahad and the speaker of these words (Sir Bors) do at last see the Grail, we remember also that Galahad pays for the privilege with his life, and that the Grail is never brought back to Arthur's court. At this stage in his development Morris was convinced that idealism was usually doomed to failure.

Another most important theme in *The Defence of Guenevere* is again the preservation of the past. Some critics have felt that Morris's sole intention was to bring to life people and situations of medieval history and legend. Laurence Perrine says of the eponymous poem:

Morris has merely taken one of Malory's characters in a moment of stress and brought her intensely alive. His task has been not to excuse or to blame, but to vivify.[10]

The theme of 'Concerning Geffray Teste Noire' is precisely the act of artistic animation. The narrator, waiting in an ambush, finds the bones of a murdered man and woman. He proceeds to imagine their story, and to cover their bones with metaphorical flesh. He conjures up a picture of the lady:

> I saw you drink red wine
> Once at a feast; how slowly it sank in,
> As though you fear'd that some wild fate might twine
> Within that cup, and slay you for a sin.
>
> And when you talk your lips do arch and move
> In such wise that a language new I know
> Besides their sound; they quiver, too, with love
> When you are standing silent.   (l. 80)

As an extension of this imaginative re-creation the narrator has the bones buried in a fine tomb. The image is familiar, and as usual the attempt to create permanence by art is contrasted with the realities of time and death. The final words tell us that the sculptor who carved the figures on the tomb is dead, and the narrator himself is approaching death. In a further irony, the narrator asks his hearer to tell the story to Froissart, so that it may be immortalized in the *Chronicle*; but the tale is not in Froissart at all, although the circumstances of the ambush are to be found there. Morris is as sceptical as ever of the possibilities of art capturing and preserving the past.

The image of suspended animation and sterility is strongly present in *The Defence of Guenevere*. 'The Blue Closet' was inspired by a water-colour by Rossetti, and describes two women trapped in a castle from which they can escape only in death. In the poem 'Golden Wings' the opening is an evocation of happiness. Within a walled garden is a castle where sorrow never comes, and where men and women live a peaceful, idyllic life. One of the women, however, is unsatisfied, and longs for her lover to come to her from outside the charmed enclosure. Eventually she goes out to seek him. This action, in some unspecified way, brings violence and sorrow within the castle walls. The final image is of the immobility of death:

> Inside the rotting leaky boat
> You see a slain man's stiffen'd feet.　　(I. 123)

Jehane, the heroine, hears a song before she attempts to escape from the castle; its theme is Arthur on the magic island Avallon, unable to die but nevertheless growing old. As long as he remains there Arthur has eternal life, but it is a futile existence; he is only waiting for the moment when he can break out of the island and act again in the world. This seems to be Jehane's desire too, but her rejection of the unchanging life of the castle leads to her death and the destruction of the beautiful place. This extremely complex poem is concerned with the problem of a good which is incapable of development opposed to an evil which is destructive but contains elements of life-giving force. Is Jehane right to seek love at the cost of her life? Although the prose 'Golden Wings' is not directly connected with the poem of the same name, failure of aspiration is common to both.

This cursory glance at some of the poems in *The Defence of Guenevere* is designed to show that they express many of the same preoccupations as the early stories. Although there are some happy endings in the book, the general feeling is one of depression and disillusion. Images of imprisonment, bondage, coldness and death are constantly present. On the surface of the poems are the colour and glitter of their medieval settings, but their meaning is in opposition to this decorative façade. The last poem in the sequence is taken from 'Frank's Sealed Letter', where it is a song sung by the statuesque and heartless Mabel. Now it is called 'In Prison':

> all alone,
> Watching the loophole's spark,
> Lie I, with life all dark,
> Feet tether'd, hands fetter'd
> Fast to the stone,
> The grim walls, square-letter'd
> With prison'd men's groan. (I. 145)

Morris had spent several years writing about the futility of artistic or practical attempts to improve life, and the sterility of escape into the only thing which delighted him, the past. It is not perhaps surprising that after *The Defence of Guenevere* he published nothing for nearly ten years.

CHAPTER 2

'The dread eternity': *The Earthly Paradise*

Morris's ten-year silence may be partly explained by his doubts about the usefulness of art. It is also possible that he was discouraged from publishing by the critical reaction to *The Defence of Guenevere*, which was in general extremely unfavourable. Reviewers complained of the poems' obscurity, formlessness and general lack of relevance to contemporary life; the notice in the *Athenaeum* (probably by H. F. Chorley) declares that *Guenevere* 'shows how far affectation may mislead an earnest man towards the fog-land of Art'.[1] Although there were a few favourable comments (notably a review in the *Literary Gazette*, probably by Richard Garnett)[2] sales of the book languished. Perhaps Morris felt that the reception of his poems justified his artistic pessimism.

He did not, however, stop writing. Morris's literary work during the twenty years which followed *The Defence of Guenevere* may be seen partly as a quest for a viable form which would adequately embody the things he still felt it necessary to say, despite his reservations about art. After 'Golden Wings' he abandoned prose fiction until the early 1870s, when he attempted a novel with a contemporary setting. He gave this up in disgust, describing it to Burne-Jones's sister-in-law Mrs Baldwin as 'a specimen of how not to do it'.[3] Immediately after finishing *The Defence of Guenevere*, he embarked on a series of dramatic poems entitled *Scenes from the Fall of Troy*, in which he traces the disillusionment of the Trojan heroes and the destruction of their city. This work was also left unfinished. In 1872 appeared *Love is Enough: or, the Freeing of Pharamond*,[4] another dramatic poem formally related to the medieval morality play. It shows considerable mastery and inventiveness in dealing with metrical patterns, but the argument and characterization are unconvincing. Having lost faith in romance, Morris seems at this period of his life unable to weld form and content into a satisfying whole.

Yet at this time he produced the book which was to bring him lasting fame as a poet. During the 1860s he was working on a series of narrative poems based on classical and medieval themes, and in 1867 he published the first of these: *The Life and Death of Jason*, an epic in seventeen parts. It had grown too long for its place in the proposed collection and was issued separately as a test of public and critical opinion. It was well received, and Morris's next publications were the twenty-four tales which make up *The Earthly Paradise*. This appeared in three volumes between 1868 and 1870, and was an immediate and pronounced success. It established Morris's reputation as one of the foremost poets of his day. The long and elaborate work appealed to the Victorian taste for substantial narrative poems; it was welcomed especially for its presentation of Greek myths in a form suitable for family reading. Gone from Morris's style were the unsettling complexities, hiatuses and vividly startling images found in *The Defence of Guenevere*. Instead he had concentrated on producing a clear and simple narrative line. More recent critics have tended to reverse the early reviewers' judgements, preferring the idiosyncrasies of *Guenevere* to the admittedly sometimes soporific blandness of the *Earthly Paradise* narratives. Yet, as so often with Morris, surface smoothness and technical skill belie certain tensions which may be detected when the poems are more rigorously examined. *The Earthly Paradise*, despite the early reviewers' opinions, is not a consolatory or undemanding work. On the contrary, through plot, imagery and structure the book requires its reader to face the problem of time and to consider the value of man's constant search for a way of evading time's depredations – the theme so important in Morris's early poetry and prose. And as in those earlier works, the prevailing emotion is one of cynical distrust in the face of any claim that man can find a refuge from the process of change. Once again we are asked to consider the role of the artist, he whose creations may be seen as potentially untouched by time. As before, Morris can react only ambiguously to any such suggestion.

Yet in order to discuss these ideas he chooses again a form based on medieval models. In a poem concerned radically to examine concepts of escapism, he still searches in the past for the stories and the literary structures which provide the basis for his own art. By doing so he aligns himself with those in his poems who – perhaps fatally – turn from their own time to search elsewhere for patterns by which they hope to order their lives. In criticizing their response, Morris ironically calls into question the validity of his own artistic practice.

I

Morris claimed Chaucer as a source of inspiration for *The Earthly Paradise*, and the arrangement of the poems owes something to *The Canterbury Tales*. In the Prologue, we are transported from the dreariness of modern England to a 'nameless city in a distant sea' (III. 3), inhabited by a race of Greek origin which retains its language, religion and customs. To this island comes a band of men who, many years before, fled from the Black Death then devastating Europe to seek the fabled land of undying bliss, the Earthly Paradise. They tell to their Greek hosts the story of their wanderings and miseries, and are offered a home on the island. They and the elders of the city arrange to meet twice monthly for a feast, at which one of the Greeks or one of the Wanderers will tell the others a tale. There then follow twenty-four stories, twelve of Greek and twelve of medieval European provenance, supposedly told at the feasts which take place during a whole year. Volume One contains the stories for March to August, Volume Two (published in 1869 with the imprint of 1870) those for September to November, and Volume Three those for December to February.

This carefully organized framework allows Morris plenty of scope to tell his favourite stories. The Prologue, however, does not merely provide a plausible excuse for collecting together twenty-four disparate tales. It announces the theme of the entire work, to which all the other poems will relate. It opens with some of Morris's most-anthologized lines:

> Forget six counties overhung with smoke,
> Forget the snorting steam and piston stroke,
> Forget the spreading of the hideous town;
> Think rather of the pack-horse on the down,
> And dream of London, small and white and clean. (III. 3)

The reader, thus exhorted to clear from his mind his modern problems and the ugliness of nineteenth-century industrialization, is taken first to Chaucer's London (much idealized) and then to the beautiful island of the Greeks. The tale we hear is of men who also attempted to escape from the horrors of their own period, though in their case freedom is to be attained by actual physical activity, not through aesthetic experience. Menaced by the plague, the Wanderers decide to flee from Norway to find the Land of Everlasting Youth. By doing so they are initiating a search for something more than a refuge from a specific evil, the Black Death. Their goal is a land where death itself can be evaded. This becomes clear when Rolf, the leader of the Wanderers, remembers his feelings of delirious delight when he believed they were approaching the land they desired:

> Ah, then it was indeed when first I knew,
> When all our wildest dreams seemed coming true,
> And we had reached the gates of Paradise
> And endless bliss, at what unmeasured price
> Man sets his life, and drawing happy breath,
> I shuddered at the once familiar death.   (III. 28)

The Wanderers wish to escape from their own mortality. They learn, in pain and sorrow, that no such escape exists. The Prologue shows Rolf and his companions undergoing a series of adventures which teach them that their quest was in vain. By the time they reach the Greek island Rolf has accepted the futility of his desire, and can look back ironically on his former self. He begins his story with the gloomy words:

> Masters, I have to tell a tale of woe,
> A tale of folly and of wasted life.   (III. 6)

Yet he still feels the old fear of death, the old wish to find an escape from it.

Morris has taken up his former theme of the difficulties and dangers of retreat into the past, and extended it into a discussion of escapism in general. To do so he uses the image of an Earthly Paradise, which he first employed when Svend and his brethren sailed away to find a new land in the west. The concept of a place on earth where men lived an idyllic life, free from death and pain, was present in Hebrew and classical mythology, and was taken up with enthusiasm by medieval writers. St Brendan and Alexander the Great were supposed to have found it; the author of Mandeville's *Travels* claimed to have approached very near. Medieval stories abound with such places as the magic island

Avallon, the Celtic Tír na n-Óg or Land of the Young, and the land from which the hero's lover comes in Marie de France's *Lai of Lanval*.[5] The Earthly Paradise stands in Morris's poem for the object of man's escapist aspirations; it is a symbol of mankind's longing for a better life. Morris, however, as in the story 'Golden Wings' and the *Guenevere* poems, was concerned to show how a harsh reality conflicts with the romantic desires of his heroes.

Morris wrote two almost completely different Prologues to *The Earthly Paradise*. The first version, unpublished in his lifetime, is written in the jaunty, four-stress ballad metre which he perfected in *Guenevere* and has vivid imagery in the style of the earlier volume. In this poem the adventures of the Wanderers are similar to those of sailors in Irish legend who sought the Land of Everlasting Youth. They visit a series of islands, where they see various mysterious and magical sights or have strange adventures. One land is frozen in a state of suspended animation; on another stands a city eternally burning but never consumed. In the second version of the Prologue there are none of these episodes from mythology. Instead the story is told in a spirit of prosaic realism. It is as if Morris were denying himself any potential escape into poetic fantasy, just as the Wanderers are denied release from death. They sneak away from their plague-ridden city, afraid that those who have to stay and die will prevent them leaving. This scarcely seems a propitious opening to a romantic quest. Soon after their departure they meet in the English Channel the royal fleet of King Edward III and have an audience of him. The king offers them glory and excitement in his service, but they reject this legitimately chivalrous way of life in favour of their search. Their adventures are in no way romantic. On one island they find a dying king exposed on a hill-top, surrounded by the embalmed bodies of his servants. The appearance of the Wanderers causes the old man's death from shock. They suffer great physical hardship, and are continually involved in battles with unfriendly natives. Understandably, some of the Wanderers decide to give up the quest and sail home; others settle in the lands they have reached, take native wives, and resign themselves to a life of privation. Nicholas, who had the most intense vision of Paradise, sees his wife killed by savages, and himself dies just before the remnant of the band finds a final asylum in the Greek island. There is a tone of weary bitterness throughout this first poem; if it stood alone, one might see Morris as writing a dire warning against all aspiration, since hope is sure to be destroyed by cruel reality.

In one sense this is what he is doing in *The Earthly Paradise*, but his point of view is less simple than has so far been implied. The Prologue is not the only part of the sequence to deal with the futile search for immortality. All the succeeding poems are part of an extended meditation on the theme.[6] Some of the stories clearly relate directly to the quest of the Wanderers, notably 'The Story of Ogier the Dane' and 'The Hill of Venus' (based on the Tannhäuser legend), in both of which the hero does find an Earthly Paradise. In others the theme of 'the heart's desire' is dealt with in more general terms. In some tales the heroes seek the attainment of earthly bliss through love. The two kings whose stories are told in 'The Son of Croesus' and 'The Doom of King Acrisius' find that, like the Wanderers, they cannot evade fate. Morris unites his stories both by their related themes and by a series of recurrent images. The most important of these is Paradise itself, presented in terms of a garden with a fruitful tree and a fountain or river. This traditional description appears in its pure form in the Garden of the Hesperides in 'The Golden Apples', and in horrible parody in the western island where Perseus kills Medusa (in 'The Doom of King Acrisius'). In many of the poems lovers meet in a garden; the adulterous Queen Sthenoboea attempts to entrap Bellerophon in an artificial garden with a golden tree and statues of animals. Traditionally, to win the fruit of Paradise one had to kill the guardian of the tree, which was a snake or monster. This image of evil and death, which suggests the difficulties which have to be overcome by the seeker after happiness, appears throughout the sequence in various guises. Both Perseus and Bellerophon kill a monster during their adventures; a monster attempts to prevent the consummation of Admetus's marriage to Alcestis; and in 'The Lady of the Land' the heroine herself appears as a dragon. On this occasion the hero has to kiss the monster instead of killing it, in order to release the Lady from her enchantment. He cannot bring himself to do so, and the story ends unhappily.

Thus this hero is the antithesis of all the successful dragon-slayers, as the snaky-haired Medusa is an ironic counterpart of all the beautiful heroines.

All the prevailing images are to be found in the first version of the Prologue. The Wanderers, for instance, fight with lions to save women who have been left, like Andromeda, to be devoured by the beasts; the battle takes place in a valley made beautiful by streams and wells and fruit-laden trees. This congruence of images makes clear the close relationship between the Prologue and the other poems. In the second version of the Prologue much of the linking imagery has disappeared. The Paradise symbol remains, however, for on the banner of one of the Wanderers' ships is painted the 'green, gold-fruited tree of Paradise' (III. 26). On the ship's sail appears the image of a lion. The unpublished Prologue ends with an unambiguous statement of the narrator's didactic aim in telling the remaining stories:

> Ye shall be shown how vain it is
>   To strive against the Gods and Fate,
> And that no man may look for bliss
>   Without an ending soon or late. (XXIV. 170)

Morris eventually chose to avoid such a dogmatic expression of the purpose of his twenty-four tales, yet they remain closely related, in theme and imagery, to his opening discussion of the difficulty of escape.

When we turn to the tales themselves, we find at first that the tone is less sombre than in the Prologue. In the opening stories, supposedly told during spring, love is sometimes triumphant. In 'Atalanta's Race' the hero Melanion has to run a race against his beloved in order to win her. The penalty for losing the race is death. Knowing that he is unlikely to beat Atalanta, Melanion contrives to win by distracting her attention, at crucial moments of the race, by throwing down in front of her three golden apples, the gift of Venus. Thus he is able to defeat her, to evade death and to gain his heart's desire. Golden apples are, of course, important components of the Paradise motif. Melanion achieves his goal, it is suggested, because he is prepared to face death – indeed, to run strongly towards it – for the sake of his desire. In later stories the need to be prepared to die in the quest will be symbolized in the battle with the monster; many of the heroes will be less able than the youthful and hopeful Melanion to come to terms with potential destruction.

'Atalanta's Race' is one of the few poems in *The Earthly Paradise* with an unequivocally happy ending. Yet even here shadows fall over the lovers' bliss. The elders listening to the story take a rather sceptical view of the value of Melanion's prize:

> the end of life so nigh,
> The aim so little, and the joy so vain.   (III. 105)

After the March stories this emphasis on the fragility of man's earthly happiness is increasingly present. Perseus wins Andromeda, but the tale of their love is undercut by the suggestion that it cannot last:

> Love while ye may; if twain grow into one
> 'Tis for a little while; the time goes by,
> No hatred 'twixt the pair of friends doth lie,
> No troubles break their hearts – and yet, and yet –
> How could it be? we strove not to forget;
> Rather in vain to that old time we clung,
> Its hopes and wishes round our hearts we hung;
> We played old parts, we used old names – in vain;
> We go our ways, and twain once more are twain.   (III. 229)

Disillusionment soon takes a strong hold on the tales, although some do still have a temporarily happy ending. (In the case of Psyche the happiness is permanent, but she cannot find it on earth; she must lose her humanity and become a goddess.) In 'The Love of Alcestis' the heroine gives up her life for her husband, but Hercules does not, as in the legend, wrestle with death for her soul; she cannot return to life. In 'The Lady of the Land', as already mentioned, the lover fails to win his lady, being too terrified of the dragon shape she is forced to assume. Even when the lovers in a story do seem to achieve happiness, somewhere a jarring note is struck. When Acontius gains Cydippe, the priests of Diana show their cynicism about love:

> O fools, who know not all has sworn
> That those shall ever be forlorn
> Who strive to bring this thing to pass –
> So is it now, as so it was,
> And so it shall be evermore,
> Till the world's fashion is passed o'er.   (V. 154)

At the end of 'Bellerophon in Lycia' the hero attains his heart's desire when he marries Philonoë, and feels:

> even as a man new made a God,
> When first he sets his foot upon the sod
> Of Paradise.   (VI. 277)

Yet the narrator immediately concludes the story with a lament that men, and love, fail in the end:

> That use, and long days dropping one by one,
> As the wan water frets away the stone,
> Should change desires of men, and what they bring,
> E'en while their hearts with sickening longing cling
> Unto the thought that they are still the same,
> When all they were is grown an empty name.   (VI. 277)

In *The Earthly Paradise* lovers can evade change only for a fleeting moment.

The most interesting of the stories in *The Earthly Paradise* are those in which the hero, unlike the Wanderers, finds the land of eternal happiness. They show the same variations in tone as the love stories, and are full of similar ambiguities. The Garden of the Hesperides, in 'The Golden Apples', naturally conforms most exactly to type, with its enclosure, stream, fruitful tree and guardian serpent; Hercules is successful in his attempt to gain the apples. The other heroes do not find their adventures so easy. The hero of 'The Land East of the Sun and West of the Moon', having lived with his fairy lover in her magic land, finds himself bereft of his beloved and of Paradise and has to seek for many weary years to regain them. He does at last find the Land East of the Sun and awakens his lover from the spell of immobility under which she had been held. Bharam, in 'The Man Who Never Laughed Again', is less fortunate. Unable to control his curiosity, although warned against the adventure, he enters a mysterious cavern through a locked door and finds himself in a beautiful land, where he marries the queen. A song implies that she and Bharam will enjoy everlasting bliss. Then a familiar fairy-tale motif is employed to darken the end of the story. The queen goes on a journey, forbidding Bharam to open a locked room. Of course he can no more resist this temptation than he could the first. He enters the chamber and drinks from the cup which he discovers there. He falls into a swoon, and

wakes outside the cavern, on the wrong side of the locked door
to which he no longer has the key. From that day to the end of
his life he never laughs. At one stage of Bharam's story, when he
has tried to put out of his mind the cavern and its adventure, his
desire for an ideal happiness is contrasted with life in the real
world:

> So amidst thoughts of pleasant life and ease,
> Seemed all things fair that eve; the peasant's door,
> The mother with the child upon her knees
> Sitting within upon the shaded floor
>
> ...
>
> at that sight those sweet vague hopes and wild
> Did he cast by, and in the darkness smiled
> For pleasure of the beauty of the earth,
> For foretaste of the coming days of mirth. (v. 177–8)

Yet Bharam cannot maintain his confidence in the satisfaction
of purely earthly joys, and his search for the dream of eternal
happiness ends in disaster – because he cannot control his
longing for something even better. Morris was interested
throughout his life in mankind's deep-rooted desire for a better
state, a greater happiness; signs of this theme are present in the
Oxford and Cambridge Magazine stories, and it remains one of
Morris's preoccupations until the final prose romances.
Through Bharam's unhappy search, Morris seems to be suggesting that man can only gain happiness by remaining content with
life as it is. Such appears to be the message also of 'The
Wanderers' and of many other poems in *The Earthly Paradise* –
the search for bliss is doomed not necessarily because it does not
exist, but because man is incapable of accepting and resting in
happiness when he finds it. Yet this restlessness, as Bharam
discovers, is as natural as the first impetus to take up the quest.
Indeed, it is the same impulse, eternally to seek what is beyond
and never to be content with what is. The pain that results from
our unending search for the unattainable is Morris's major
theme in *The Earthly Paradise*.

Another hero in the sequence who reaches the undying land is
Ogier the Dane, and like John in 'The Land East of the Sun ...' he
remains there at the end of the poem. Ironically, however, Ogier
is not seeking Avallon when he finds himself there. At the end of
a long and fruitful life he is wrecked on the Lodestone Rock, and

believes himself about to die. With a stoicism unusual in Morris's heroes, he accepts the fact of death as one of the gifts of God and looks forward to being received into Heaven:

> though his flesh might fear
> The coming change that he believed so near,
> Yet did his soul rejoice, for now he thought
> Unto the very heaven to be brought.   (IV. 221)

Instead he is wafted to Avallon to be the lover of Morgan le Fay. The glorious life he lives with Morgan (whose name, to those who know the Arthurian legends, carries a distinct suggestion of evil) is described at some length, but the narrator has to take considerable pains in his attempt to convince us that unchanging felicity is not, eventually, boring:

> everything was bright and soft and fair,
> And yet they wearied not for any change,
> Nor unto them did constancy seem strange.
> Love knew they, but its pain they never had,
> But with each other's joy were they made glad
>   ...
> Nor need they struggle after wealth and fame;
> Still was the calm flow of their lives the same,
> And yet, I say, they wearied not of it.   (IV. 234)

After a hundred years of this passionless Paradise, Ogier returns for a while to France to help the country against its enemies. He quickly forgets Avallon and is betrothed to the queen. She is the most attractive character in the poem. Discovering that the secret of Ogier's youth lies in the magic ring he wears, she resists the temptation to take it for herself and reign (like Morgan) in everlasting beauty. She chooses instead the pains and delights of earthly love. In doing so she also accepts the inevitability of change, old age and mortality – all of which Ogier is preserved from by the magic ring. He too seems content to live in an imperfect world; soon we are told that he no more remembers Avallon:

> Than the hot noon remembereth of the night,
> Than summer thinketh of the winter white.   (IV. 250)

In other parts of *The Earthly Paradise* the land of everlasting bliss is described by images of summer, while night and winter are associated with normal human life. Here, however, the eternal island is represented by night and winter, while real life has the qualities of daylight and sunshine. Morris seems to be standing the basis of the whole sequence on its head; he appears to be suggesting that an Earthly Paradise might not be desirable after all. Morgan eventually comes to fetch Ogier on his wedding morning and takes him back to Avallon. As they go she, the queen of Paradise, turns from Paris with a sigh. Does she too regret the loss of her mortality?

In the early prose tales and in *The Defence of Guenevere* Morris had been concerned with man's tenuous hold upon individual identity when this is assailed by time and change. He had offered solutions to the problem which were based on an acceptance of the processes of time rather than on a struggle to evade them. Through memory and history, in understanding one's own past and that of one's race, perhaps through re-enacting the past as Florian does in 'The Hollow Land', integration and security can be achieved. Alternatively, there is the possibility of searching for the new – a process favourably contrasted, in 'Svend and his Brethren', with a sterile embracing of a dead past. In *The Earthly Paradise* this image of a potential haven, a place of bliss to be sought for as a release from the evils of one's present existence, becomes the main focus of Morris's attention. Svend presumably succeeded in the quest; but in *The Earthly Paradise* the land of promise is much more elusive. Some seekers never find it. Others, like Bharam, find it and lose it. For Ogier, however, the tragedy is even greater. For him the golden land is attainable but unsatisfactory. It provides eternal youth, undying love. But in its changelessness, is it sterile? Only in 'real' France, where love is transitory and life finite, can deeds of heroism be performed.

Standing at the half-way point in *The Earthly Paradise*, 'Ogier the Dane' brings into focus one of the sequence's most important themes. Many of the work's heroes see time, change and death as their ultimate enemies. They seek a release from process. But we may remember that in Morris's early fiction stasis was an attribute of evil. At the centre of his vision of human life lies the paradox that although man is subject to terror in the face of mortality, it is death which makes youth, love and beauty so valuable. Morris's most characteristic poetic mood, at least in the period of *Guenevere* and *The Earthly*

Paradise, is a poignant sadness in contemplation of transitory earthly delight. Like his heroes, he longs to grasp and retain beauty, to preserve it from inevitable decline. Yet he knows that beauty is confirmed and magnified by its juxtaposition with the forces of change and our knowledge of its certain destruction:

> Ah, what begetteth all this storm of bliss
> But Death himself, who crying solemnly,
> E'en from the heart of sweet Forgetfulness,
> Bids us 'Rejoice, lest pleasureless ye die.'   (III. 82)

Thus time becomes both something to be escaped from, if possible, and also something to be welcomed as the agent of the very happiness it threatens. In *The Earthly Paradise*, and particularly in 'Ogier the Dane', Morris uses the image of a quest for eternal bliss in an unchanging land to remind us of the complex nature of our response to time. He warns us that to escape from time and change might, even if it were possible, result not in delight but in weariness and lifelessness.

The sequence, full as it is of characters who seek eternal life, contains one figure who cannot die. For Medusa, her destroyer Perseus is welcome as her deliverer from the torments of an undesired immortality.

II

It will by now be clear that *The Earthly Paradise* is by no means to be read merely as a collection of undemanding narratives. It is a work full of complexities and, fittingly, embodies them in a sophisticated structure. As the tales unfold, the reader must relate them not only to each other but also to the Prologue and to the story of the Wanderers. Each pair of tales is framed by short passages which place the stories according to the month of the year in which they are told and which record the reactions of the listeners to each narrative. Sometimes the narrator is named. Thus each story on the theme of the Earthly Paradise is ironically counterpointed by our knowledge that many of the story-tellers themselves are disappointed searchers after eternal bliss. There is also another point of reference which draws our attention away from the historical/mythical past in which the stories are told. Each month is characterized by a three-stanza lyric describing the changing aspect of nature as the months progress. These poems are assigned to no narrator and have no specific chronological reference either to the supposed date of the framing narrative or to any other period. Their style tends less towards medieval pastiche than that of the other *Earthly Paradise* poems. They have a certain timelessness too in that, although a shadowy story can be discerned if all twelve are read in sequence, their major function is reflective rather than narrative. They ensure that we consider the major tales in the context not just of the Prologue but also of an experience which reflects every man's relationship to nature and the seasons. Thus *The Earthly Paradise* seeks to universalize its message.

As might be expected, the mood of the 'months lyrics' is initially one of youthful hope – like Melanion's in the first March story. The poet (conventionally) sees the spring as an image of his own eager, vigorous enjoyment of life. March promises that winter is over and the poet looks forward to the delights to come. By May his longings seem to have been satisfied, since the lyric speaks of the arrival of love. June appears to provide a haven of peace and mutual affection. Indeed, the setting of the June poem – an inland stream 'whose hamlets scarce have names', comfortably secluded from 'the city's misery' (IV. 87) – is clearly another version of the Earthly Paradise. Like the other Paradises, therefore, its presentation is not lacking in ambiguities. Though it is far from the sea which as we have seen is an image in the book for the troubles and pains of living, there are hints that its idyllic quietness may not last:

> Calm is the sky with harmless clouds beset,
> No thought of storm the morning vexes yet. (IV. 87)

The poet is aware that his existence here is a 'rare happy dream' from which he may one day awake. Even earlier he was alerted to the knowledge that his happiness would be transitory. Amid the hope of the March poem is adumbrated the conviction, typical of Morris, that pleasure is only delightful because of the presence of death which will destroy it. In May the narrator sees a pageant celebrating the coming of love; but creeping along at the end of the procession are the ominous figures of Old Age and Death. So the poet's joy is precarious, menaced by change and mortality. And it is threatened also by an inability of the poet himself fully to accept it. In the face of death he might be expected to take an attitude of *carpe diem* – indeed, he believes in the March poem that he is being counselled to do precisely that. Yet he finds it difficult to obey, since even in moments of great joy he discovers himself restlessly longing for something even better:

> Ah, love! such happy days, such days as these,
> Must we still waste them, craving for the best. (IV. 187)

To live for today might be an answer to the problem of mortality, but it appears to be impossible. With these hints of the ephemeral and unsatisfactory nature of earthly delights, therefore, the 'months' poems provide yet another variant on the central thematic concern of *The Earthly Paradise*. By September the poet is already lamenting the loss of past joys; by December love is only a dream.

The 'months lyrics', then, express once more the futility of man's attempts to retain happiness. They do so chiefly by bringing into focus an aspect of the theme which was approached in 'The Story of the Unknown Church' and which now becomes of central importance. Unlike *The Earthly Paradise* tales themselves, which concentrate on narrative accounts of the loss of love or the failure of heroism, the 'months lyrics' are mainly concerned with the relationship between man and nature. It will be remembered that in 'The Story of the Unknown Church' the cornfields hiding almost all evidence of the existence of the church indicated the weakness of man's creations compared with the power of nature. The juxtaposition of the deceptively permanent-looking stone cross and the deadly nightshade plant containing the seeds of its own renewal was also related to this idea. In the 'months' poems our attention is brought pointedly to the contrast between man's dreams and hopes and the natural process. The relationship is a complex one. Early in the sequence the following of winter by spring and summer seems to confirm the poet's optimistic attitude to life. Soon, however, the evolving of the seasons insistently reminds him that like the year he too is moving from youth to old age and death. (The movement from spring to winter relates both to a single year in the poet's life and to his life as a whole.) It is reassuring to know that June will follow on the heels of the spring months; it is painful to realize, in September, that the best moments have irrevocably passed by. The fruitful trees (again the image is of the golden apples of Paradise) only mock the poet's sadness, for he himself is unfulfilled and can only look back, not forward to new life:

> Look long, O longing eyes, and look in vain!
> Strain idly, aching heart, and yet be wise,
> And hope no more for things to come again
> That thou beheldest once with careless eyes!
> Like a new-wakened man thou art, who tries
> To dream again the dream that made him glad
> When in his arms his loving love he had.   (v. 1)

In the poems of the winter months change becomes a recurrent preoccupation. The poet's mood wavers between two responses. Sometimes he attempts to reconcile himself to the loss of youth, seeking a calm and passionless withdrawal from the anguish of life and love. He claims to desire rest and release from the pain which being a feeling human being seems to involve. At other moments he rejects quietism, asserting that his humanity lies in his restless longing, his constant reaching out for emotional commitment even when it brings pain: 'How can I have enough of life and love?' (v. 122). In both these moods he finds his misery exacerbated by the contrast between him and the natural world. He cannot forget the process of time and live only for the moment, as the joyous birds do in the March poem, for he is inescapably aware of his own finite existence. Nature, on the other hand, is both constantly changing and eternally the same. As was implied by the nightshade image in 'The Story of the Unknown Church', growth involves death and rebirth; spring will return and new birds will sing in place of the old ones. For man alone an individualistic self-consciousness makes this natural process a horror, rather than an acceptable cycle:

> Yea, I have looked and seen November there;
> The changeless seal of change it seemed to be,
> Fair death of things that, living once, were fair;
> Bright sign of loneliness too great for me,
> Strange image of the dread eternity,
> In whose void patience how can these have part,
> These outstretched feverish hands, this restless heart? (v. 206)

In this most poignant expression of the theme, the November lyric, is summed up the central problem of the 'months' poems and of the whole *Earthly Paradise*. Nature is both changing and changeless. To mortal men, however, change can bring only the death of the personality – the 'dread eternity' in which passion can have no place. Such dissolution is unacceptable – but inescapable.

From such feelings stems the search of the Wanderers for an Earthly Paradise: a state in which nature has been arrested at a moment of beauty and from which change has been abolished. Yet if they find it, will they not lose what makes it valuable, their knowledge of time's process? And if life involves growth, the changeless Paradise can be no more than death-in-life. There is no solution, it seems, to this dilemma. In *The Earthly Paradise* Morris has developed ideas which were important in his early work. There he dramatized his awareness that to seek solace in the past for modern problems might be futile. In *The Earthly Paradise* this insight is extended. We are asked to recognize the longing, which all men share, to transcend the limits of our humanity, to achieve a state in which time and change cease to be threatening. To do so, Morris suggests, would be to cut ourselves off from nature, to become alienated from the sources of our own being. At this stage of his life, he seems to have seen no resolution to this problem. Time and change remain enemies against which the individual battles in vain.

As a young man Morris greatly enjoyed Shelley's poem 'The Skylark'. One reason for this rather uncharacteristic appreciation of a Romantic poem may have been that it expresses the pain caused by man's status as an intelligent animal, in contrast to the unselfconscious bird:

> We look before and after,
> And pine for what is not:
> Our sincerest laughter
> With some pain is fraught:
> Our sweetest songs are those that tell of saddest thought.[7]

These sentiments are remarkably similar to those with which Morris was for so long preoccupied. The tone of sadness which is detectable even at the happiest moments of *The Earthly Paradise* is the result of his feeling that we are doomed to suffer from the effects of our own human awareness.

III

In *The Earthly Paradise* Morris is once again concerned with problems of time, change and death. It will perhaps have been made clear already that his discussion of these themes is not effected by a logical progression of thought. The order and selection of the stories was to some extent random, as can be seen by comparing Morris's advertisement for *The Earthly Paradise* in *The Life and Death of Jason* with the eventual series. Of the twenty-four tales promised in the advertisement, only sixteen found their way into the finished work. Six of the others were written, or at least begun, and the other two never materialized at all. In Volume One of *The Earthly Paradise* Morris specified the twelve tales he intended to print in Volume Two, but again the list underwent considerable alteration before the two remaining volumes appeared.[8] Morris thus published the first half of his book without knowing precisely what was going to be in the second half. He also shows no desire to unify his poem by such obvious poetic devices as the use, perhaps, of a single metre. Some of the stories are in the heroic couplets of the printed Prologue, others in four-stress couplets, and the rest in rhyme royal. There is no detectable pattern in the choice of metre. Although most of the classically based poems are in rhyme royal or heroic couplets, one is in the ballad metre; similarly half of the medieval stories are told in four-stress couplets, but the rest are written in the other two forms. Morris is careful not to juxtapose two tales in the same metre, but otherwise his choice of style seems as random as his selection of story.[9] Yet all this does not detract from the essential unity of *The Earthly Paradise*. Its unity is based not on the relationship of one story to another, but on the connection of each one with the central theme. The subject of each tale has a bearing on the idea of the escape from death presented in the Prologue. The poems are further bound together by the recurrent images. This means that although, for instance, 'The Love of Alcestis' and 'The Lady of the Land' are coupled as the poems for June, they should not necessarily be compared with one another; instead both should be referred back to the Prologue and the governing idea. In fact, of course, the poems do comment on each other; we contrast Alcestis's willingness to die for her husband with the hero of 'The Lady of the Land', who cannot break the spell by kissing the dragon. Yet these two poems relate just as closely to those others in the sequence where the image of the monster is strongly present. Apart from the fact that the early tales seem on the whole less gloomy than the later ones, there is no reason why the order of the stories could not have been completely different.

Morris is here using a technique common in medieval literature, but which was later superseded by the Aristotelian desire for artistic unity and clarity. Eugène Vinaver has pointed out that in medieval romance the formal principle is one of association rather than logical progression. The adventures are not related serially; a second will begin before the first has ended, and so on, in a constantly expanding accretion of stories without beginning, middle or preconceived end. Vinaver reminds us that in medieval visual and literary art, 'order and perfection were synonymous with the elaboration of the material, with its multiplication and its development, whereas to us terms such as order and perfection naturally suggest a process of selection and simplification'.[10] This doctrine was called *amplificatio* or *auxesis*, and prescribed 'a linear or horizontal extension, an expansion or an unrolling of a number of interlocked themes'.[11] This description could be applied with precision to *The Earthly Paradise*. Like the authors of medieval romance, Morris explains nothing and never appears in his own person to direct the responses of his readers (except perhaps in the Introduction and Epilogue). Having stated his theme in the Prologue, he proceeds to illustrate it by a collection of poems, each of which relates to the central idea in a different way. This artistic method gives Morris considerable freedom. He can comment both favourably and unfavourably on the concept of escapism: suggest in one story that Paradise is infinitely desirable, and in another that if reached it might prove disappointing. He can indicate that the wish to escape is a universal passion, while reminding us that some people may seek not everlasting life, but unattainable death. Some of his heroes gain happiness; others fail in the quest. Relieved from the pressure of an authorial control, Morris's readers are obliged to analyse their varying responses to the material, and discover for themselves where they stand in relation to the concepts dealt with in the poem. Morris provides no answers; as in his early work, he poses questions and then surrounds his readers with ambiguity and paradox, in which they must come to their own conclusions. Morris has of course given his work a more restricting framework than that of the medieval romances by using the device of the months and the changing seasons as a unifying element. Yet this merely adds to the paradoxes and the freedom, for when the poem ends in February a new year is about to begin; and there is no reason why the narrators should not start again on another twenty-four stories. There is no finality in the poem, no necessary end. In this way the structure of the work is made to relate directly to the aspect of life with which the poem is concerned. The stories and images remind us that the ultimate end of all life is death, but that even from death new life can spring. The greatest sin of the Wanderers is their desire to stop the process of eternal and cyclical death and re-creation, preferring a static immortality. Thus the organizational framework of the poem, lacking the sense of an inevitable beginning and end, mirrors the work's main theme.

Morris has attained the goal which he seems to be seeking in other literary works of this period, that of welding form and content into one whole. It is significant that he is able to do so by the use of a medieval art form; he has found that the style to which he is emotionally drawn is a valid means of expression for nineteenth-century ideas. He could not make this connection in his earlier work, when he seemed to be struggling to force the romance form to contain concepts alien to its structure. Having succeeded in *The Earthly Paradise*, however, Morris does not develop his new-found mastery of form and expression. Instead, he tries other forms which are far less congenial to him: a contemporary novel, and a medieval morality play which attempts to convey a secular, visionary ideal (*Love is Enough* is the nearest Morris ever came to an endorsement of escapism). One reason for his renewed literary failure may be found in his attitude towards art itself, which in *The Earthly Paradise* appears only to provide yet another method of evading reality.

IV

One of the recurrent images in *The Earthly Paradise* is that of a stone figure, or a living person turned to stone. The goddess Venus appears in several stories not only in her own shape, but also as a statue, which may come to life to help her worshippers or to confound her enemies. Thus when Psyche is borne away to be married to a monstrous lover, the statue of Venus is seen to smile. In his earlier work Morris used the image of a man embracing a statue to represent the idea that it is dangerous and unproductive to invest all one's emotional capital in the past. In *The Earthly Paradise* the statue image is related once more to the belief that escapism leads only to a sterile death-in-life. In the unpublished Prologue the Wanderers reach an island where the people, like those in 'Svend and his Brethren', are frozen into immobility. The Wanderers find one of their own ships already in the harbour, with its crew similarly petrified. They themselves fall into a charmed sleep when they eat food from a banquet laid out in the city. While he is in this drugged sleep, Rolf has a dream which seems to emphasize the central conviction around which the whole poem is based. He dreams that he has entered Paradise at last, but only after crossing a black river which clearly symbolizes death. Then he is snatched away from Paradise to a land of eternal youth, but finds that the inhabitants are full of misery and long only for death. The dream warns Rolf that one cannot evade death, for it is only by submitting to mortality that one may attain any kind of lasting happiness. This theme is carried into the main body of the work in the story called 'The Writing on the Image', in which an impious treasure-seeker penetrates into a subterranean cavern. There figures of dead men and women sit surrounded by gold and jewels. The interloper's personal heart's desire is wealth, and he tries to steal the ornaments; but when he attempts to prise from the floor a great green stone, a wooden statue of an archer comes horribly to life and shoots an arrow at the jewel. This extinguishes the light and seals the vault, dooming the seeker to die there. This tale is one of several which remind us not to mistake for Paradise a place or way of life which cannot change.

The image of statues reminds us of the theme of death-in-life which is a central concern of *The Earthly Paradise*. It also has another function. It is used to continue the discussion about the value of art which Morris began (using images of tombs) in his early stories. This discussion opens at the very beginning of the work. Preceding the Prologue are some introductory stanzas in which the poet seems to be speaking for himself. In words which recall Morris's youthful rejection of the idea of working for social change, he disclaims any intention of altering society by his poetry:

> Dreamer of dreams, born out of my due time,
> Why should I strive to set the crooked straight?   (III. 1)

Indeed, he could not even if he wished:

> I cannot ease the burden of your fears,
> Or make quick-coming death a little thing,
> Or bring again the pleasure of past years,
> Nor for my words shall ye forget your tears,
> Or hope again for aught that I can say,
> The idle singer of an empty day.   (III. 1)

All he can do is create transient illusions, like a magician who could make spring appear at one window, summer at another and autumn at a third, but who could not destroy the drear winter which was the reality. By his art he can appear to offer release from the constraints of time, making past present and winter spring. The stories he tells, however, are lies and deceits, for they come through 'the ivory gate' (III. 1) which in Virgil's Avernus was the exit for false dreams. In this introduction the Paradise motif appears for the first time, as the poet declares that he cannot create a refuge from real life by his art, however much he would like to:

> Who strive to build a shadowy isle of bliss
> Midmost the beating of the steely sea.   (III. 2)

In the Prologue Nicholas recommends to his companions:

> That we to gain that sure abode of bliss
> Risk dying in an unknown landless sea.   (III. 13)

The verbal echo emphasizes the point made in the Introduction, that the poet's art is often another form of escape from life, an Earthly Paradise. We are discouraged at the outset from believing that it can be anything but a false retreat. In this same spirit those characters in Morris's early poetry and prose who tried to evade death and decay through art were doomed to disappointment.

In 'Pygmalion and the Image', the concept of a statue coming to life reappears to continue the exposure of the limitations of art. When we first see the sculptor he is famous for his statues of

71

the gods, and is inclined to despise and avoid the company of women. He grows tired of creating images of the gods, however, and decides to turn instead to carving the figure of a real woman. As he progresses his work becomes an obsession, and he gradually falls in love with his own creation. He fights against the feeling, knowing its futility, but cannot overcome it. Morris's previous artists attempted in vain to make a permanent representation of living men and women. Pygmalion in contrast has found that the very immutability of his statue has become a curse, because he cannot breathe life into it. Being himself subject to death, he has fallen in love with 'the form of immortality' (IV. 195). Eventually he thinks of praying to Venus. He goes to her temple, where the statue before which he falls is one he has carved himself – an irony of which he is well aware. Returning home, he finds to his delight that Venus has brought the image alive, and that the statue loves him. Yet love holds pains as well as pleasures, as his mistress reminds him:

> For now I love thee so, I grow afraid
> Of what the Gods upon our heads may send –
> I love thee so, I think upon the end.   (IV. 207)

While he loved a statue, Pygmalion was at least assured that his mistress would always remain the same. Now that she is alive she is subject to death, and may even cease to love him. Morris is emphasizing the fact that perfection can only be sought outside life, that living things cannot be unchanging. He is also implying that art can only be effective if it too is recognized as existing at a remove from life.

In his early work Morris suggested that art which attempted to reproduce the values of the past was doomed to failure, because the artefact, like human life, had to submit to the process of decay and death. Perfection was impossible; therefore to seek solace in an artistic expression of past ideals was a dangerous self-deception. In 'Pygmalion' he alters the focus, and criticizes the value of any type of art, whether concerned with the past or with contemporary society. As early as 1855 he had indicated that his own preference was for literature as far removed as possible from the problems of real life. In a letter to Cormell Price he tried to analyse the pleasure he felt in reading Shelley's poem 'The Skylark':

most beautiful poetry, and indeed almost all beautiful writing makes one feel sad, or indignant, or – do you understand, for I can't make it any clearer; but 'The Skylark' makes one feel happy only; I suppose because it is nearly all music, and that it doesn't bring up any thoughts of humanity: but I don't know either.[12]

Educated by Carlyle, Ruskin and Kingsley, Morris had enough of a social conscience to feel disturbed by artistic representations of human suffering, but preferred not to have his philanthropic emotions painfully aroused. Art was therefore best when it did not contain any uncomfortable commentary on real life. Thus as a young man Morris was close to indulging in the very escapism which he criticized in his own writing. No doubt it was his awareness of his tendency to retreat from life into art which enabled him to explore the theme of escape so carefully. That he knew his danger is clear from his words to Cormell Price in 1856, when he was excitedly contemplating a new venture – studying painting under Rossetti. Looking forward to the labour involved (he was still working all day in an architect's office) he declared:

I was slipping off into a kind of small (very small) Palace of Art.[13]

One reason why Morris loved medieval art was because it was restful; it was far enough removed from the struggles and problems of everyday life to provide adequate relaxation. When he came to write his own poetry and prose, it was easier to slip into the romance convention with which he was thoroughly familiar than to force out a new form which would relate to the contemporary society he hated. Yet he knew that to withdraw from the real world was a denial of life. In *The Earthly Paradise*, which is about escapism, he was concerned with this problem as it affects the artist.

Pygmalion turns from the creation of imagined gods and goddesses to the portrayal of a real woman, feeling that this will make his art more relevant to his own needs. The statue is so successful, however, that he tries to put it into a relationship with himself which falsifies its status as a work of art. Art is only perfect when divorced from reality. To gain his desire he is forced to pray to his own statue of Venus, thus returning for help to the purely imaginary creation which he had previously rejected as irrelevant. His prayer seems to be answered, yet when the statue comes alive – when art becomes indistinguishable from life – it is unsatisfactory. This story confirms Morris's feeling that art and life are best kept apart. Art is destroyed by too close a contact with reality, and in the end it is the work of fantasy which helps the artist most. In the Epilogue to *The Earthly Paradise* Morris takes up the Pygmalion image again, to remind us that we could have no delight in the story if we did not carefully distinguish it from reality:

> all those images of love and pain,
> Wrought as the year did wax, perfect, and wane,
> If they were verily loving there alive,
> No pleasure to their tale-tellers could give.   (VI. 329)

The listeners, in the linking narratives, see the stories as 'pictures', as a 'painted veil' (III. 239); distance is necessary for the tales to be effective.

Perhaps it was an inability sufficiently to distance his story which led Morris to abandon his novel, begun in 1871. In the conventions of romance he found a support for his imagination; the stylization of character and incident natural in the romance form gave him a freedom which he could not make use of when he had first to create his own, convincingly contemporary characters. He attempts on one occasion to elaborate his heroine's character by describing her eyes:

amidst apparent aquiescence they would be cold with disdain, amidst apparent coldness they would be tender, O how tender, with love; amid apparent patience they would burn with passion; amid apparent cheerfulness they would be dull & glassy with anguish no lie or pretence could ever come near them.[14]

The effect is to overload the features of an ordinary woman with a weight of meaning which they cannot support. Like Pygmalion's struggle to extract reciprocal feeling from his statue, Morris's effort to portray character in this pictorial, schematic way is a failure because it destroys the conventions of the art form he is using. His heroine becomes an image rather than a person, and is thus at odds with the descriptions of ordinary life in which she is placed. When, however, Morris begins with a romance heroine, who has already been refined into a typical rather than a realistic figure, he can make her actions and appearance express psychological complexity without causing a split between what she is and what she represents. It was to be several years before this aspect of Morris's genius was to reach its full flowering in the late prose romances. In the early 1870s he was well aware that he had not yet found his natural form of expression. He wrote to Louisa Baldwin of his novel:

'tis nothing but landscape and sentiment: which thing won't do.[15]

The sort of art which he was equipped to produce was, he knew, essentially remote from reality, and at this time he found it difficult to believe that it could be productive of anything but a momentary, purely sensual delight.

V

Early reviewers of *The Earthly Paradise* seemed to endorse Morris's view when they took the evocation of Chaucer's London at the beginning of the Prologue at its face value. They praised the poems for taking their readers beyond real life into a dreamy, relaxing, romantic world. The comments on Volume Three in the *Spectator* begin:

Whither shall a reader turn in these days who longs to escape for a while from all the toil and clamour and strife of the world, and to roam at will in pleasant places, where nothing shall remind him of the doubtful battle-field where after a short breathing-space he must again bear his part?[16]

The answer, of course, is that such a reader will find in *The Earthly Paradise* 'not how to face cares, but how to forget them'.[17] The poet Alfred Austin discussed Morris in one of his articles on 'The Poetry of the Period' in *Temple Bar*, and declared that he had:

surrendered himself wholly to the retrospective tendency of his time ... He ignores the present, and his eyelids close with a quiet sadness if you bid him explore the future.[18]

Austin recognized that the search for the Earthly Paradise was itself a metaphor for this withdrawal from the world. Like the other contemporary reviewers, however, he failed to see that Morris was producing not escapism, but a criticism of it. As a young man Morris had realized that a love of the past might lead to a retreat from reality, and had reminded his readers that such a retreat would be unproductive. In *The Earthly Paradise* he is even more certain that mankind is constantly in search of ways to evade unpleasant truth. He insists that escape is impossible.

One may wonder why Morris, feeling as he did about art, should have taken the trouble to compose a poem like *The Earthly Paradise*. It would surely have been more consistent for him to have given up poetry altogether and concentrated entirely on his practical occupation as a designer of fabrics, glass and wallpapers. The answer to this question may be found in certain lines of *The Earthly Paradise* which show that even while he was writing he was beginning to develop a different feeling about the possibilities of art. Between the Prologue and the lyric for March is another short poem, which obscurely indicates that the author feels there may be some useful purpose in writing and reading his old stories. He takes up the image of the seasons from the Introduction, and suggests that the far-away land of the imagination from which he draws his tales not only delights in the spring, summer and autumn which were created by the conjuror. It also:

> hath little fear
> For the white conqueror of the fruitful year.   (III. 81)

If winter, in the Introduction, stood for unpleasant reality, its presence here may indicate that (in some as yet unspecified way) the stories are effective when brought into relationship with real life. The linking narrative between the stories shows that the Wanderers and the Greeks feel that the tales have some connection with their own history, although they usually serve only to increase their melancholy and remind them of death. The idea of a valid connection between art and life is developed further in 'The Land East of the Sun and West of the Moon'. This story is given yet another framework, of a man called Gregory the Star-gazer who dreams the events of the narrative. His dream is in three parts. In the first, he is at a Christmas feast listening to a stranger telling the story. In the second, he becomes this narrator; and finally he himself seems to be the hero of the story. As the tale thus grows more and more closely interwoven with Gregory's personality, we are told that in the dream he 'dealt with his own miseries' (V. 85). The suggestion is that the imaginary adventures of the hero relate to, and even act beneficially on, problems in Gregory's real life. At the end of the tale Gregory does not seem to have gained much of value from his dream, but we have been asked to consider the possibility that art may after all be able at least to provide us with fictional analogues for our own sorrows.

This tentative assertion of value in art is developed, appropriately, in the winter section of the book. It is initiated in the lyric for December. As the old year passes, the poet regrets the loss of former joys in the tone of muted anguish with which we are by now so familiar. In the third stanza, however, a new suggestion seems to be made. The poet feels that if one clings firmly to life and love and refuses to reject the past, some hope may be discovered even though he knows no reason why it should be so:

> Though nought of good, no God thou mayst discern,
> Though nought that is, thine utmost woe can move,
> Though no soul knows wherewith thine heart doth yearn,
> Yet, since thy weary lips no curse can learn,
> Cast no least thing thou lovedst once away,
> Since yet perchance thine eyes shall see the day. (VI. 1)

This, we may remember, was the message of 'Frank's Sealed Letter'. The narrative which immediately follows is the story of Hercules's successful search for the Earthly Paradise and his seizure of the golden apples. He too sets an admittedly unformulated optimism, a largely blind trust in the value of heroism, against the weary sameness of the life of the passive Hesperides. These nymphs are isolated from the changing world beyond Paradise; they do not even tell stories of noble deeds that take place there, clearly believing such actions to be futile and frivolous. So enervated do they seem by their eternal felicity that they cannot even react to Hercules's destruction of the guardian serpent and his plucking of the golden apples, but remain stoically silent and motionless. Their view of time perceives it as an unceasing cycle of repetition:

> all things, changed by joy or loss or pain,
> To what they were shall change and change again. (VI. 12)

And they warn Hercules against the apples which, they say, bring a curse with them. Hercules is unmoved. He sees the world not as controlled by a cyclical process of repetition but as progressing towards an ultimate end. This linear movement requires his heroism – his great actions will in some way be of use to those who come after him:

> But this I know at least: the world shall wend
> Upon its way, and gathering joy and grief
> And deeds done, bear them with it to the end;
> So shall it, though I lie as last year's leaf
> Lies 'neath a summer tree, at least receive
> My life gone by, and store it, with the gain
> That men alive call striving, wrong, and pain. (VI. 13)

He employs his physical prowess to break, in noisy violence, the calm of the magic island as he kills the monster which protects the tree. His story seems to suggest that mighty actions about which heroic tales can be woven – 'deeds for folk to tell' (VI. 14) – have after all some positive value. Like Svend, he stands for progress and change rather than the passivity which can lead to death-in-life.

It will have been noticed that Hercules expresses his perception of the usefulness of his life to future generations in organic imagery which contains a reference to the changing seasons. Morris, as we have seen, uses imagery of statues and cold stone when discussing the failure of art adequately to relate to reality. He also, earlier in *The Earthly Paradise*, shows man alienated from the natural world. Hercules, however, is not so alienated; he seems to be able to contemplate his individual dissolution by relating his heroism to the life of future generations as if it were fertilizing their own actions. This is an important new emphasis in Morris's poetry and one which is reinforced in several ways in the last volume of *The Earthly Paradise*. In the Envoi to the whole work he again uses organic, rather than stony, imagery to express a belief in the usefulness of his artistic creation. He is addressing his book:

> if indeed
> In some old garden thou and I have wrought,
> And made fresh flowers spring up from hoarded seed,
> And fragrance of old days and deeds have brought
> Back to folk weary; and all was not for nought.
> – No little part it was for me to play –
> The idle singer of an empty day. (VI. 333)

Though he is vague about the precise value of 'old days and

deeds', he does seem to feel that they are recalled for some purpose. The vision of himself as 'idle singer' is now an ironic refrain rather than a statement of resigned acceptance of impotence on the part of the poet. The lyric for February, the final month of the story-telling year, likewise suggests a guarded optimism. The dreary landscape seems to hold no promise of spring. Yet there is corn in the fields, though we cannot see it; and in the final lines the 'changeless change', so terrifying in November, is at last transformed into a sign of hope:

> Shalt thou not hope for joy new born again,
> Since no grief ever born can ever die
> Through changeless change of seasons passing by? (VI. 175)

The poet is perhaps moving nearer to an integration with nature; at least he is no longer anguished by his perception of it.

This new hope is indicated also in the final story, 'The Hill of Venus'. It is Morris's version of the Tannhäuser story. The hero finds earthly life stale and unsatisfying, and seeks instead the delights of the Venusberg. He lives with Venus in her Paradise for some time, but eventually (like Ogier and Bharam) he returns to the real world. Unlike previous heroes, he actively chooses to return, because he finds the 'never-ending, hopeless day' (VI. 302) of Paradise ultimately sterile; he has nothing left to wish for. Here again is the warning against death-in-life. Yet the world can only offer him the prospect of its destruction, for he finds that everyone is looking forward with terror to the millennium which they believe is imminent. In despair, he goes to the Pope, to seek assurance from him of some everlasting peace and hope available through God's mercy. The Pope, horrified by his story, declares that there is no more chance of Walter's redemption than of his own wooden staff bursting into flower. Walter departs, mindlessly flinging himself back into the Venusberg, and Morris briefly tells us of the horrors he experiences in that changeless land, which has now become Hell.

Had the story ended here, it would have been the most pessimistic of all the tales. Walter finds Paradise, but it is as terrible in its timelessness as the changing and doomed earth. Yet there is more to come. The Pope begins to regret that he gave Walter no comfort. While he is thinking about his lost penitent, he suddenly realizes that a change has come over his staff:

> For lo, in God's unfaltering timeless spring,
> Summer, and autumn, had that dry rod been,
> And from its barrenness the leaves sprang green,
>
> And on its barrenness grew wondrous flowers,
> That earth knew not; and on its barrenness
> Hung the ripe fruit of heaven's unmeasured hours.   (VI. 325)

The heaven from which the branch has come shares the same attributes as the Venusberg and the other Earthly Paradises: it is 'timeless', hours pass there uncounted, winter is excluded and the other seasons exist concurrently rather than serially. The staff grows not just flowers but leaves and fruit as well. In most of Morris's poetry and prose at this period such an image, as we have seen, would be presented hedged about with ambiguity. It would represent either unattainable fantasy or an evasion of life and death which would ultimately be perceived as sterile. Here, however, along with the idea of timelessness are unmistakable assertions of growth, development and movement. The dry, barren rod is transformed, springs into flower, produces fruit. At last, at the very end of the sequence, the flowering tree of Paradise has come to earth in glorious reality.

The hope hinted at here is of course only a fragile one, if set against the overwhelming emphasis of the rest of *The Earthly Paradise*. Walter has found no comfort, on earth or in the Venusberg, and the Pope dies when the glory of Paradise is revealed. Yet the message is of forgiveness. The final image of 'The Hill of Venus' is a powerful indication that the dream can after all be discovered on earth; the conflict between fantasy and reality need not result merely in disillusion.

VI

I have suggested that the central theme of *The Earthly Paradise* is the process of change. Morris examines the tendency of man to try to hide from the knowledge of his own mortality; and clearly states his view that such escapism is a criminal evasion of the growth and development which alone constitutes genuine life. Yet for most of the poem he appears unable to suggest a valid alternative. His imagery, the repetitive use of his typical softly falling cadence, the melancholy which pervades story and style in *The Earthly Paradise*, all indicate his regret at man's inability to make any kind of vigorous challenge to time's inexorable process. This results in an alienation from nature, portrayed in the numerous unnatural Paradises and in the 'months lyrics'. Its other concomitant is a regrettable dichotomy between man's creative power and the reality which he attempts to portray; art is divorced from life and can offer little to those who seek its consolations. In every way man's ephemeral personality and creativity are mocked by time and change.

The Earthly Paradise is a fine expression of these ideas; but, not surprisingly, it is hardly invigorating reading. Some of the stories seem to slide to a halt under the weight of their own languor and melancholy. Morris's feeling that he could create little of value in literature, first discernible in the early stories and poems, is in danger of causing him to give up altogether. Yet towards the end of the work there are hints that his mood is changing. Hercules asserts the value of heroism and appears to be more integrated with nature than the other heroes; the Envoi claims some value for the literary creation itself. Upon these foundations are to be built the insights into the nature of history and time and man's relationship to them which will free Morris into his greatest literary achievements, the prose romances of his final years. The rest of this study will attempt to demonstrate the process of this releasing.

One of the saddest phrases in Morris's work occurs in the poem 'Golden Wings', in which the minstrels sing of 'Arthur, who will never die, / In Avallon he groweth old' (I. 118). As I suggested in the previous chapter, this image of futility relates to Jehane's unconsummated love and the pain of her existence in the charmed but for her emotionally sterile land. Arthur has evaded death but is gradually losing his heroic strength. It is the plight of all who seek to escape. If his literature is to show the same forceful vitality as his design work, Morris must find a way of reconciling man's dreams of happiness with the real world in which he has to act. Only then will the past and the future offer anything but mockery of man's petty and ephemeral aspirations. One place where Morris began to discover a new attitude to heroic activity was in the Norse sagas, in reading which he took his first step on a return to romance as a valid art form.

CHAPTER 3

'The dawn that waketh the dead':
Sigurd the Volsung

Romance deals in idealized figures, in clear and stylized distinctions between good and evil, hero and villain. Its happy ending requires (at least for the duration of the story) that writer and reader share a belief in the tendency of good to overcome evil and in the ability of the hero radically to improve his society. And for Morris, who was only happy when drawing inspiration from the past, the romance distancing necessitated an acceptance of the value of that past when transmuted into art. As we have seen, all these requirements are only ambiguously part of Morris's creative approach up to the period of *The Earthly Paradise*. 'The Hollow Land' and the prose 'Golden Wings' indicate his doubts about the concept of heroism as a valid and productive motive for action. His inability to write stories with unequivocally happy endings shows his uncertainty about any ultimate vindication of good at the expense of evil – a feeling linked to his deep apprehension of the destructive force of mutability. His obsession with the past results in suggestions that art is fallible, futile and deluding, since it can deal powerfully with neither past nor present.

Yet by the end of his life Morris was writing formal romances, using medieval models, about successful heroes. From the late 1860s to the 1880s the history of his literary work is that of a gradual but inexorable progress towards romance. There were, I believe, three main influences which combined to make this possible. One was the literature of the northern races, especially the Icelandic sagas, with which he became familiar in the original language in the 1870s. These stories had much to teach Morris about the relationship of art to life and about heroism; it is no accident that the final volume of *The Earthly Paradise*, with its hints of a more hopeful artistic philosophy, also contains the sequence's two stories taken from Icelandic sources. Linked with his study of Icelandic was an increasingly extensive knowledge of trends in philological and mythological research; and this combined with his love of the sagas to allow him a newly positive view of the value of artistic representations of the past. Finally, his terror in the face of time and change, so obvious in *The Earthly Paradise*, became transformed when he embraced Socialism. It is my intention to show how these three influences, closely interwoven, govern the quintessential style, structure and ethos of the late romances.

The main influences on Morris's literary work in the 1870s were Icelandic sagas and Norse mythology and legend. Although he had known something of the sagas and the *Edda* in translation since he was a young man, when he read them in the original language they made a great impression on him. In the poems he based on Icelandic sources may be traced his gradual change of heart about the value of art and of the past; when these ideas were reinforced by an acquaintance with new theories about history and mythology, Morris produced in *Sigurd the Volsung* a poem whose mood differs greatly from that of *The Earthly Paradise*. A study of *Sigurd* will show that it was an essential step in Morris's progress towards romance.

I

Morris first came into contact with northern literature as a young man. 'The Hollow Land' has an epigraph from the *Nibelungenlied*, quoted from Carlyle's essay on the poem.[1] Another of the early stories, 'Lindenborg Pool', was inspired by part of Benjamin Thorpe's collection of northern religious legends and folk-tales, *Northern Mythology*. By the time Morris met, in 1868, the Icelandic scholar Eiríkr Magnússon he was well versed in Icelandic literature in translation. According to Magnússon, Morris had read Bishop Percy's translation of *Introduction à l'Histoire de Dannemarc* (1755–6) by Paul Henri Mallet, which as *Northern Antiquities* had been originally published in 1770 and reissued by Bohn's Antiquarian Library in 1847. He also knew *Icelandic Poetry* (1797) by Amos Cottle and Benjamin Thorpe's translation of the *Elder Edda* (1866). The first saga to be translated into English had appeared in 1861: *The Story of Burnt Njal*, issued by George Webbe Dasent. Morris had read both this and the same author's *The Story of Gisli the Outlaw* (1866). Magnússon's account continues:

From modern books of travel on Iceland he was surprisingly well up in the geography of the island, and from Bishop Finn Jonsson's 'Historia ecclesiastica Islandiae' he had mastered the main features of the general history of the country. (VII. xvj)[2]

This indicates that Morris already had a considerable interest in Icelandic culture. When he began to study the language his enthusiasm became passionate. He began with *Gunnlaug's Saga*, a short tale written at the same time as the great sagas and serving as a useful introduction to the study of Icelandic. The pattern of Morris's joint work with Magnússon was soon established. After each lesson Magnússon wrote out a literal translation of the passage they had read, which he then returned to Morris for emendation. This became the printer's copy. In January 1869 'The Saga of Gunnlaug the Worm-tongue and Rafn the Skald' appeared in the *Fortnightly Review*. Later that year *Grettis Saga: the Story of Grettir the Strong* was published, and by the autumn Morris had finished his version of the *Laxdaela Saga*, 'The Lovers of Gudrun', which was printed in Volume Two of *The Earthly Paradise*. In 1870 Morris and Magnússon issued the first English translation of the *Volsunga Saga*, called *The Story of the Volsungs and Niblungs with Certain Songs from the Elder Edda*. The pace did not slacken; in 1871 Morris contributed 'The Story of Frithiof the Bold' to the *Dark Blue*, and in 1875 he and Magnússon published *Three Northern Love Stories and Other Tales*.[3] In 1876 Morris's fascination with Norse literature culminated in his epic poem *The Story of Sigurd the Volsung and the Fall of the Niblungs*. Although this signalled the end of the first frenzy of activity, Morris never lost his deep love of Icelandic literature. Between 1891 and 1895 he collaborated with Magnússon on the first five volumes of The Saga Library.[4] Besides these published works, other pieces bear witness to the influence on Morris of Icelandic culture. They include an illuminated manuscript of his translation of the *Eyrbyggja Saga*, which he gave to Georgiana Burne-Jones in the early 1870s, and a number of short poems, some of which were published in *Poems by the Way* (1891).

Morris was always capable of exceptional amounts of work, but the volume of Icelandic-influenced literature which he produced in this period shows what a remarkably strong hold was taken on him by Norse writing. The burst of creativity which it induced indicates that in Icelandic poetry and prose Morris found some quality which corresponded to a specific emotional and artistic need. To discover the nature of that need, it may be helpful to compare two of the poems in *The Earthly Paradise* which are based on Norse legend. One was written before he came into contact with the Icelandic language, the other in his first flush of enthusiasm for the sagas. The difference between them may point to the reasons why Morris found Icelandic literature so artistically liberating.

'The Fostering of Aslaug' appeared in *The Earthly Paradise* after 'The Lovers of Gudrun', but May Morris implies that it was written, or at least conceived, before Morris's general interest in the sagas developed into intimate knowledge. It is based on the version of the story in Volume One of Thorpe's *Northern Mythology*.[5] Thorpe laconically relates how Aslaug, the daughter of Sigurd and Brynhild, is brought up in poverty and obscurity. The Viking Ragnar, son of King Sigurd of Sweden, berths his ship near Aslaug's cottage; he is struck by her beauty and attempts to seduce her. When she refuses him, he offers her marriage, and is forced to keep his promise because she will not sleep with him until after the wedding. The couple return to Sweden. There Ragnar, who still believes that his wife is a peasant's daughter, plans to divorce her so that he can marry a princess. Aslaug reveals her noble lineage, which causes Ragnar to renounce his new love; but, says Thorpe, 'from that time Aslaug became fierce and vindictive, like all of her race'.[6] Morris turns this rather grim and cynical story into a tender vindication of the power of true love. His poem stresses that Aslaug is released by Ragnar's affection from a life of misery; it makes no mention of Ragnar's desire for a more suitable wife, nor of Aslaug's growing harshness of character. The lovers' bliss will be terminated only by Ragnar's heroic death in battle. While sentimentalizing the story, Morris makes the heroine into a delicately beautiful maiden who walks among trees and flowers in communion with nature:

> into the wood
> She turned, and wandered slim and fair
> 'Twixt the dark tree-boles
> . . .
> The wild things well might gaze their fill,
> As through the wind-flowers brushed her feet. (VI. 38)

This description is completely different in tone from Thorpe's simple statement that Aslaug was 'distinguished for her understanding and beauty'.[7] 'The Fostering of Aslaug' is one of the few poems in which Morris's tendency towards romantic escapism leads him to distort completely the emphasis of his source.

When we turn to 'The Lovers of Gudrun' the atmosphere is entirely different. While 'Aslaug' is written in ballad-metre, 'Gudrun' is given the more weighty heroic couplet. (The only other medieval poem in *The Earthly Paradise* to have this form is the pivotal story 'Ogier the Dane'.) In the introductory lines the Wanderer who tells the tale emphasizes the strength and stoicism of the Icelanders, bred no doubt by the harsh aspect of their homeland:

> Strong, uncomplaining, yet compassionate
> . . .
>   a strange and awful land
> Where folk, as in the hollow of God's hand,
> Beset with fearful things, yet fearing nought,
> Have lived their lives and wondrous deeds have wrought.
>
> (v. 250)

The opening of the tale, Guest's prophecy to Gudrun about her four husbands, marks the story as one of those dealing with the impossibility of escaping fate. The narrator grimly announces that he is about to tell 'how the sky blackened, and the storm swept down' (v. 252) on the unsuspecting protagonists. Morris's main concern in 'Gudrun' is to show how the principal characters (Gudrun, her husband Bodli and her former fiancé Kiartan) meet and face up to their doom. This time there is no softening of the story,[8] and Morris faithfully copies from the saga the pathos and pain of the final scene, where Gudrun, old and blind, remembers the passion and strife of her youth. The suggestion that men must learn to face danger and death with fortitude pervades the entire *Earthly Paradise*; what is new in 'Gudrun' is the method which Morris uses to express his idea. Instead of drawing attention to his theme in a medieval way, by the use of images such as the dragon, Morris emphasizes his point simply by concentrating on the reactions of the characters at moments of stress. Moreover, while in other poems of *The Earthly Paradise* we are asked to deduce the emotional state of a character by his actions, in 'Gudrun' Morris attempts to give an

insight into the motives and psychology of the chief figures in
the poem. After Gudrun's marriage to Bodli and the unexpected
return of Kiartan, her state of mind is analysed in a quiet un-
medieval manner:

> she forgot those eyes
> What they were now, all dulled with miseries;
> And she forgot the sorrow of the heart
> That fate and time from hers had thrust apart.
> Still wrong bred wrong within her; day by day
> Some little speck of kindness fell away,
> Till in her heart naked desire alone
> Was left, the one thing not to be undone.
> Then would the jealous flame in such wise burn
> Within her, that to Bodli would she turn,
> And madden him with fond caressing touch. (v. 337)

This presentation of the emotions of a sexually thwarted
woman would be totally out of place in any of the other poems
in *The Earthly Paradise*.

Many reviewers noticed this new attempt by Morris to dissect
the minds of his characters. The critic of the *Pall Mall Budget*
pointed out the difference between the poems in Volume One of
The Earthly Paradise and those in Volume Two:

the emotional elements are realized with a far greater intensity and
expressed with a far greater vehemence in most of the present poems
than in any of those of the former volume. The versified Saga of
Gudrun, which forms the last and longest of the narratives here given,
is in its intention a half tragic, half epic study of fate and passion ...
having a quite modern subtlety and involution of emotion thrown into
it, both where the characters speak for themselves and where the poet
analyzes for them.[9]

The new poems, he concludes, have a 'more pronounced and
developed humanity'[10] than those in the preceding volume. The
review in the *Spectator* also declared that in 'Gudrun' Morris
had 'put forth new and unexpected strength'.[11] It would be
wrong to suggest that Morris had never before been interested in
passion and emotion; the Browning-influenced poem 'The
Defence of Guenevere' offered the reader a psychological study
as vivid as anything in 'Gudrun'. Yet, as the reviews make clear,
since *The Defence of Guenevere* Morris had become less and
less concerned with analysing the mental states of his characters. As we have seen, he felt that it was not the place of art to

87

attempt such an analysis. Now, under the influence of the Icelandic saga, he produced a poem in which for the first time since *The Defence of Guenevere* his main focus was on the passions and motives of a human being, expressed not in images but through an examination of the mind of that character.

By reading the sagas Morris discovered that it was after all possible for art to deal directly with the actual thoughts of real people. He was aware that his poetry had taken a new turn. In a letter to Swinburne he commented:

the book would have done me more credit if there had been nothing in it but the Gudrun, though I don't think the others quite the worst things I have done. Yet they are all too long and flabby, damn it!... Acontius I know is a spoony, nothing less, and the worst of it is that if I did him over a dozen times I know I should make him just the same.[12]

It is impossible not to agree with this criticism of 'The Story of Acontius and Cydippe', which is perhaps the most languorous of Morris's love stories. Clearly, he recognizes the contrast between this kind of 'flabby' writing and the new tautness and emotional realism he was attempting in 'Gudrun'. As might have been expected, he at first went rather too far in the opposite direction; 'Gudrun' is almost unique in Morris's work in the degree of introspection and analysis he allows into his story. Modern translators of the *Laxdaela Saga* have suggested that it differs from the other classical sagas by 'the extent to which the author describes the actual emotions felt by his characters'.[13] Morris added considerably even to this amount of personal feeling. The most notorious example of his elaboration occurs when Kiartan returns from abroad and hears of Gudrun's marriage to Bodli. In the saga we are told:

He now heard about Gudrun's marriage and showed no sign of emotion at the news.[14]

In Morris's poem Kiartan delivers himself of a twenty-line lament, beginning:

> O blind, O blind, O blind!
> Where is the world I used to deem so kind,
> So loving to me? O Gudrun, Gudrun.   (v. 320)

This extravagance, however, is that of a poet joyously rediscovering a form of expression he had once felt compelled to repudiate. Closer contact with the sagas gave Morris an admiration for their stylistic reticence as well as the depth of emotion to be found in them. At this stage he was enjoying to the full his new freedom to present in art the real feelings of ordinary people. Art and life were coming into contact again, through the influence of the sagas which used actual events as the basis for their stories.

Nineteenth-century scholars (like modern ones) were by no means unanimous about the degree of historical accuracy which could be ascribed to the sagas. Nevertheless it was agreed that they were organized around a core of objective truth. The persons and places mentioned by the saga authors did exist, and the national events which provide a framework for the stories (for example the conversion of Iceland to Christianity in the year 1000) could be verified from other sources. To Morris, accustomed to base his stories on old legends, the sagas gave a new impetus towards the use of actual life as the foundation for art. The characters in the sagas, though some of them achieved heroic stature, were the ordinary inhabitants of the country going about their everyday business. Njal is the hero of his saga not because of any outstanding physical prowess but because of his wisdom, self-restraint and quiet courage in the face of death. The sagas are concerned with what Dorothy Hoare calls 'the general life'.[15] When Morris found that nevertheless they stirred him more than any stories he had ever read, he was forced to reconsider his ideas about the unreality of art. Moreover, not only did they turn into art the ordinary lives of tenth- and eleventh-century Icelanders, they were also surprisingly relevant to the preoccupations of nineteenth-century Englishmen. In the Preface to their translation of the *Grettis Saga* Morris and Magnússon commend to the modern reader 'the dramatic power and eager interest in human character, shown by our story-teller' (VII. xxviij). In their Preface to the *Volsunga Saga* the translators suggest that a reader prepared to take the trouble to overcome any unfamiliarity of style and setting 'will be intensely touched by finding, amidst all its wildness and remoteness, such startling realism, such subtilty, such close sympathy with all the passions that may move himself to-day' (VII. 286). Morris has by now radically reconsidered his idea that it was not the place of art to relate to reality, and praises the sagas for their accurate descriptions of archetypal human emotions.

Perhaps it was the influence of the sagas which led Morris to attempt his own version of a work of art dealing exclusively with the real lives of real people. I have already discussed his unfinished novel, in which he was unable successfully to combine his habitual use of romantic symbolism with naturalistic description. It seems possible that he wished (for only the second time in his career) to base a literary work on the actual life of his contemporaries because he was at this time so absorbed by the Icelandic sagas. The strength of the impression they made on him is demonstrated by this struggle to write in a mode which he found uncongenial. It is also interesting that at this point Morris returned to prose as a fictional medium, a form which he had not used since the prose 'Golden Wings' and would not employ again until his propaganda romance *A Dream of John Ball* (1886–7). His attempt to emulate the style of the sagas failed, however, because his mind continued involuntarily to turn towards the atmosphere of romance. If the sagas were to be truly fruitful in Morris's creative life, they would have to provide him not only with a renewed faith in the ability of art to deal with reality, but also with a conviction that it could do so through his preferred medium, that of romance. This sounds impossibly paradoxical; but the sagas could and did provide both these insights. We have seen that Morris felt that the sagas related very closely to contemporary passions; a closer analysis of precisely how this was effected will demonstrate Morris's growing realization that romance could after all be useful.

II

One reason why the sagas gave Morris a renewed faith in the ability of art to deal with real problems was that his discovery of Icelandic literature coincided with a period of crisis in his personal life. The story of his wife Janey's relationship with Rossetti is now well known; having rented Kelmscott Manor jointly with Rossetti, Morris left the lovers together there while he made his two trips to Iceland, in a brave attempt to allow Janey the freedom he believed was her right. The cost to his own feelings, however, was considerable. He found that reading the sagas enabled him to face his emotional difficulties, when he related his own struggles to those of the saga heroes. In the sonnet which he prefixed to the *Grettis Saga*, Morris expresses his despair of doing any really valuable work:

> A life scarce worth the living, a poor fame
> Scarce worth the winning, in a wretched land,
> Where fear and pain go upon either hand.   (VII. xxxvj)

Yet in a world of the dead and the dying, the memory of Grettir's heroism comes to the poet as a bringer of comfort and much-needed companionship:

> Nay, with the dead I deal not; this man lives,
> And that which carried him through good and ill,
> Stern against fate while his voice echoed still
> From rock to rock, now he lies silent, strives
> With wasting time, and through its long lapse gives
> Another friend to me, life's void to fill.   (VII. xxxvj)

In a second sonnet on the same subject, unpublished in Morris's lifetime, the personal relationship between poet and hero is even more strongly emphasized:

> At least thy life moved men so, that e'en I,
> Thy mother's wail in the lone eve and drear,
> Thy brother's laugh at death for thee, can hear –
> Hear now nor wonder at her agony
> Nor wonder that he found it good to die –
> Speak, Grettir, through the dark: I am anear.   (VII. xix)

In yet another poem written as an introduction to *Grettis Saga*, and later published as 'To the Muse of the North' in *Poems by the Way*, Morris analyses further the process by which the sagas brought him comfort; he begs the Muse to:

> Let some word reach my ears and touch my heart,
> That, if it may be, I may have a part
> In that great sorrow of thy children dead.   (IX. 116)

He alleviates his own sorrows by sharing in those of the saga heroes. Since he invokes the Muse of the sagas to bring him this consolation, it is clear that it comes to him specifically through art.

The idea of turning to twelfth-century literature for solace in one's emotional crises contains more than a hint of the escapism against which Morris had battled so fiercely in *The Earthly*

Paradise. Yet precisely what excited Morris about Icelandic literature was its uncompromising vigour. The sagas helped him to come to terms with his own problems by showing him how the heroes of old faced their difficulties with extreme stoicism. From his first contact with the sagas, as the introductory lines to 'Gudrun' show, it was this aspect of the Icelandic character which most impressed him. In his later comments on Icelandic men and society he continually stresses the importance of courage in the Northman's attitude to life. In 1877 he wrote about the *Njala Saga* to Georgiana Burne-Jones:

What a glorious outcome of the worship of Courage these stories are.[16]

When in 1883 he gave his Socialist colleague Andreas Scheu a brief history of his life, he remembered the impact of the sagas in their original language:

the delightful freshness and independence of thought of them, the air of freedom which breathes through them, their worship of courage (the great virtue of the human race) ... took my heart by storm.[17]

In a lecture given in 1887 on 'The Early Literature of the North – Iceland', Morris again isolates this facet of the Icelandic character:

Self-restraint was a virtue sure to be thought much of among a people whose religion was practically courage: in all the stories of the north failure is never reckoned as a disgrace, but it *is* reckoned a disgrace not to bear it with equanimity...[18]

Morris had always been sceptical of the practical value of escapism; the sagas inspired him with a desire to take a more positive course, and face up to his problems with a fortitude like that of the Icelandic heroes.

Icelandic literature provided Morris with a new stoicism. It did so by showing him that heroism was not, as he had thought, possible only in the world of romance, but could be found just as easily in ordinary life. The concept of heroism aroused intense interest among the Victorians. Its champion was Carlyle, whose lectures *On Heroes, Hero-Worship, and the Heroic in History* (1841) would almost certainly have been read by the young Morris. Carlyle's contention was that Europe had sunk to its present level of disorder and revolution because men had ceased to exercise the faculty of hero-worship and turned instead to profitless speculation and the chimera of equality. Man had to seek out the best and the highest, and bow down to it when he found it; only when a nation was ruled by its wisest man would it realize its true potential:

Find in any country the Ablest Man that exists there; raise *him* to the supreme place, and loyally reverence him: you have a perfect government for that country.[19]

For lesser men, wisdom consists in obeying the commands of the ablest man. Carlyle habitually dealt in certainties, and other authors who trusted in what they believed to be immutable creeds could write without excessive difficulty about the development of the modern hero. Kingsley and Charlotte Yonge drew portraits of the Christian hero (Lancelot in *Yeast* (1848) or Guy in *The Heir of Redclyffe*) and Disraeli offered for his readers' admiration the young man inspired by a political faith (the eponymous hero of *Coningsby* (1844) and Charles Egremont in *Sybil* (1845)). Yet for some writers the nature of heroism, and even its very existence, was more problematic. In *Vanity Fair* (1848) Thackeray wrote 'A Novel Without a Hero'; he wondered sardonically whether the concept of heroism retained any value in the mid-nineteenth century. Tennyson seems to have been certain of Sir Galahad's heroic stature, but by the time he wrote the final *Idylls of the King* he tended to create instead an atmosphere of weary disillusion. 'The Last Tournament' (first published in the *Contemporary Review* in 1871) shows how Arthur's court has lost its original idealism and is being destroyed from within by the failure of its knights to live up to the chivalrous standards of their leader. *The Idylls of the King* end with the death of the hero.[20]

In his youthful work Morris had also been doubtful about the value of heroism. As we have seen, he tended to be sceptical when discussing the conventions of chivalry and the concept of heroic action. In *The Earthly Paradise* he obsessively reminded his readers that whatever joy his heroes obtained would be rudely cut short by death. In his reading of the sagas, however, he found a race whose heroism was of a kind he could understand and admire. Men became heroic not by an impossible transcendence of their situation but by facing up to and making the best of it. In the letter to Georgiana Burne-Jones on the *Njala*

Saga already referred to above, Morris reminds her of the characters in the saga whom he most admires, highlighting the ordinary nature of their nevertheless heroic actions:

the exceeding good temper of Gunnar amidst his heroism, and the calm of Njal: and I don't know anything more consoling or grander in all literature (to use a beastly French word) than Gunnar's singing in his house under the moon and the drifting clouds ... or Skarphedinn's death; or how Flosi pays the penalty for the Burning, never appealing against the due and equal justice, but defending himself and his folk stoutly against it at every step.[21]

Good temper, calm acceptance of death, self-control in the face of adverse legal judgement – here were forms of heroism which Morris could accept, and which were obviously relevant to contemporary life. Part of Morris's excitement when he came to read the sagas stemmed from the fact that they showed how a love for tales of heroes could be reconciled with a feeling that art should be of practical value. The Icelanders did not seek to escape from the problems of life, but attained greatness because of the way they faced them. Heroism was possible, therefore, even in the unromantic world which Morris found so uncongenial. When he was able to believe this, he could turn to romance in a spirit of understanding. He could recognize that to talk of heroes was to discuss qualities which were as important to his readers as to medieval adventurers.

III

The sagas suggested to Morris that art could deal with reality without being invalidated, and that heroism could still exist in the modern world. The logical outcome of these new ideas would have been a work showing the heroic spirit operating in a contemporary setting. This was perhaps what he was attempting when he began his novel. When it failed, he had to think again. He was temperamentally capable only of producing literature which was based on the art of the past, just as his decorative work was firmly grounded on medieval and ancient styles. If he was to be released into writing true romance, which would have to be set in a period remote from his own, he needed to be convinced that the past could have a direct bearing on the present. He had found that he could be helped and comforted by stories of the past. Was there any guarantee that this was a universal truth? Could he write of the past with an assurance that other men would find in his fiction the values he had discovered in the sagas? During the period of his Icelandic studies, Morris does seem to have reached the conclusion that he could rely on his readers to see the relevance of the past to their own situations. One of the factors which persuaded him of this was his understanding of recent developments in historical research. Earlier in the century the connection between past and present had been described chiefly in moral and ethical terms; but by the 1870s this attitude had been largely replaced by a concentration on more organic links. Studies of nineteenth-century customs, laws, social organization and language all explained the contemporary manifestations as developments from the culture of the past. This view would have been familiar to Morris, because of its prevalence in the work of writers on Norse mythology and society.

As early as 1755 Mallet had felt it necessary to begin his history of Denmark with a book on the lives of the Norsemen. In the Preface to his *Introduction à l'Histoire de Dannemarc* (as translated by Percy in the Bohn edition of 1847) he justified himself as follows:

is it not well known that the most flourishing and celebrated states of Europe owe originally to the northern nations, whatever liberty they now enjoy, either in their constitution, or in the spirit of their government? For although the Gothic form of government has been almost every where altered or abolished, have we not retained, in most things, the opinions, the customs, the manners which that government had a tendency to produce?[22]

Before Mallet's work became widely available in England, it was used by a popularizer of Northern legend called Grenville Pigott as the main source for his book entitled *A Manual of Scandinavian Mythology*. He published it in 1839, and was very conscious of the fact that he was breaking new ground. The Preface opens:

The Mythology of the ancient Scandinavians ... has hitherto excited but little attention in this country.[23]

Like Mallet, he justifies his interest by reminding his readers of the close connection between the Northern way of life and modern customs. The Danes were neighbours and conquerors of the Anglo-Saxon population of England:

a short retrospect will suffice to shew, that the religion of Odin must have exercised a great and lasting influence on the character and institutions of the inhabitants of Great Britain.[24]

When knowledge of Icelandic history and culture began to spread in England, readers were continually reminded that the Norsemen who wrote the sagas and believed in the gods of Asgard were the ancestors of modern Englishmen. In an article on 'Iceland in the Year One Thousand' in *Fraser's Magazine* for 1852, the inhabitants of Iceland were described as follows:

notwithstanding the fierce and savage character of their daily life, we may detect among them, perhaps more clearly than in Norway itself, the germs of more than one of the great sources of European civilization.[25]

Two years later the *Westminster Review* contained an article about a number of German books on Norse mythology, in which the connection between Icelander and Briton was made more specific. The religion of Odin:

might be called *English* or *Saxon* with as much right as *Scandinavian*: it was the religion of the whole Teutonic race.[26]

By 1866 a reviewer of Sir Edmund Head's *Viga-Glum's Saga* could concentrate on the similarities between the hero and contemporary Englishmen, confident that:

Many readers will find in this rough landlord of olden time a mirror of the natural English character untempered by modern civilization.[27]

The article concludes with the statement that the more we know about Icelandic literature and life:

the more clearly shall we understand the history of our ancestors and the deep-laid bases of our national character.[28]

Here was historical justification for Morris's feeling that the literature of the North was deeply relevant to modern life.

There was also, however, a further sense in which even the strange mythology of the Norsemen was inextricably linked with the thought-patterns of nineteenth-century men. It was pointed out by, among others, the German refugee Karl Blind, in an essay on 'Germanic Mythology' in the *Contemporary*

Review. He begins with an idea that had become commonplace, that we use the names of our ancestors' gods in daily conversation. The days of the week, and many English place-names, are based on the Norse pantheon. After these comfortingly familiar remarks, Blind continues by discussing 'some facts which at first sight appear rather startling'.[29] There are disconcerting similarities, he points out, between Germanic and Christian religious symbolism. Both systems refer to a flood, baptism, the sign of the cross, a dying god, a traitor and the return of the god inaugurating a Golden Age. Despite Gladstone's theory – expressed for example in *Juventus Mundi* (1869) – that these resemblances were caused by God's partial revelation of Christian truth to the pre-Christian peoples, scientific study revealed that the true explanation was a racial link which could be traced back into the far-distant past. It was, incredibly, possible to 'establish a clear connection between the mythology of our Germanic ancestors and that of the Aryan stock in India, at the time when the Vedas were composed – that is, probably, thousands of years before Christ'.[30] Blind ends with a plea for further study of these phenomena, so that the gloom of superstition might be cleared away and human progress no longer impeded.

Blind was in fact rather behind the times in his suggestion that the study of comparative mythology was a new one. By the early 1870s, when he published his article, examination of ancient mythological systems had been for nearly twenty years an expanding academic field in England. Even before this period, men had been made familiar by their predominantly classical education with the Greek and Roman myths, and had felt the need to explain how they were produced. As well as Gladstone's theory of pre-Christian revelation, there was the euhemeristic view that the gods and heroes had once been real people, and that myths could be explained as garbled versions of historical facts. Other commentators believed that myths were symbolic, describing natural phenomena in allegorical language. Karl Otfried Müller wrote a book in defence of this theory which was translated into English in 1844 as *Introduction to a Scientific System of Mythology*. All these ideas, however, were challenged by the mythologists who based their studies on philological research, and it was they who began to make connections between classical mythology and the myths of the Norsemen.

The science of comparative philology made its first appearance at the end of the eighteenth century, when students of Sanskrit began to notice similarities between this Indian language and the European tongues Latin and Greek. As Sanskrit texts became more readily available, scholars gradually discovered that there was a family relationship between Sanskrit, Latin, Greek, Celtic and the Teutonic dialects; all were sister languages, which could be traced back to a single common ancestor. This was the language spoken by an ancient tribe before it split up to form the Hindu, Greek, Teutonic and Celtic races. Several names were suggested for the family of languages and the tribe which spoke their mother-tongue. The name which was most popular in England was coined by a German scholar who lived and worked in Oxford, Friedrich Max Müller. He gave to the ancient tribe and its language the title 'Aryan'.

Max Müller did more than anyone to give academic respectability to the science of philology. He was the first holder of the Chair of Comparative Philology at Oxford, which was created especially for him in 1868. A modern biographer of Max Müller has declared that the scholar's books and articles:

not only established the concept of an Indo-European family of languages more firmly, but they also popularized it in a manner nobody else rivalled.[31]

One of Max Müller's most important contributions to philology was his suggestion that an understanding of language could lead to a true explanation of the origin of mythology. His studies of the language of the Aryans convinced him that they were a rational and civilized people, who already possessed the concept of a single omnipotent deity. Yet it was clear that long after the division of the Aryan tribe into the separate Indo-European nations, myths were current among these races which seemed to imply that they had regressed from their primitive rationality to a degraded polytheism. Max Müller was particularly affronted by the story of Zeus's mutilation of his father Chronos; how, he asked, could such a revolting tale have gained credence among the descendants of the logical and humane Aryans? To explain how the monotheism of the Aryans was transmuted into the mythological system of the Greeks, Max Müller suggested that myths were the result of linguistic distortion.

The Aryans did not believe in a sun-god, but were obviously concerned to describe such natural phenomena as the sun-rise. At that early stage of its development, their language was inevitably vivid and metaphorical; abstract and emotionally neutral terms were non-existent. Similarly, neuter forms were unknown; the words for 'sun' and 'dawn', for example, would have respectively masculine and feminine gender. This meant that a simple statement of fact such as 'the sun-rise follows the dawn' would be linguistically impossible. The Aryans would have to express the idea metaphorically, and say 'the shining one hastens to embrace the woman who gleams'. Phrases such as this passed into the language of the Aryans' descendants. Over the centuries, however, the meaning of these descriptions of natural events was forgotten. The terms for 'sun' and 'dawn', 'the shining one' and 'the one who gleams', were mistaken for proper names; the Greeks, for example, forgot that 'Daphne' was a synonym for 'dawn' and turned the phrase 'Apollo pursues Daphne' into the basis for a mythological story about a sun-god and a beautiful nymph. Max Müller called this process a 'disease of language',[32] and believed that it was universally responsible for the existence of mythology. He first put forward this theory in an article on 'Comparative Mythology' in the 1856 volume of *Oxford Essays*, and it was a central aspect of his later publications.[33]

Max Müller did not only take examples from Greek mythology to substantiate his contention. He believed that the natural phenomenon which most often gave rise to mythology by means of linguistic misunderstanding was the rising and setting of the sun, because of the awe with which the Aryans viewed the body which gave them warmth and light. It followed that a great many tales not only about gods but also about heroes could be seen as metaphorical descriptions of the career of the sun. This solar myth was common in the legends of many European and Indian peoples:

The idea of a young hero, whether he is called Baldr, or Sigurðr, or Sîfrit, or Achilles, or Meleager, or Kephalos, dying in the fulness of youth, a story so frequently told, localized, individualized, was first suggested by the Sun, dying in all his youthful vigour either at the end of a day, struck by the powers of darkness, or at the end of the sunny season, stung by the thorn of winter.[34]

One of Max Müller's examples is the story of how 'Sigurðr, as the solar hero is called in the *Edda*',[35] kills the dragon Fafnir, who embodies the powers of darkness and has stolen away the gold as Pluto stole Persephone:

The vernal sun wins it back, and like Demeter, rich in the possession of her restored daughter, the earth becomes rich again with all the treasures of spring.[36]

Sigurd's release of Brynhild represents the spring returning with the warmth of the sun. Eventually, however, the sun comes under the influence of the 'nebulous regions'[37] symbolized by Gudrun and the Niblungs. Sigurd is killed while asleep at the winter solstice, and the sun's cycle of increasing power and subsequent decline has been completed for another day or another year.

The belief that many of the myths and legends of European races were versions of the rise and setting of the sun became known as the 'solar mythology theory'. In 1870 George Cox, one of Max Müller's disciples, published a two-volume work dealing exhaustively with the philologically based study of mythology and entitled *The Mythology of the Aryan Nations*. In Cox's view such figures as Arthur, Beowulf and Charlemagne, as well as Sigurd, were all solar heroes. He discusses at some length the solar basis of the *Volsunga Saga*:

the whole myth of Volsung and his children is but a repetition, in all its phases, of that great drama of Greek mythology which begins with the loss of the golden fleece and ends with the return of the Herakleidai. This drama represents the course or history of the sun in all its different aspects.[38]

Sigurd is the sun, Brynhild the dawn and Gudrun the evening twilight:

It is the old tale, repeated under a thousand different forms. The bright dawn who greeted the newly risen sun cannot be with him as he journeys through the heaven; and the bride whom he weds in her stead is nearer and more akin to the mists of evening or the cold of winter.[39]

The theory of solar mythology thus linked the Norse legends with Greek mythology, and postulated a common origin for the theological systems of all the Indo-European nations.

Reactions to this theory were naturally mixed. Some people accepted it wholeheartedly; one correspondent quoted by the classical scholar F. A. Paley was convinced that Red Riding Hood was a solar heroine.[40] Others, such as the historian Edward A. Freeman, were more sceptical. He was prepared to admit that the gods of Greek mythology could be explained as metaphors for the sky and the sun, but was less certain about the heroes of legend:

what I cannot bring myself to admit is that Oidipous, Achilleus, Odysseus, Paris, and a crowd of other heroes, are all the sun also.[41]

Yet he realized that Max Müller and the other philologists had suggested new ways of looking at the customs and institutions of modern man; he felt that comparative philology:

will be found to be the true key to wide fields of political history, a key that will show us that the Aryans left their first home, not only with a common stock of language and legend, but with a common stock of political institutions.[42]

It was generally accepted that Max Müller's discoveries had cast new and vital light on the problem of the origin of mankind, and had established connections between peoples formerly considered distinct. Max Müller himself demonstrated in 'Comparative Mythology' his knowledge that his views were revolutionary:

To us, man is no longer this solitary being, complete in itself, and self-sufficient; man to us is a brother among brothers, a member of a class, of a genus, or a kind, and therefore intelligible only with reference to his equals.[43]

He continues:

the human soul ... stands before our mind in quite a different light since man has been taught to know and feel himself as a member of one great family.[44]

Karl Blind also saw that the new philological research, which linked man to his fellows in a way not dreamt of before, was akin to recent developments in other sciences. He gives as an example the work of Darwin. Blind explains that:

We live in an age in which the human mind endeavours to trace all things and ideas to some early germ, or root. It is done in language, in literature, in physiology, in religion.[45]

Darwin showed how in nature plants and animals were dependent on each other for existence. Comparative philology suggested that Englishmen and Hindus had come from the same tribe and had their thinking moulded by the same language. Mythological studies were proving that even men's conceptions of God were not unique to each nation but part of a unified response to the wonders of nature and based on a common feeling of religious awe in the face of the unknown. The whole tenor of such researches was to discountenance the idea that man, especially the Victorian Englishman, was in any way isolated from or more perfect than the rest of creation. It follows that if, for instance, the ancient Scandinavians were not only our historical ancestors but also, like us, a section of the great Teutonic branch of the Aryan nations, it was impossible to consider them as remote from or irrelevant to modern life. If Morris was at all affected by the work of Max Müller, Cox and their supporters, he must have found there all possible justification for basing his writing on that of the medieval Icelanders.

IV

It is impossible to be certain precisely how much Morris knew about comparative philology and the solar mythology theory. That he was interested in this branch of scholarship is clear from his own words. In a paper read to the seventh Annual Meeting of the Society for the Protection of Ancient Buildings in 1884, he spoke of two new sciences which had revolutionized historical research, namely philology and archaeology. He continued:

Of the first of these instruments, deeply as I am interested in it, and especially on the side which, tending towards comparative mythology, proclaims so clearly the unity of mankind, of this I lack the knowledge to speak.[46]

Thus while claiming only a layman's understanding of the theory, he shows that he has grasped its essential implication. On several occasions in 1884 Morris discussed what he saw as the new concept of history, and showed that he accepted the idea of an organic link between past and present. In the address previously quoted he explained that up to the present time only two historical periods had been thought worthy of study, namely classical antiquity and post-Renaissance Europe. Now the new historical methods were casting light on ages once dismissed as barbaric, and revealing an ordered progress of civilization:

The mists of pedantry slowly lifted and showed a different picture; inchoate order in the remotest times, varying indeed among different races and countries, but swayed always by the same laws, moving forward ever towards something that seems the very opposite of that which it started from, and yet the earlier order never dead but living in the new.[47]

In a lecture given earlier in the same year, the first of two on 'The Gothic Revival', Morris declared that in recent times:

a new science grew up, almost a new sense one may say, and real living history became possible to us; not a dry string of annals, not a mere series of brilliant essays or comparisons between the past and the present; but a definite insight into the life of the bygone ages.[48]

It seems highly likely that one influence which helped him to this belief was comparative philology and mythology.

It would have been possible for Morris as an undergraduate to attend Max Müller's lectures in Oxford.[49] He was, as we have seen, inspired in his early work by Thorpe's *Northern Mythology*, which in its opening section deals with the etymology of Norse words. In later life Morris gave high praise to *Teutonic Mythology* by Jacob Grimm, finding the book by the great philologist 'crammed with material for imagination'.[50] In Morris's library were, besides Thorpe and Grimm, two copies of *Teutonic Mythology* by the Swedish scholar Viktor Rydberg, translated in 1889 by the American Ambassador to Copenhagen, Rasmus B. Anderson.[51] These books, all of which accept the Aryan theory, indicate that during the 1880s Morris came into contact with the ideas I have been discussing. Although there is no proof that he discovered them earlier, it would seem likely that he read, for instance, a review entitled 'Myths of the Aryans' in the *London Quarterly Review* for October 1870. The article discusses Cox's *Mythology of the Aryan Nations*, Gladstone's *Juventus Mundi*, Ruskin's *The Queen of the Air* (1869) and Morris and Magnússon's translation of the *Volsunga Saga*. The critic is sympathetic to the solar mythology theory, and describes the story of Sigurd in these terms:

Fafnir is the Python of the north ... He appears to represent the malignant power of the earth that steals Brynhild (the summer) and her treasure, and guards them with barriers of ice and volcanic fire.[52]

He ends by emphasizing the unity of the Aryan race and of its literature and religion:

Wherever the branches of the Aryan race are found, there also is found the Aryan mythology. In spite of differences of form, such as are to be expected from the moulding of Ionian rhapsodists, of Keltic bards, and of Norse skalds, the materials of all are evidently the same, and these materials are preserved to us in the incoherent phrases of the Vedic hymns.[53]

Whether or not, however, Morris read this particular article, it is certain that he was influenced during the 1870s by the theory of solar mythology. For proof we have only to turn to his poem *Sigurd the Volsung*, in which the imagery attached to the hero might have come directly from the pages of Max Müller or Cox.

The Story of Sigurd the Volsung and the Fall of the Niblungs is in several ways a turning-point in Morris's literary development. His last long poem, it was, he believed, his greatest achievement, the work by which he wished to be remembered.[54] Yet it was not so much a summing up of what had gone before, as a first step in the direction of the romances which completed Morris's literary canon. In *Sigurd* Morris drew together the various strands of the Icelandic influence on his thinking. The poem deals with the concept of heroism, and does so in the spirit of acceptance and admiration which Morris had learnt from the sagas. It is set in the past, but gone are the ambivalent and ironic images of tombs, statues and death-in-life which once permeated Morris's poetry and embodied his sceptical attitude to literature based on the past. The poem looks not backwards but forwards, to a glorious future. Optimism, tentatively embraced at the end of *The Earthly Paradise*, becomes a ruling force in Morris's poetry, and he is thus prepared for the possibility of writing true romances. Finally, the poem uses images of cosmic significance taken from Aryan mythology, which give *Sigurd* a universal and timeless relevance more extensive than anything Morris had previously attempted. Linked with these Aryan references is a feeling that art not only can but must relay to its audience fundamental truths about human existence. Far from seeing art as separated from real life, Morris is in *Sigurd* expressing a belief in the artist as preserver and transmitter of ultimate realities.

v

According to Eirikr Magnússon, Morris was not greatly impressed by the *Volsunga Saga* when he read it for the first time. Magnússon translated it during the summer of 1869 and sent his version to Morris, who was staying with his wife Janey at Ems. In a letter Morris describes the saga (of which he had as yet only read the early sections, the story of Sigmund and Signy) as 'rather of the monstrous order' (VII. xx). When he had finished Magnússon's translation, however, he became fascinated by the saga. Magnússon recalled him:

in a state of great excitement, pacing his study. He told me he had now finished reading my translation of the 'grandest tale that ever was told'. (VII. xx)

This extreme enthusiasm may also be traced in Morris's letter written in December 1869 to the American writer Charles Eliot Norton. The letter ends with Morris's regret that he could not use the *Volsunga Saga* as the subject for a modern imaginative work:

I had it in my head to write an epic of it, but though I still hanker after it, I see clearly it would be foolish, for no verse could render the best parts of it, and it would only be a flatter and tamer version of a thing already existing.[55]

His reaction to Wagner's temerity in choosing the story as the basis for his opera cycle similarly emphasizes the sublimity of the saga and the fact that modern treatment tended to trivialize it:

I look upon it as nothing short of desecration to bring such a tremendous and world-wide subject under the gaslights of an opera ... the idea of sandy-haired German tenor tweedle-deeing over the unspeakable woes of Sigurd, which even the simplest words are not typical enough to express![56]

By October 1875, however, when he began work on *Sigurd*, Morris had changed his mind about the possibility of creating a modern epic based on the *Volsunga* story. Perhaps he realized that in the tale of Sigurd he had found a theme perfectly fitted for the expression of his new ideas about heroism.

Even before his birth Sigurd is marked out as a mighty man, and when he is born his step-father King Elf greets the baby with prophecies of greatness. From an early age the young hero has a sense of his vocation; receiving from his mother the shards of his father's sword, he foresees that when new-forged they will be used in the service of the gods:

> They shall shake the thrones of Kings, and shear the walls of war,
> And undo the knot of treason when the world is darkening
>   o'er. (XII. 92)

When he has killed Fafnir and come to the height of his power, his fame is world-wide:

> So fares the tale of Sigurd through all kingdoms of the earth,
> And the tale is told of his doings by the utmost ocean's
>   girth. (XII. 162)

Yet the noble Sigurd is fated to live unhappily and to die by treachery. He is beguiled by Grimhild, Queen of the Niblungs, into forgetting his love for Brynhild and instead marrying Grimhild's daughter Gudrun. Having thus broken his vows of faith to Brynhild, he adds to his guilt by wooing her on behalf of his brother-in-law Gunnar and tricking her into accepting him. He does so in ignorance that he once loved her himself, but the action alone is enough to seal his fate. Brynhild, in revenge for the double deception, provokes Gunnar, Sigurd's sworn brother, into having Sigurd murdered. His dying words are a cry to Odin, wondering whether his heroism has earned him any reward:

> I have done and I may not undo, I have given and I take not again:
> Art thou other than I, Allfather, wilt thou gather my glory in
>   vain? (XII. 230)

This is the central problem of *Sigurd the Volsung*. If the glory of a hero leads only to an ignominious death, is it in any way worthwhile? Has Sigurd any assurance that his courage and might have not been wasted? Before he read the sagas, Morris would perhaps have concluded that Sigurd's death was nothing but a tragic destruction of potential. Now, however, he is able to come to a somewhat different conclusion.

First Morris must define precisely what constitutes Sigurd's heroism. To do so he sets up a picture of a world where evil and violence are paramount. The poem is organized around a series of parallel events. In the opening section, the story of Sigurd's father Sigmund and his sister Signy, Signy's wedding leads to an invitation from her husband to her father and brothers, asking them to feast with him. When they arrive at his hall they are ambushed and murdered. After many years Sigmund, the only surviving brother, revenges himself on Siggeir and the hall is burnt by Signy. As the story progresses these events are repeated, in various combinations. Sinfiotli, son of Sigmund and Signy, is murdered by Sigmund's wife because he slew her brother. Sigmund's marriage to his second wife Hiordis leads to his death in battle, fighting against one of her rejected suitors. We have seen how the marriages of Sigurd to Gudrun and Gunnar to Brynhild precipitate the murder of Sigurd. In the final book Gudrun has remarried, and persuades her husband Atli to invite her brothers to a feast. When they arrive she watches them being massacred by Atli's soldiers, in revenge for their killing of Sigurd. Then she kills her husband and sets fire to his hall. The story of Sigurd is thus only a part of a cycle of bloodshed and revenge, and there seems no reason why the violence should not continue for ever.

The recurrent evil in the world is symbolized in the poem by a series of images which Morris took from his source and expanded into powerful motifs. Savage violence is represented by the image of a wolf. Sigmund is left in the forest to be killed by wolves, and escapes only by becoming 'wolfish' (XII. 21) himself and tearing the beast with his teeth. Later he and Sinfiotli turn into werewolves and learn how to abrogate their humanity in order to carry out their task of revenge. When persuading her son Guttorm to kill Sigurd, Grimhild gives him a magic drink containing, among other ingredients, 'the heart of the ravening wood-wolf' (XII. 227). Another kind of evil evoked in *Sigurd* is that which works by stealth and cunning. This is represented by two images. Gunnar the oath-breaker is killed by being flung into a snake-pit, and the snakes are called 'images of guile' (XII. 296). The other image is that of a snare, net or trap which may envelop the unwary. Siggeir lays a 'death-snare' (XII. 13) for Signy's family. When Sigurd goes to war on behalf of the Niblungs, we hear:

Now spread is the snare of treason, and cast is the net of guile,
And the mirk-wood gleams with the ambush, and venom lurks at
  the board. (XII. 160)

This phrase links the net image with that of the poisonous serpents. These are only a few examples of the way three images – wolves, snakes, nets – create an atmosphere of brooding evil throughout the poem. Sigurd must contend against this if he is to be truly a hero.

At first it seems as if he is going to succeed. The wolf imagery is never connected with him. He rejects the cunning symbolized by the images of snakes when he kills the dragon or worm Fafnir. He also kills the treacherous Regin, despising the 'tangled web' (XII. 117) of evil in which the Dwarf sought to entwine him. In the saga Sigurd avenges his father before killing Fafnir; in Morris's poem he never attempts to do so. He tries instead to break the pattern of retribution which controls everyone else in the poem. Yet although he is proof against savagery, he can be overcome by cunning. Grimhild takes away his memory by a drink in which are mingled:

> a tangle of strange love,
> Deep guile, and strong compelling.   (XII. 166)

Later he tells Brynhild that he was caught in an 'eyeless tangle ... the snare for our feet fore-ordered' (XII. 222–3). Sigurd is a hero because he attempts to destroy the cycle of recurring evil, but he is doomed to be captured after all in the net of deception and to become a deceiver himself. The fact that his failure is foretold by Gripir the seer adds to the feeling of inevitability: Morris seems to be returning to his familiar view that heroism is futile.

Morris has given us a picture of a world in which heroic actions are vain attempts to halt a process of repeated evil. Instead of leaving the problem there, he suggests in this poem the possibility of good ultimately outweighing evil. Even at the moment of their greatest happiness, Sigurd and Brynhild are aware that sorrow may overtake them. Sigurd asks:

> what were the fruit of our lives if apart they needs must
> pass? (XII. 147)

She echoes his question, but hints also at an answer:

> what fruit of our life-days, what fruit of our death shall be?
> What fruit, save men's remembrance of the grief of thee and
> me? (XII. 147)

In 'The Golden Apples' Hercules made a similar suggestion, that the memory of his heroism might be of use to later generations. In *Sigurd* this process is explained further. When Sigurd awakens Brynhild on Hindfell he asks her to teach him wisdom. In the saga she responds with a series of rather predictable remarks about not getting drunk and avoiding involvement with another man's wife. In Morris's version of the scene she turns instead to the subject of heroism, and gives Sigurd advice about the spirit in which he should meet the dictates of fate:

> Know thou, most mighty of men, that the Norns shall order all,
> And yet without thine helping shall no whit of their will befall
>
> . . .
>
> And the night of the Norns and their slumber, and the tide when
> the world runs back,
> And the way of the sun is tangled, it is wrought of the dastard's
> lack.
> But the day when the fair earth blossoms, and the sun is bright
> above,
> Of the daring deeds is it fashioned and the eager hearts of
> love. (XII. 126)

To understand these rather cryptic sentences, we must remember the context of Norse mythology in which Morris is writing. The 'night of the Norns' is Ragnarök, the last battle in which gods and men will be united in the fight against the evil powers of the world. When evil has been destroyed, at the cost of the lives of many gods and men, a new world will be born and the dead god Baldur will return to rule over a new Golden Age. This is 'the day when the fair earth blossoms'. It was usually believed that heroes who had died in battle were taken to Valhalla, to form part of Odin's host on the day of Ragnarök. Morris here makes Brynhild alter the traditional conception, by claiming that the actions of men on earth contribute either to the ultimate good or evil of the world. Sigurd must suffer and die, but his death is valuable because the heroism with which he accepts it will add to the stock of earthly good and hasten the coming of the Golden Age:

> a gift to the Gods hast thou given,
> And a tree for the roof and the wall in the house of the hope that shall be,
> Though it seemeth our very sorrow, and the grief of thee and me. (XII. 127)

This is the point of Sigurd's death-cry; he is asking whether Odin has in fact accepted the gift. Although he receives no reassurance, the reader does. The lament for the dead lovers asserts that they have brought closer the Golden Age:

> They are gone – the lovely, the mighty, the hope of the ancient Earth:
> It shall labour and bear the burden as before that day of their birth:
> It shall groan in its blind abiding for the day that Sigurd hath sped,
> And the hour that Brynhild hath hastened, and the dawn that waketh the dead:
> It shall yearn, and be oft-times holpen, and forget their deeds no more,
> Till the new sun beams on Baldur, and the happy sealess shore. (XII. 244)

Mankind will be supported while it waits for Ragnarök by the memory of Sigurd and Brynhild's heroism, and by the hope of ultimate happiness which their story awakens in the hearts of those who hear it. As in 'The Golden Apples', but now with positive clarity, a view of time as cyclical, repetitive, has been set against the hero's concept of time as progressive, moving towards an end. Much more firmly than in the *Earthly Paradise* story, cyclical time is perceived as connected with recurrent evil. But more powerful is the opposing heroic vision, which now in *Sigurd* is given extended and telling expression. Morris surrounds with images of hope an apocalyptic belief in the eventual triumph of good over evil.

A feeling that the world is a theatre of battle between good and evil had been implicit in Morris's poetry before *Sigurd*. It was because evil appeared to be winning that he, and his characters, felt the need to escape to an Earthly Paradise where only good could exist. Present also was the idea that to withdraw from the world took one beyond the reach of good as well as evil; the Paradise, even if attainable, was a sterile limbo of non-being. In *Sigurd* Morris states emphatically that good and evil are inter-mingled and can be separated only at the cost of denying one's humanity. Regin the Smith, one of the Dwarfs born before the creation of man, tells in Book Two how his people once lived without sorrow, memory or love, knowing no difference between good and evil. Then the gods came from Asgard, and with them hope and fear entered the world. Men began to understand the arts and crafts of civilization; they learnt both how to cure the sick, and how to poison their enemies. Morris turns the story of the compensation demanded from the gods for the death of Regin's brother Otter into an ideological conflict. The Dwarfs wish to overcome the gods and return the world to the condition of the Golden Age, in which both pleasure and pain were unknown. Yet if the gods abdicate, although the earth will cease to be torn by violence, it will lose also laughter and poetry:

> And there shall be no more kings, and battle and murder shall fail,
> And the world shall laugh and long not, nor weep, nor fashion the
>   tale. (XII. 80)

Regin desires to use the wealth of Anvari's gold, when Sigurd has obtained it from Fafnir, to enforce a return to the Golden Age and to destroy the rule of the gods. He wishes to make good and evil once more indistinguishable so that morality and heroism become impossible. The birds warn Sigurd not to allow this to happen:

> Arise! lest the world run backward and the blind heart have its
>   will,
> And once again be tangled the sundered good and ill;
> Lest love and hatred perish, lest the world forget its tale,
> And the Gods sit deedless, dreaming, in the high-walled heavenly
>   vale. (XII. 116)

Sigurd kills Regin to prevent this retrogression. The rest of his life is devoted, as we have seen, to deeds which will hasten the coming of the future Golden Age, when Baldur returns and the earth is new-made. The fact that this regeneration is certain makes *Sigurd* Morris's first really optimistic poem. He has come to believe that the Earthly Paradise is indeed attainable, not by

escaping from reality but by facing up to it. Here at last is a
world-view which might enable an author to write within the
convention of romance.

VI

As he begins to look forward with hope to the future, Morris is
released from his ambivalent attitude towards the past. In the
portrait of Regin he condemns, as usual, an unthinking idealization of former ages. It is as impossible as it is undesirable to turn
the world back to what it used to be. However, the hero who is
working for the future happiness of mankind may be supported
by the knowledge that others have suffered and endured before
him, just as Morris was encouraged by reading the story of
Grettir. When Sigurd is born, King Elf links past and future as he
thinks of the baby's potential greatness. He revolves in his
mind:

> the years and their building and burden, and toil of the sons of
>   man,
> The joy of folk and their sorrow, and the hope of deeds to
>   do. (XII. 65)

In his death-song Gunnar comforts himself by recalling the
creation of mankind, and asserts his conviction that the gods
have a purpose for the world. The generations of man are born
and die like the transient phenomena of nature, but new life is
constantly being formed:

> they changed their lives and departed, and came back as the
>   leaves of the trees
> Come back and increase in the summer: – and I, I, I am of these;
> And I know of Them that have fashioned, and the deeds that have
>   blossomed and grow;
> But nought of the Gods' repentance, or the Gods' undoing I
>   know. (XII. 298)

Gunnar's individual fate is unimportant; it is merely part of the
constantly repeated cycle of birth and death which has been
ordained for the whole natural world. In *The Earthly Paradise*
the revolving of the seasons caused men to despair because it
reminded them of their own transience. In *Sigurd* the action of
time is reassuring, because in living and dying men are part of

the process which will eventually culminate in the Golden Age. The organic imagery found in *The Earthly Paradise* becomes insistent in *Sigurd* as an expression of this idea. A survey of the quotations from the poem already employed will suggest the frequency with which the heroes, especially Sigurd, are associated with natural imagery. Both Sigurd and Brynhild speak of their lives and love as potentially fruitful; the culminating Ragnarök is described as 'the day when the fair earth blossoms'; Gunnar, like Hercules in 'The Golden Apples', is comforted in the face of death by imagining the great heroes returning to earth, reborn like next year's leaves, and speaks of 'deeds that have blossomed and grow'. There are no hints now of stony immobility, no pictures of a hero (like Arthur in the poem 'Golden Wings') unable to return from death-in-life to valuable earthly activity. The (literally) overarching symbol of the organic power of heroic action is the tree, which is one of the poem's dominant images. The opening description of the Volsungs' hall stresses that its chief wonder is the living tree which provides its central pillar: the Branstock, from which Sigmund draws Odin's sword to initiate the feud between the Volsungs and the Goths. As he does so he is compared to a tree:

Like the best of the trees of the garden, when the April sunbeams fall
On its blossomed boughs in the morning, and tell of the days to be. (XII. 8)

After his revenge on Siggeir he recalls his sister Signy and remembers that she sacrificed herself 'that the Volsung kin might blossom and bear the fruit of worth' (XII. 42). He believes that he himself is an 'after-summer seed' (XII. 42) ensuring the continuance of his almost obliterated race. The fruit of the seed, of course, is the mighty hero Sigurd. In language reminiscent of biblical references to Christ as the Rod of Jesse, Hiordis prophesies that her yet to be conceived son will be a 'stem' (XII. 51) growing from the loins of Sigmund. When the baby is born he is described as the 'latest flower' of the Volsungs (XII. 62) and likened to a great tree:

They said: 'The earth is weary: but the tender blade hath sprung,
That shall wax till beneath its branches fair bloom the meadows green.' (XII. 65)

Brynhild cautions Sigurd to be sure that he acts wisely so that his actions will bear heroic fruit:

Be wise, and cherish thine hope in the freshness of the days,
And scatter its seed from thine hand in the field of the people's
   praise;
Then fair shall it fall in the furrow, and some the earth shall speed,
And the sons of men shall marvel at the blossom of the
   deed. (XII. 126)

If he succeeds, she tells him in lines already quoted, he will become like the Branstock: mightily upholding his kindred as a great tree supports the walls and roof of a hall. As in 'The Hill of Venus', then, transforming power is described in terms of growing and blossoming. What has changed since Morris wrote *The Earthly Paradise* is that he has acquired a newly unambiguous belief that men can channel that power usefully and successfully through their actions. The vegetable imagery suggests that this is achieved as the result of a unity between the hero and nature.

In both scientific and historical research of the mid-nineteenth century considerable stress was laid on the defining of organic links – between species, races, historical periods. We have seen how both racial and social characteristics of the English were described as developments from those of the Scandinavian people; and how the Aryan language came to be understood as a mother-tongue from which grew modern Indo-European speech. Scientists similarly sought proof of unity between organisms; Darwin is only one of those who cast new light on the links between man and the rest of the natural world.[57] Morris has clearly found in these ideas a valuable corrective to his former fear that tales of the past might be merely escapist fantasy. If past and present, like man and nature, are so necessarily involved with one another, he no longer needs to apologize for taking a subject from the past, nor to hedge his medieval tale around with ironies about the uselessness of ancient stories. In the letter about Wagner quoted above, it will be remembered, Morris spoke of the sorrows of Sigurd as something which only 'typical' words could express. He is approaching here another of the concepts of romance, that a work of art may show truths which are valid for all time, rather than describe a particular period or individual. Romance does not reflect the temporary and external appearance of things, but aspires to embody a deeper reality that is eternally relevant. In *Sigurd* Morris is more concerned with heroism than with the hero himself. He is attempting to alert his readers to a process which is timeless because constantly repeated. Sigurd's life and death is important as one man's struggle against evil. It is also an example of a basic element in the life of mankind, a story which must be acted out in one way or another by every human being. Above all, it reflects the process of fruition and decay and the promise of new birth which is at the centre of the natural world. Both men and nature endlessly perform the same drama. To suggest this idea to his readers, Morris makes use of Max Müller's solar theory and turns Sigurd into an image of the sun.

In the saga, Sigurd is most often described with reference to the gold he won from Fafnir, and especially as the wearer of a golden suit of armour. These descriptions were one reason for Max Müller's identification of Sigurd with the sun. Morris systematically elaborates the motif. The hero is born at daybreak, and is hailed by one of King Elf's men as 'Dawn of the Day' (XII. 66). His sword is likened to the sun shining through the clouds of evening. Even before he kills Fafnir he is described as 'golden' (XII. 107), and Regin has to shield his eyes from his glory as he might from the sun. The battle between Sigurd and Fafnir is consistently described as a conflict between light and darkness, and he kills the dragon as the sun rises:

> he laughed at the heavens above him for he saw the sun arise,
> And Sigurd gleamed on the desert, and shone in the new-born light,
> And the wind in his raiment wavered, and all the world was bright. (XII. 110)

The language here is such that one has difficulty in knowing whether Sigurd is reflecting the rays of the sun or is lit by a radiance of his own. When Sigurd arrives in Lymdale, he appears to the folk there like the rising sun:

> All eyes are turned to beholding the eastward-lying glade,
> For thereby comes something glorious, as though an earthly sun
> Were lit by the orb departing, lest the day should be wholly done;
> Lo now, as they stand astonied, a wonder they behold,
> For a warrior cometh riding, and his gear is all of gold. (XII. 141)

These examples could be extended at will, for the whole poem is moulded by the conception of Sigurd as a solar hero. Opposed to him are the Niblungs, whom Morris, like Max Müller, sees as images of darkness. They are 'the Cloudy People' (XII. 306), and we are told:

> they deal with the wind and the weather; in the cloudy drift they
> dwell. (XII. 131)

In contrast with the golden-haired and gold-clad Sigurd, they have black hair and wear blue-black armour. When Sigurd and Brynhild meet for the first time after their marriages, Grimhild stands between them:

> e'en as the rainless cloud
> Ere the first of the tempest ariseth the latter sun doth shroud,
> And men look round and shudder, so Grimhild came between
> The silent golden Sigurd and the eyes of the mighty
> Queen. (XII. 200)

The prevalence of these images ensures that when Sigurd and Gunnar change shapes, and Sigurd's glory is literally obscured by the darkness of Gunnar's appearance, the action relates to a wider context than merely the betrayal of Sigurd's individual faith. We are seeing the sun hidden by clouds; the light which gives life to the world made invisible by darkness. Sigurd himself sees the distortion of truth which results from the shape-changing in terms of clouds drawing across the sky:

> cloudy of late were the heavens with many a woven lie,
> And now is the clear of the twilight, when the slumber draweth
> anigh. (XII. 214)

This reference to evening and the setting sun emphasizes the connections which we are asked to make between Sigurd's death and the end of the day. Gunnar dies at daybreak, as the darkness is lifted by the promise of a new sun.

Morris also links Sigurd with Baldur, the dying god of Norse mythology who was himself seen as a solar hero by Max Müller. When Sigurd first rides his horse Greyfell, he is described thus:

> Lo, lo, the horse and the rider! So once maybe it was,
> When over the Earth unpeopled the youngest God would pass;
> But never again meseemeth shall such a sight betide,
> Till over a world unwrongful new-born shall Baldur ride. (XII. 97)

When he arrives at Lymdale the men wonder:

> Are the Gods on the earth? did the world change yesternight?
> Are the sons of Odin coming, and the days of Baldur the
>   bright? (XII. 141)

Like Karl Blind, Morris in *Sigurd* also looked further than Norse
mythology and made some other comparisons. There are
several places in the poem in which Sigurd is likened to Christ.
When he is born, King Elf asks Hiordis's women:

> Of a King new-born do ye tell,
> By a God of the Heavens begotten in our fathers' house to
>   dwell? (XII. 65)

As Sigurd is about to slay the serpent (symbol of Satan in
medieval literature) he is told by Odin to dig a pit and await the
dragon there:

> be as the dead for a season, and the living light abide! (XII. 109)

When he has killed Fafnir, we are told that 'he leapt from the pit
and the grave' (XII. 110). These phrases remind us of biblical
references to the death and resurrection of Christ. After the
murder, the Niblungs repent that they rejected Sigurd:

> For he, the redeemer, the helper, the crown of all their worth,
> They looked upon him and wondered, they loved, and they thrust
>   him forth. (XII. 232)

This also seems to reflect the words in St John's Gospel about
the inability of Christ's people to accept his sacrifice.[58] Finally,
at the end of the poem the serpent is again linked with Satan
when Gunnar is killed by the oldest of the snakes. It is described
as:

> of the kin of the Serpent once wrought all wrong to nurse,
> The bond of earthly evil, the Midworld's ancient curse. (XII. 298)

This could apply to the Midgard serpent, but it could equally
well be a reference to the serpent of Genesis. Gunnar cannot
withstand him, but Sigurd–Christ overcomes the snake and,
like the sun, rises again.

Morris could not, I believe, have published in 1876 a poem
thus linking his Norse hero with Baldur, Christ and the sun
without expecting his readers to realize the connections with

the theories of Aryan mythology. He needed to make these references because when writing *Sigurd* he no longer saw himself as a simple story-teller providing temporary escape or entertainment. In *The Earthly Paradise* he had tentatively suggested that art might on occasions relate very closely to the reality of a human situation, as Gregory the Star-gazer found his own problems mirrored in the tale of 'The Land East of the Sun and West of the Moon'. Now this concept has matured. Morris undoubtedly loved the story of Sigurd because of its heroic fantasy, its excitement, pathos and exhilaration. Yet it was not solely because it appealed to his delight in adventure that he first translated it and then used it as a basis for an epic poem. He felt that it was a story which embodied basic and essential insights about life and death, good and evil, which it was his duty to offer to modern English readers. It was part of their Aryan, and specifically Teutonic, inheritance. This is hinted at in the Preface to the translation of the *Volsunga Saga*, which ends with these words:

this is the Great Story of the North, which should be to all our race what the Tale of Troy was to the Greeks – to all our race first, and afterwards, when the change of the world has made our race nothing more than a name of what has been – a story too – then should it be to those that come after us no less than the Tale of Troy has been to us. (VII. 286)

It may be recalled that Cox, for instance, interpreted the tale of Troy as another Aryan solar myth. Morris has been taught by the mythologists that a story, a myth, may express by its structure and imagery the most fundamental truths of existence. We are asked to read *Sigurd* with our minds open to the relevance of his story to our own, since we are involved in the same struggle.

When he wrote *Sigurd* Morris had come to believe that it was the duty and privilege of the artist to express anew for his generation certain ultimate truths. He must also help men to remember the deeds of the heroes of the past, so that they may be inspired to play their part in the eternal struggle. Two of the aspects of civilization which Regin wishes to destroy are memory and poetry. He must not be allowed to do so, lest men forget that their lives are part of the progress of the world. The artist may forcibly assert what men are in danger of denying:

that time and change are not enemies of human achievement, for by their agency the final happiness is brought closer. In *Sigurd* Morris finally and resoundingly rejects the feeling that as a poet he is nothing but the 'idle singer of an empty day'. The day is empty no longer, and the singer has a specific and indispensable task to perform.

VII

For Morris, *Sigurd the Volsung* paves the way towards romance. In writing it he discovered the value of heroism, the relevance of the past to the modern world, the inspirational potential of story and the duty of the artist to his readers. All these insights receive their most potent expression in the romances of his last years. It only wanted one more event to spur Morris to the writing of romance. He needed to find the story around which his writing could organize itself, the theme to which he was to give form. When he embraced Socialism in 1883 he was presented with his subject, and from that point his vocation as a romance writer began to flower into maturity.

CHAPTER 4

'A true conception of history': the political romances

After the publication of *Sigurd the Volsung* in 1876 there was another ten-year period during which Morris wrote very little poetry or prose fiction.[1] His next major literary work was the prose story *A Dream of John Ball*, which appeared as a serial in the *Commonweal* between November 1886 and January 1887, and as a book in 1888. This work may be said to inaugurate the final creative period of Morris's life, in which he turned more and more exclusively to the writing of prose romances.

Several reasons may be suggested for Morris's long silence, after the epic heights of *Sigurd the Volsung*. One may simply have been lack of time, for in the 1880s Morris's already busy life took on an added commitment when he began actively to interest himself in current affairs. In 1876 he was prominent in the agitation to prevent England from going to war against Russia in support of the Turkish Empire in the Balkans. In March 1877 he wrote a letter to the *Athenaeum* protesting against the restoration of Tewkesbury Abbey, which led to the formation of the Society for the Protection of Ancient Buildings. In December of the same year he gave his first public lecture, on 'The Decorative Arts: their Relation to Modern Life and Progress'.[2] In 1883 Morris joined the Democratic (later the Social Democratic) Federation, and from this time to the end of his life he was deeply involved in the task of spreading Socialist ideals by every possible method: lecturing, speaking on street corners, writing for and editing magazines and organizing the work of the various groups to which he belonged. One might imagine that even Morris would have been unable to find a free moment in which to continue his literary activities. This may be partly true; yet he did manage to produce a translation of the *Odyssey*,[3] and in the last few years of his life he became as prolific of literature as he had been in the period of his excitement over the Icelandic sagas. More serious than lack of time was a feeling that he had nothing left to write about. In a letter to Georgiana Burne-Jones in 1879 he explained that he was not writing because he had no suitable subject:

to write verse for the sake of writing is a crime in a man of my years and experience.[4]

In 1882 he explained to the same correspondent that he could not enjoy Swinburne's poem *Tristram of Lyonesse* because it was 'founded on literature, not on nature'.[5] He went on convincingly to reject any notions of 'art for art's sake' which he might once have entertained:

in these days the issue between art, that is, the godlike part of man, and mere bestiality, is so momentous, and the surroundings of life are so stern and unplayful, that nothing can take serious hold of people, or should do so, but that which is rooted deepest in reality and is quite at first hand: there is no room for anything which is not forced out of a man of deep feeling, because of its innate strength and vision.[6]

If Morris could not find a vital and forceful theme, he was not prepared to write at all.

The immediate motivation behind the composition of *A Dream of John Ball* was less exalted than one might have expected. Morris's son-in-law Henry Halliday Sparling tells us that Morris found he needed a serial story for the *Commonweal* and asked a colleague to write one, suggesting as a subject the history of Wat Tyler. The colleague refused, claiming he lacked the epic faculty. Morris burst out in reply:

Epic faculty be hanged for a yarn! Confound it, man, you've *only* got to tell a *story*!

To prove how easy it was, he produced *A Dream of John Ball*.[7] Yet the work was clearly prompted by more than a need to fill up space in the *Commonweal*. When Morris became a Socialist he found a faith which he felt it was his duty to spread to as wide an audience as possible. At first he was content to do this by the same methods as his fellow workers, and he continued to take his full share in the arduous and sometimes dangerous work of proselytizing until forced by ill health to curb his activities. However, in *A Dream of John Ball* and *News from Nowhere* (1890) Morris expressed the feeling that he was also able to bring a specific and individual skill to the service of Socialism. *News from Nowhere* is particularly concerned with the position of art in a Socialist society, and with the contribution a writer could make to the coming of the Socialist millennium.

In the previous chapter I suggested that two of the strands which would combine to form Morris's romances – his acceptance of the organic unity between past and present and a renewed belief in the force of heroic action – were provided by his reading of the sagas and related historical and mythological research. By the time of *Sigurd* the ambivalence about these two concepts so prevalent in the early prose and poetry has been very largely transformed into affirmation. Yet the third problem which dogged Morris's literary work, that fear and uncertainty about the future so poignantly expressed in the symbol of the futile search for an Earthly Paradise, is not fully solved in *Sigurd*. Though that poem is concerned with hope, it approaches it in terms of a mythical Ragnarök which lacks clarity and precision of description and may seem less than adequately powerful when set against the recurrent scenes of death and disaster which it is intended to mitigate. Morris is not yet willing to contemplate a potential Paradise that is truly earthly, attainable in fact rather than in mythology.

The Socialist faith as embraced by Morris confirmed his belief in the relevance of the past to the present; and it stressed also the need for heroic action in the present. Most vitally, for Morris, it offered him a newly convincing vision of future happiness. The Socialist vision was of no vague or metaphorical Paradise; on the contrary, it perceived that not only was the Earthly Paradise possible, its achievement was actually historically inevitable. When Morris had grasped this, he became able to reconcile past, present and future in a conjunction that enabled him to look on the operation of time not with regret or terror, but with eager hope. Thus the final condition for writing romance – a conviction of the value of the happy ending – was provided; Morris was free to pour his literary talents into the form with which for so long he had had such a tentative relationship.

Morris's return to prose fiction commences with the two Socialist propaganda stories, neither of which is a true romance though both have romance elements. From there he went on to begin the series of romances which was to end only with his death. This chapter will relate the Socialist stories to the first three romances, in an attempt to show how the political convictions of Morris's later years were the spur to his new literary mastery.

I

Some of Morris's most precise references to contemporary theories of history occur, as we have seen, in his lectures of 1884. This was the year after he joined the SDF; and together with ideas about the past there can be found in the lectures a view of the future which illustrates a political, as well as an historical and mythological, influence on Morris's thinking. He suggested that the Gothic revival was symptomatic of a new attitude:

the historic method of looking at life and the hopes for the future of mankind: for us as I have before hinted there is no longer a brief period of perfection dropped down into a world no one knows how or why ... we have done with all that for ever, and have grasped the idea of the unity and continuous life of man, in which change and growth are always present.[8]

Morris accepted the Marxist belief in historical necessity; in the Socialist insistence on the need for a clear understanding of historical process he found the final answer to his old doubts about the uses of the past. He explored his new historical certainty in a series of articles written in collaboration with E. Belfort Bax and published in the *Commonweal*. 'Socialism from the Root Up' traces the history of European civilization from the first grouping of individuals into tribal associations, to the Paris Commune of 1871: a survey of the past seen as a necessary preliminary to the second part of the series, an analysis of Marxist economic theory and a manifesto of the aims of scientific Socialism.[9] In October 1886 the series had reached the so-called Utopists Owen, Saint-Simon and Fourier. In terms reminiscent of Engels's *Socialism, Utopian and Scientific* (published in French in 1880), Morris and Bax criticize the Utopists for failing to understand the inevitability of change. After this essay the survey breaks off until February 1887; but in the meantime Morris published *A Dream of John Ball*. Seen in this context, *John Ball* is revealed as a fiction whose aim is to discourage its readers from making the same mistake as the Utopists. It is an illustration of the forces of historical necessity.

The narrator of *A Dream of John Ball* is transported, in a dream, to a Kentish village in the fourteenth century. He is present at a speech made by John Ball, one of the leaders of the Peasants' Revolt, and at a battle between the villagers and the sheriff's men-at-arms. From the beginning the dreamer feels almost completely at home in the medieval setting. He emphasizes that after the first few minutes he feels no surprise at the landscape and architecture, although they are so different from what he is used to; he accepts his new clothes, recognizes various medieval social customs and is able to understand the language. Above all, he has no difficulty in becoming part of the rebellion. He even knows the password. Naturally Morris himself might well have felt at home in a fourteenth-century village. The point, however, is to stress the close connections between the men who took part in the Peasants' Revolt and a nineteenth-century Socialist. He feels at one with these villagers because his objectives are the same as theirs; he too is a fighter for freedom and a good life for all. The fact is made plain, and the historical references extended, when the dreamer tells a tale to his friends in return for their hospitality. The story he chooses is an Icelandic one. When it is told one listener praises the Icelanders and wishes for such men in England. Another replies:

such men have been and will be, and belike are not far from this same door even now. (XVI. 224)

The linking of past, present and future in this sentence takes up some earlier words of the dreamer, when before he began his story he felt that the mead he was drinking had 'deepened my dream of things past, present, and to come' (XVI. 223). These suggestions prepare us to listen to John Ball's speech at the village cross with an understanding of the relevance of his words to the modern struggle. He talks of his desire for freedom, the abolition of the distinction between rich and poor and the life of peace and plenty which will come after the revolution. Readers of Morris's story were fighting for the same things. The dreamer makes the point specifically:

The political romances

men fight and lose the battle, and the thing that they fought for comes about in spite of their defeat, and when it comes turns out not to be what they meant, and other men have to fight for what they meant under another name. (XVI. 231–2)

Nineteenth-century Socialists may see themselves as direct ideological as well as physical descendants of the fourteenth-century peasants, and as engaged like them in the continuing class struggle.

The leading aspect of John Ball's doctrine is the importance of fellowship. It is necessary for men to love and serve each other; indeed, if they isolate themselves from other people they are already suffering the tortures of the damned:

fellowship is heaven, and lack of fellowship is hell: fellowship is life, and lack of fellowship is death. (XVI. 230)

Men are the fellows not only of their friends and neighbours, but of all those who will come after them. John Ball tells his followers that even if they die they will still be part of the revolution:

he who doeth well in fellowship, and because of fellowship, shall not fail though he seem to fail to-day, but in days hereafter shall he and his work yet be alive, and men be holpen by them to strive again and yet again. (XVI. 233)

We may remember here the similar sentiments which Morris expressed in *Sigurd the Volsung*. There he suggested that every right action added to the stock of goodness in the world and hastened the coming of the Golden Age. Now Socialism has given him a faith in a revolution which will swiftly create a Golden Age in England. Men of goodwill in former ages have already furthered its appearance, because they too were part of the historical process which makes the Golden Age inevitable. This is the message of *A Dream of John Ball*, and it is further embodied in the discussion between John Ball and the dreamer with which the book closes. After the battle, an example of fellowship in action, the bodies of the dead are laid in the church, and John Ball watches them during the night. He has divined something strange in the person of the dreamer, and asks him to talk with him. They begin by discussing life and death, and what constitutes immortality. The dreamer believes that he will live wherever men exist, because of his humanity:

though I die and end, yet mankind yet liveth, therefore I end not, since I am a man. (XVI. 265)

Although as a priest John Ball believes in a more personal immortality, he also feels that his actions will affect the lives of men on earth in future generations. Here is the heroic concept of Hercules and Sigurd, now clearly articulated in a political context. John Ball asks the dreamer to tell him whether his hope will be fulfilled. The dreamer then explains to him – in Marxist terms – the process of social history from the Peasants' Revolt to the nineteenth century, showing that although John Ball's actions do lead to the end of villeinage other forms of slavery are substituted, so that men remain divided into oppressors and oppressed. Yet eventually the time will come when people begin to understand the reasons for their subjection, and the aims of John Ball's fellowship will be united with the hope of the Socialists:

thy deeming of folly and ours shall be one, and thy hope and our hope; and then – the Day will have come. (XVI. 286)

Although for the dreamer the events he relates are in the past and for John Ball they are in the future, the same end is sought by both men.

In 'Frank's Sealed Letter', thirty years before, Morris had considered the possibility that either memory, or an imaginative experience of a fictional past, might enable someone productively to order his future activity. That story, however, ended before we were allowed to see any practical results of the narrator's insights and their virtue appeared ambiguously asserted. Fired now by a conviction of an ultimate Socialist victory, Morris returns to the theme of the past, embodied in a fictional narrative, stimulating action which will itself bring closer the future good. This time there is no ambiguity: 'the Day will have come'.

Towards the end of *A Dream of John Ball*, the priest says to the dreamer:

scarce do I know whether to wish thee some dream of the days beyond thine to tell what shall be, as thou hast told me, for I know not if that shall help or hinder thee. (XVI. 286)

The political romances

One vision of the future which Morris considered extremely unhelpful was a book published in 1888 by the American author Edward Bellamy, called *Looking Backward, 2000–1887*. When he read this account of a Socialist state in which conscription of labour is combined with a seemingly benevolent paternalism, Morris was horrified; May Morris remembered her father saying that 'if they brigaded *him* into a regiment of workers he would just lie on his back and kick' (XVI. xxviij). The immediate outcome of his reading of Bellamy was a restrained but disapproving review of the book in the *Commonweal* for 22 June 1889. Later Morris provided an antidote to Bellamy's ideal of vastly expanded State Socialism, by looking into the future himself and producing his own Utopia, *News from Nowhere*. It ran in the *Commonweal* from January to October 1890.

In *The Earthly Paradise* Morris briefly offered his readers an escapist vision of 'London, small and white and clean' (III. 3), the London in which Chaucer could be found working at the quayside. In *News from Nowhere* he returns to this fantasy; for his imagined London of the twenty-first century is characterized by a return to fourteenth-century customs and fashions. The dreamer, experiencing the future as in *John Ball* he was transported into the past, finds a society in which industrialization has been swept away. London is once again a group of villages, small and largely rural communities where craftsmanship thrives. There are no factories, no railways (though there are rather mysterious but pollution-free 'force-barges' for river transport); in both clothing and architecture the people employ styles much closer to medieval patterns than to nineteenth-century ones:

There were houses about ... so like mediaeval houses of the same materials that I fairly felt as if I were alive in the fourteenth century; a sensation helped out by the costume of the people that we met or passed, in whose dress there was nothing 'modern'. (XVI. 23)

So like the dreamer in *John Ball*, William Guest the narrator of *News from Nowhere* feels to some extent at home in the new society – not because it reminds him of his own time but because it reminds him of the past.

Central to the book, then, is a blending of past and future. This occurs on several levels in addition to the medieval appearance and craft-based economy of the people of Nowhere.

The political romances

The Socialist society is aware of the need to remember its past. Certain buildings are preserved, including the Houses of Parliament which are used as a manure store. And an old man in the British Museum relates to Guest the history of the revolution, which some at least of the people of Nowhere believe should be remembered. Ellen, who is in many ways the chief spokesman of the new age, values accurate knowledge of the past, since it helps to safeguard against any idealization of history which might lead to dissatisfaction with the present. So Guest becomes for his companions a source of information about their past, as they are for him a vision of his possible future. The dreamer himself is at the centre of a more personal blending of chronologically disparate periods. Old Hammond the historian (who is 105 years old) sits in a room containing furniture chosen by his father which resembles that designed by Morris's firm; and when they meet, Guest has the feeling that he is looking into a mirror. Is this a grandson of the dreamer? Met in the future, he provides an organic, as well as an ideological, link between Guest and the Socialist Paradise. Another link is the old house which is the goal of a journey up the Thames. It is Morris's home Kelmscott Manor, to which Morris himself had twice travelled by boat from Kelmscott House in Hammersmith; an engraving of the Manor appeared as the frontispiece when *News from Nowhere* was published in book form. The house was old when Morris acquired it; in Nowhere it represents a genial past which has stored up all the goodness of former ages for the added joy of the present. Ellen describes it thus:

It seems to me as if it had waited for these happy days, and held in it the gathered crumbs of happiness of the confused and turbulent past. (XVI. 201)

Thus the Utopian vision of the future constantly refers back to the past, whether of memory or history, and unites it with the future.

In the early stories merging of past and present was accompanied by images of whirling and shifting which made the fluidity and flux of time something disturbing and destructive. In *The Earthly Paradise* remoteness from time guaranteed security from dissolution but entailed sterility. In *News from*

Nowhere time's process becomes benevolent. Thus the artist's predilection for inspiration from the past is no longer suspect. In July 1884 Morris reviewed in the magazine *To-day* the summer exhibition at the Royal Academy. There he states his conviction that the only original works are, paradoxically, those by artists who understand the paintings of the medieval masters:

Anyone who wants beauty to be produced at the present day in any branch of the fine arts, I care not what, must be always crying out 'Look back! look back!'[10]

Socialism completed the work begun by the sagas, freeing Morris from his long doubts about the value of his own particular artistic style to a modern age.

His new confidence is reflected in the discussion in *News from Nowhere* about the kind of art most appreciated by the Socialist society. Some of the people have read Victorian novels; and though Ellen's grandfather retains an obstinate admiration for Thackeray, this is as unusual as his tendency to regret the passing of old-fashioned competition. Dickens, the fantasist and idealist, is much more to the taste of Nowhere. On the whole, however, the people believe that the novel is dead. Novels, with their sociological and psychological realism, can only be written about people who are unhappy; since no one is unhappy in Nowhere, novels have become impossible. In any case they were never actually realistic, despite their claims, for fiction always falsified reality:

there was a theory that art and imaginative literature ought to deal with contemporary life; but they never did so; for, if there was any pretence of it, the author always took care ... to disguise, or exaggerate, or idealise, and in some way or another make it strange. (XVI. 102)

And even those novels which professed to deal honestly and in reforming spirit with social problems, always failed ultimately to live up to their pretended aims:

towards the end of the story we must be contented to see the hero and heroine living happily in an island of bliss on other people's troubles; and that after a long series of sham troubles (or mostly sham) of their own making, illustrated by dreary introspective nonsense about their feelings and aspirations, and all the rest of it; while the world must even then have gone on its way, and dug and sewed and baked and built and carpentered round about these useless – animals. (XVI. 151)

The political romances

These ideas (expressed here with an ironic Earthly Paradise motif) relate closely to Morris's views as presented in a lecture on 'The Society of the Future', given at Ancoats, Manchester, in 1888. After the revolution, he said, the need for modern realistic novels would be removed:

You see you will no longer be able to have novels relating the troubles of a middle-class couple in their struggle towards social uselessness, because the material for such literary treasures will have passed [a]way.[11]

So the people of Nowhere turn instead to legend and fairy-story, covering the walls of the Bloomsbury banqueting hall, for example, with pictures based on tales from Grimm. In language reminiscent of Stevenson's justification of romance as adult play,[12] Old Hammond explains that 'it is the child-like part of us that produces works of imagination' (XVI. 102). His kinsman Dick agrees. Stylization, rather than realism, is what is required of art:

surely it is but natural to like these things strange; just as when we were children, as I said just now, we used to pretend to be so-and-so in such-and-such a place. That's what these pictures and poems do; and why shouldn't they? (XVI. 102)

Through such imaginings the people of Nowhere express their child-like delight in their surroundings; only thus can they relate artistically to their perfect society.

Morris, of course, was not writing in Utopia. But these views about the inevitable decline of the novel colour all his romances. He had come to believe that those aspects of art which he criticized in his early stories and in *The Earthly Paradise* – its ephemeral nature and its tendency to distort the realities it pretended to describe – were specific attributes of the novel. Artists must reject the ugly world around them; as he states in 1891, in an address to mark the opening of an exhibition of Pre-Raphaelite painting in Birmingham:

When an artist has really a very keen sense of beauty, I venture to think that he can not literally represent an event that takes place in modern life. He must add something or another to qualify or soften the sordidness of the surroundings of life in our generation. That is not only the case with pictures, if you please: it is the case also in literature.[13]

This is not, however, a drawback – quite the contrary. By looking for inspiration in the past, the artist links himself onto the historical development of the art of the people, without which his creativity will be stifled:

one reason why there is much to be said for that Art which deals with the life of the past, or rather with the artist's imagination of it, is because only so can the artist have at his back in the form of history anything like that traditional combined idea of Art which once was common to the whole people.[14]

The other reason why it is not only allowable, but necessary, for an artist to work from an understanding of the past is that only by doing so is he made free of the sordid, transient trappings of nineteenth-century capitalist society. Art should not slavishly mirror the miseries of the present time, but should deal instead with the eternal truths which must be studied in a wider context of past and future. In the Preface to an edition of *Medieval Lore* by Robert Steele, printed in 1893, Morris explains how past and future are linked in the minds of those who believe in the progress of society:

at the present time those who take pleasure in studying the life of the Middle Ages are more commonly to be found in the ranks of those who are pledged to the forward movement of modern life, while those who are vainly striving to stem the progress of the world are as careless of the past as they are fearful of the future.[15]

To take inspiration from the past was not escapism, but quite the opposite; it was the only way of being in touch with the future. The people of Nowhere were right to revere Grimm, because through his work they could approach their own lives with more accuracy than they could have found in a realistic novel.

Artists who accepted these theories had a great task to perform, for on them lay responsibility for rousing people to action. In *News from Nowhere* this concept of the role of the artist is made explicit. Old Hammond, having given the dreamer the story of the revolution, says:

Who knows but I may not have been talking to many people? For perhaps our guest may some day go back to the people he has come from, and may take a message from us which may bear fruit for them, and consequently for us. (XVI. 135)

The political romances

At the end of the story the dreamer takes up the challenge, hoping that 'if others can see it as I have seen it' (XVI. 211) the new society will arrive all the sooner. The book itself is the outcome of his commission from Old Hammond. On several occasions during the 1880s Morris declared a belief in the inspirational properties of art. In a lecture on 'Socialism: the End and the Means', given in 1886, he stressed the need for idealism if men were to be able to set the end for which they worked above the weariness of their present struggle. If they:

can be shown the glorious end and made to feel it in their hearts, will it not transfigure for them that dulness and weariness aforesaid, change its relative proportions, at least make it seem small and easy to bear?[16]

In this lecture he does not say specifically that the ideal may be presented by art, although this is implied. In an earlier lecture, however, he did state unambiguously that stories and pictures might inspire men. He discusses first the subjects which make the best art, and decides that they are themes of heroic self-sacrifice and service to the cause of 'the future welfare' of the race. He continues:

Take note, too, that in the best art all these solemn and awful things ... impress the beholder so deeply that he is brought face to face with the very scenes, and lives among them for a time; so raising his life above the daily tangle of small things that wearies him, to the level of the heroism which they represent. (XXII. 176)

Although this lecture was delivered in 1881, its sentiments are appropriate to the romances which Morris was soon to begin. He believes that art can inspire men to work without faltering towards an ideal; and the method by which this is effected is the telling of stories about men of past ages who also fought present evils for the sake of a future good.

Socialism reinforced feelings that Morris already entertained about the nature of the artist's sources of inspiration and his duty to his readers. It gave these still rather unformed thoughts a purpose and direction; Morris had a goal to aim for, and he brought his literary art, like everything else he possessed, to the service of his ideal. If we consider all the various ideas about literature which Morris held in the 1880s, we shall see that only the romance form could adequately embody them. Romance must be set in a period remote from that of the reader, and is ideally suited for an historical theme. Romance is not concerned with contemporary phenomena, but can nevertheless discuss the most important subjects because it deals in symbols and images rather than with social details belonging to any one age. Finally, romance is by nature idealistic, and may very easily become inspirational. *A Dream of John Ball* and *News from Nowhere* are not romances.[17] They are too obviously concerned to convert their readers to a specific point of view to attain the detachment of true romance. Yet they demonstrate that Morris was ready to write in the romance form. Indeed, he could have written in few other ways if he was fully to express in his literature his artistic and political convictions.

II

Between writing *A Dream of John Ball* and *News from Nowhere*, Morris began his series of prose romances. The first was published in December 1888 (with the imprint of 1889); it was called *A Tale of the House of the Wolfings and all the Kindreds of the Mark*.

For his first romance Morris turned for his setting not, as might have been expected, to medieval England, but to a more remote time and place. The Wolfings are a family group, or *gens*, within a larger Gothic tribe, living in the foothills of the Alps in the second or first century BC. The tale is of their first meeting with the Romans in battle; the Romans are defeated and the Wolfing Hall saved from destruction largely through the efforts of the leader of the gens, Thiodolf, who dies in the final assault. Morris goes to considerable pains to create the atmosphere of the clearing in the forest which is the Wolfings' home. He details at some length the social and political organization of the tribe, even emphasizing their law of exogamy, and minutely describes the Wolfing Hall itself. So convincing was his picture of Gothic life that when the book was published a German professor wrote to enquire where Morris had obtained his new information about conditions in the Mark. Morris responded with characteristic vehemence:

'Doesn't the fool realise', demanded Morris at the top of his voice, 'that it's a romance, a work of fiction – that it's all LIES!'[18]

The political romances

Yet despite his forceful rejection of the idea that he had written anything but a work of imagination, Morris shows throughout *The House of the Wolfings* that he possessed a good deal of knowledge about the early Goths. May Morris says that this was a period:

which had a great fascination for the writer [Morris], who read with critical enjoyment the more important modern studies of it as they came out. (XIV. xxv)

Why, then, did he choose this particular setting for his first romance? The answer may help to clarify his intention in this work, and in all the later romances.

We have seen that Morris was well informed about developments in historical research during his lifetime. We have seen also that his love of Icelandic literature led him to the work of philologists and mythologists, in particular of those scholars who were exploring the religion of the early Teutonic tribes. By 1888 he would have been able to read in English the whole of Grimm's *Teutonic Mythology*, which he praised in 1886 when only part of this monumental work had been translated into English. While the mythologists were stressing the kinship between the Teutonic tribes and modern Englishmen, scholars in other branches of history were also claiming that aspects of contemporary life could be traced back to Teutonic origins. Constitutional historians and students of political organization were particularly quick to see links between the Mark and British democracy, while it became fashionable to trace to Gothic ancestors some of the attitudes of the English to the family, the state and the law. This idea had been put forward as long ago as 1768, when in his book *An Historical Dissertation Concerning the Antiquity of the English Constitution* Gilbert Stuart claimed that the 'foundation and principles of the Anglo-Saxon constitution, are to be found ... in the institutions and manners of the ancient Germans'.[19] Later Sharon Turner stressed the Gothic element in British life in his *History of the Anglo-Saxons* (1799–1805). Kemble's *The Saxons in England* (1849) also emphasized the Teutonic aspects of early English society. The first historian to combine a belief in the importance of the British people's Teutonic inheritance with newly rigorous scholarship was William Stubbs, whose greatest work was *The Constitutional History of England in its Origin and*

The political romances

Development (1874–8). In the Introduction he expresses an idea which was very close to Morris's heart:

the roots of the present lie deep in the past, and nothing in the past is dead to the man who would learn how the present comes to be what it is.[20]

Stubbs begins his survey of the British constitution with the descriptions of German tribes by Caesar and Tacitus, and for the best of reasons:

The English are not aboriginal ... They are a people of German descent in the main constituents of blood, character, and language, but most especially, in connexion with our subject, in the possession of the elements of primitive German civilisation and the common germs of German institutions.[21]

Stubbs discusses the importance of the family tie among the Teutons and their habit of living in village communities rather than in towns. In a section on the Saxons, he describes the Mark system, in which land was owned communally, often in a forest clearing originally formed by the settlement of one family or kinship group. All these aspects of Teutonic life are reproduced by Morris in *The House of the Wolfings*.

In 1874 also appeared *A Short History of the English People* by John Richard Green. The first history to concentrate on the people rather than on dynasties and laws, it was extremely popular; after numerous reprints it appeared in a revised form in 1888. Like Stubbs, Green begins his story with the European tribes, this time specifically the Engles. He concentrates particularly on their democratic system of government; the whole tribe met to discuss matters of importance, and Green becomes almost lyrical as he declares that these moots were the forerunners of the English Parliament:

It is with a reverence such as is stirred by the sight of the head-waters of some mighty river that one looks back to these tiny moots, where the men of the village met to order the village life and the village industry, as their descendants, the men of later England, meet in Parliament at Westminster, to frame laws and do justice for the great empire which has sprung from this little body of farmer-commonwealths in Sleswick.[22]

This belief that the British form of Parliamentary government was descended from Teutonic institutions was shared by the radical historian Edward A. Freeman and expressed, for example, in his book *The History of the Norman Conquest of England* (1867–79). He too, in his discussion of the origin of the English Parliament, refers back to Tacitus and the Teutonic tribes which that historian described. He emphasizes that the Teutonic constitution was not confined to one branch of the European family, but was 'a common Aryan possession';[23] on several occasions he draws an analogy with the customs of the Achaeans as presented by Homer. The medieval English Witenagemót was the ancestor of the modern Parliament. Like Green, Freeman allows his devotion to the idea of democracy to invest his prose with enthusiasm:

no lover of our old historic liberties can see without delight how venerable a thing those liberties are, how vast and how ancient are the rights and powers of an English Parliament.[24]

Morris seems to have been familiar with books by Green and Freeman, for he mentions them as examples of 'the new school of historians' (XXII. 319) in an article published in 1888.[25] He must have found their discussions of the origins of democracy relevant to his own developing political concern.

He would have received further confirmation of the need to understand the organization of the Gothic tribes when he became a Socialist. One of the most important books by Engels was *The Origin of the Family, Private Property and the State*, an historical survey which incorporated notes made by Marx on *Ancient Society* (1877) by the American Lewis H. Morgan. Engels's book was published in German in 1884 and not translated into English until 1902, but it seems reasonable to suppose that Morris (who knew Engels) would have been aware of the nature of its contents. The first section of 'Socialism from the Root Up' is called 'Ancient Society', and is a brief resumé of the historical development of society envisaged by Morgan and endorsed by Engels. Morgan was concerned to establish that mankind was involved in a process of social evolution, from savagery, through a period of what he describes as barbarism, to civilization. The Aryan peoples of Europe have attained civilization, although Morgan reminds his readers that there is no evidence to suggest that the evolutionary process has now been completed. Morgan discusses the forms of marriage and the family which obtain in the various stages of development, the growth of the idea of government and the institution of private property. He is convinced that the people of contemporary western civilization have inherited not only physical but also social characteristics from their ancestors:

Modern institutions plant their roots in the period of barbarism, into which their germs were transmitted from the previous period of savagery. They have had a lineal descent through the ages, with the streams of the blood, as well as a logical development.[26]

When Engels takes over Morgan's theories, he concentrates particularly on the organization of the gens – the family group typical of Middle and Upper Barbarism, into which the Teutonic tribes were divided. The gens is a group of people linked by blood; they are all descended from one ancestor by mother-right. They hold property in common, are free and equal, and are bound to defend one another's freedom. It was a community organized in this way, according to Engels, which overthrew the decadent, slave-based society of the Romans. It was able to do so because it was in the full vigour of the barbarian stage of development:

Their individual ability and courage, their sense of freedom, their democratic instinct which in everything of public concern felt itself concerned, in a word, all the qualities which had been lost to the Romans and were alone capable of forming new states and making new nationalities grow out of the slime of the Roman world – what else were they than the characteristics of the barbarian of the upper stage – fruits of his gentile constitution?[27]

At the end of the book Engels looks forward to the dissolution of present society, which is based on a reverence for private property and is doomed to destruction. Thinking of the society of the future, he describes it by quoting Morgan, adding his own emphasis:

It will be a revival, in a higher form, of the liberty, equality and fraternity of the ancient gentes.[28]

It is clear that to a Socialist who accepted Engels's doctrines, the barbarian Gothic tribes which overthrew Rome took on a very special significance.[29] Their democratic systems were the origin of modern British customs; their social organization, based on freedom and equality, community of land and a belief in blood-brotherhood, was the force which enabled them to destroy a decadent society as the Socialists wished to destroy capitalism.

Morris often spoke with enthusiasm of a return to a state of barbarism, which he believed was inevitable before the true Socialist society could be formed. In 1885 he wrote to Georgiana Burne-Jones:

I have [no] more faith than a grain of mustard seed in the future history of 'civilization', which I *know* now is doomed to destruction, and probably before very long: what a joy it is to think of! and how often it consoles me to think of barbarism once more flooding the world, and real feelings and passions, however rudimentary, taking the place of our wretched hypocrisies. With this thought in my mind all the history of the past is lighted up and lives again to me.[30]

In a lecture 'Of the Origins of Ornamental Art' in 1886 he speaks of the horror of the Romans at what they considered the anarchy of the barbarians:

but which was at the worst the Medea's cauldron from which a new and vigorous Europe was to be born again.[31]

Morris regretfully accepted the probability of a period of violent revolution before the establishment of the Socialist state. In a series of articles on 'The Development of Modern Society' in the *Commonweal* (July–August 1890) Morris compared modern society to that of the Romans, and hoped that his readers would join him in the fight against it:

So shall we be our own Goths, and at whatever cost break up again the new tyrannous Empire of Capitalism.[32]

Vigorous barbarism was better than the stagnation of bourgeois society.

With this new understanding of what the Gothic tribes meant to Morris, we may return to *The House of the Wolfings*. The importance of the carefully detailed historical setting is now clear; Morris wishes his readers to be aware of the relationship between themselves and the tribe he is describing. The first few pages of the book establish that the people of the story are a Gothic tribe, and thus the ancestors of modern Englishmen. Morris chooses for special emphasis the two aspects of Gothic life which were most important to the historians we have been considering. First he explains that the people are exogamous;

they therefore have the gentile constitution which Engels saw as the source of the Teutons' prowess. Secondly, Morris reminds us that the folk-moots by which the people govern themselves are the forerunners of modern English administrative systems:

And in each of these steads was there a Doom-ring wherein Doom was given by the neighbours chosen, (whom now we call the Jury) in matters between man and man. (XIV. 7)

A further reference defines the Wolfings as closely related to modern Englishmen. Morris describes the lamp which is kept always burning above the dais in the Wolfing Hall; it is an ancient artefact, and considered the most holy object in the Mark. It is called the Hall-Sun, and on it is modelled in gold a warrior killing a dragon and the rising sun. Anyone at all conversant with the ideas of Max Müller and Cox would immediately recognize this symbol; the Wolfings are a branch of the sun-worshipping Aryan family. All these hints of the unity between the Wolfings and Morris's readers are drawn together in the poem on the title page. There Morris sees his task as the capturing and holding for a while of the 'ancient glimmer' (XIV. I) of past days.

Morris is asking us to see ourselves mirrored in his Wolfing heroes. The reason he wishes us to make the connection becomes clear when we read further into the story. The free tribes of the Mark have to defend themselves against invading Roman legions. The descriptions of the Romans soon show how different they are from the Wolfings. The most damning criticism of them is that 'they have forgotten kindred, and have none, nor do they heed whom they wed, and great is the confusion amongst them' (XIV. 45). They are very wealthy, but the rich lords do nothing for themselves and rely entirely on slave labour. The people are not free:

mighty men among them ordain where they shall dwell, and what shall be their meat, and how long they shall labour after they are weary, and in all wise what manner of life shall be amongst them; and though they be called free men who suffer this, yet may no house or kindred gainsay this rule and order. In sooth they are a people mighty, but unhappy. (XIV. 45)

In *A Dream of John Ball* the dreamer has difficulty in making John Ball understand the concept of a free man who is dependent on his master for the materials he needs to work with in order to live. John Ball concludes that such a man cannot really be free (xiv. 272–3). The so-called free men of Rome are thus in precisely the same position as the workers under nineteenth-century capitalism; legally without masters, they are in fact no better than slaves. Morris is using the Romans in the same way as Engels had done in *The Origin of the Family, Private Property and the State*. They represent the decadent bourgeoisie, ripe for destruction by the vigorous working class. Opposed to the Romans is the fellowship of the free men of the Mark, which Morris has asked his readers to relate to themselves. The overthrow of the Romans is another moment in the history of the class struggle, like John Ball's partial victory over the barons. Morris's readers are thus reminded that they too are waging a war, and the optimistic ending gives the nineteenth-century fighters renewed hope of their own triumph.

This study of *The House of the Wolfings* has so far made it sound like another propaganda story, in the style of *A Dream of John Ball* and *News from Nowhere*. Yet although propaganda is part of Morris's intention in his first romance, he also has a less circumscribed purpose. In a rare comment on his literary work, he wrote about *The House of the Wolfings* to T. J. Wise:

It is a story of the life of the Gothic tribes on their way through Middle Europe, and their first meeting with the Romans in war. It is meant to illustrate the melting of the individual into the society of the tribes: I mean apart from the artistic side of things that is its moral – if it has one.[33]

In this book Morris is not content merely to show how a free association of comrades may overcome the forces of capitalism. He takes one member of the gens, the romance's hero Thiodolf, and uses his story to state and examine a particular problem. What happens if an individual in the tribal (or revolutionary) group discovers that his personal aspirations conflict with the needs of the fellowship as a whole? In *A Dream of John Ball* Morris exalted fellowship to the highest place among the virtues of mankind; it made the difference between Heaven and Hell. Now he recognizes that men may not always be willing to subdue their individuality for the sake of others. *The House of the Wolfings* is about this difficulty.

Thiodolf is a leader of his people. Although they do not have permanent chieftains, he is the greatest man in the Wolfing House, and is elected War-leader by the combined armies of the Mark when they go into battle. We soon discover, however, that there is a side to Thiodolf's character which is hidden from his companions. He has been involved for many years in a liaison with the Wood-Sun, a Valkyrie who has been expelled from Godhome because she has given herself to Thiodolf. The Hall-Sun, keeper of the holy lamp and named after it, is their daughter. When Thiodolf visits his mistress in the wood before leading the Wolfing warriors to war, he finds her in great misery because she foresees his death and their everlasting separation. She asks him to wear for her sake a magic hauberk, which will protect him. Both this armour and Thiodolf's liaison are linked with the idea of a betrayal of Thiodolf's loyalty to his kindred. Thiodolf has believed until now that the Wood-Sun is also akin to the Wolfings, and that in sleeping with her he has broken the law of exogamy. He is prepared to accept the consequent guilt because of his great love for her. She now informs him that he has not committed a sin after all, for he is not a Wolfing by blood; he was adopted into the House as an alien.

Having planted in his heart this doubt about his place in the fellowship, she persuades him to wear the hauberk. It soon becomes clear that it will save his life at the expense of victory for the tribe. An old man of the House of the Daylings tries to warn Thiodolf against the hauberk by telling a story of how he once traded his integrity for something he greatly wanted, and found the exchange a poor one; he knew:

> That this was the ancient pitfall, and the long expected trap,
> And that now for my heart's desire I had sold the world's
> goodhap. (xiv. 73)

When Thiodolf meets the Wood-Sun again, he has realized the nature of the choice he has to make:

> either for the sake of the folk I will not wear the gift and the curse, and I shall die in great glory, and because of me the House shall live; or else for thy sake I shall bear it and live, and the House shall live or die as may be, but I not helping, nay I no longer of the House nor in it. (xiv. 111)

He knows that the hauberk 'is for the ransom of a man and the ruin of a folk' (xiv. 111). Yet under the pressure of his love for the

Wood-Sun he does wear it in the next battle, and the effect is disastrous. At the height of the conflict he falls into a trance and is carried off the field for dead. He is thus removed from danger, but without its leader the Wolfing army is routed and nearly destroyed by the Romans. Thiodolf can see nothing of the folk around him, but imagines that the Wood-Sun is by his side and longs only to be alone with her always. Later he describes to his mistress what he felt, and emphasizes that the worst aspect of the magic was the way it took from him his sense of communion with his people:

I loved them not, and was not of them, and outside myself there was nothing: within me was the world and nought without me. (XIV. 169)

He is reduced to the position of the Roman commander, who will not risk his life 'either for the sake of the city of Rome, or of any folk whatsoever, but was liefer to live for his own sake' (XIV. 134). Thiodolf's dilemma is the choice between his personal heart's desire, his individuality, and the good of his people. By choosing life rather than self-sacrifice, he has become the embodiment of the very evil qualities against which the Wolfings are so desperately fighting.

Thiodolf has cut himself off not only from his companions, but also from the stream of history. At the beginning of the story he holds the warriors' creed that it is good to die in battle for one's people. The Wood-Sun undermines this idea by her revelation that Thiodolf is not really of the Wolfing kindred, and also by her sensible argument that he will be of more use to the Wolfing House alive than dead. In their second interview the lovers discuss the question of immortality. Thiodolf has believed until now that when he died he would still be a part of the Wolfing kindred, and would live again in each young warrior who aspired to greatness. When he looked into the future, he could not see his own grave, but the continuing life of the House:

No story of that grave-night mine eyes can ever see,
But rather the tale of the Wolfings through the coming days of
   earth. (XIV. 109)

This is the conviction which was at the centre of *Sigurd the Volsung*, and which, reinforced by the Marxist concept of history, appeared again in *A Dream of John Ball*. The actions of each good man live on because they condition the way of life of his descendants. The Wood-Sun, however, uses the individualist argument that the dead man himself cannot experience his own effect on the future history of his people, making it invalid for him:

> Nay thou shalt be dead, O warrior, thou shalt not see the Hall
> Nor the children of thy people 'twixt the dais and the
> wall. (xiv. 109)

Against this terse and rational viewpoint, Morris sets a series of images which assert the correctness of Thiodolf's belief. In *Sigurd the Volsung* he used mainly solar images to link the life of mankind to that of the natural world. Men were born and died like the sun or the leaves on the trees, and the cycles of the generations reflected those of the seasons. He similarly uses natural imagery in *The House of the Wolfings*.

The Hall-Sun speaks to the people of the way men are born and die, and live again in the future they have helped to build:

> To the world a warrior cometh; from the world he passeth away,
> And no man then may sunder his good from his evil day
>
> ...
>
> He hath lived, and his life hath fashioned the outcome of the deed,
> For the blossom of the people, and the coming kindreds' seed
>
> ...
>
>   And yet the story saith
> That the deeds that make the summer make too the winter's death,
> That summer-tides unceasing from out the grave may grow
> And the spring rise up unblemished from the bosom of the
> snow. (xiv. 87)

Before his second meeting with the Wood-Sun, Thiodolf imagines what his life will be after the war is over. He pictures himself 'partaking in the deeds of the life of man' (xiv. 105), and the actions he sees himself performing are all concerned with the cycle of the seasons: ploughing, reaping, hunting in winter. In contrast to this sense of man being at one with the changing seasons, Thiodolf's first dream when wearing the hauberk takes us back to Morris's early images of death-in-life. He finds himself speaking to a stone man, and feels as if he too is turning into stone. When he finally rejects the hauberk, he is again at one with nature:

mine eyes are cleared again, and I can see the kindreds as they are ...
Now therefore shall they and I together earn the merry days to come,
the winter hunting and the spring sowing, the summer haysel, the
ingathering of harvest, the happy rest of midwinter, and Yuletide with
the memory of the Fathers, wedded to the hope of the days to be.
(XIV. 170)

Thiodolf has renounced his individual will, and put himself
back into communion with the natural world and with the
forces of history; he can once again find pleasure in remembering his ancestors and in looking into the future. Although he is
not a blood-relation of the Wolfings, his life with and service to
them has made him one with them; he is part of the House not
by the chance of having been born there, but by reason of the
consciously willed interdependence between himself and his
fellows. His new sense of belonging extends even to his
enemies, for through his kinship with the Wolfings he is connected to every part of the earth and every living thing. At the
end of the book the Hall-Sun bids farewell to her dead father
with a reminder that he is now and forever on the right side in
the battle between good and evil. She looks forward to meeting
him again on the last day, when he will be fighting with 'the
sons of the fruitful Earth and the sons of Day' (XIV. 206) against
the powers of darkness. The story of Thiodolf is the story of how
a man achieves integration with his society, and with the whole
natural and supernatural world.

It will be clear that Morris no longer expresses terror in the
face of individual mortality. This was once a central force in his
work; but now the blending of an individual into his tribe and
their history is a matter for rejoicing, not for regret. Like Sigurd,
Thiodolf is a blossom on the tree of his people and a seed for
future generations of heroes. His desire to evade this natural
cycle led to the near-destruction of the tribe. As part of the
process, however, he contributes to the movement towards
the glorious end (for which, as in *Sigurd*, Ragnarök becomes the
symbol). Thus cyclical time and linear time are reconciled, at
last, in Morris's imagination. It is not hard to see how this
relates to his Socialist beliefs. *The House of the Wolfings* is the
first, and perhaps the most characteristic, blending of political
conviction with romance form which became Morris's chief
literary preoccupation.

The political romances

Morris's next romance was *The Roots of the Mountains*, which
was published in November 1889 (with the imprint of 1890).
The title page hints that it will be, like its predecessor, the
history of a community rather than just one man; the subtitle
adds: 'Wherein is Told Somewhat of the Men of Burgdale, Their
Friends Their Neighbours Their Foemen and Their Fellows in
Arms'. As in *The House of the Wolfings*, the opening chapter
provides a detailed geographical description of the country in
which the story is set, and an explanation of the social organization of the people. By Morgan's definition, the men of Burgdale
are in the stage of Upper Barbarism, one step higher than the
Wolfings; some of them live in a town, and they have a permanent Alderman who hands his office down to his sons. An
outline of the story also suggests similarities with *The House of
the Wolfings*. On this occasion the free Gothic kindreds of the
Dale have to withstand the encroaching Huns, who live, like the
Romans, on slave labour. Several tribes combine in the face of
the menace of the Dusky Men, and in the process of driving out
the enemy new affinities are formed and the two halves of a
long-divided tribe are reunited. The story ends with the Dusky
Men defeated, the slaves freed and the friendship between the
men of Burgdale and their allies cemented by two marriages.

The romance, as this summary indicates, is in many ways
concerned with the same themes as *The House of the Wolfings*.
Again we are shown a people historically connected with the
British race standing successfully for freedom and fellowship
against the forces of oppression and violence. Yet *The Roots of
the Mountains* does not simply repeat the motifs of the earlier
book. The first chapter is a general survey of the setting of the
story, but the second chapter opens by focusing sharply on one
of the inhabitants of the Dale. The Alderman's son Face-of-god,
of the House of the Face, is from the moment of his appearance
clearly marked out as the hero of the tale. In *The House of the
Wolfings*, although Thiodolf was the most important character,
there were long periods when he was absent from the action of
the story. The author was as concerned with the general
fortunes of the folk as with the hero's personal dilemma. In *The
Roots of the Mountains*, however, the story is told through the

consciousness of the hero. The reader very rarely knows things which are unknown to Face-of-god; when he is puzzled we share his bewilderment, and the process of his enlightenment is ours also. It is possible to imagine the story of the Wolfings told without reference to Thiodolf. *The Roots of the Mountains* is inconceivable without the central figure of Face-of-god.

Morris is moving closer to a more traditional form of romance, in which the sufferings and happiness of the hero are the central concern. One of the themes of the story is Face-of-god's growth to maturity. When the tale begins he is a young man betrothed to a maiden from the House of the Steer, from which the men of the House of the Face traditionally choose their wives. Her name is the Bride. Face-of-god has a good position in his society and is loved by his fellows, but he is not contented. He finds himself increasingly restless, and is drawn to explore the great forest which borders the Dale. On one of his forays into the wood he meets a beautiful woman called the Sunbeam, with whom he falls deeply in love. For her sake he renounces the Bride, causing her great pain and incurring the wrath of his father. His new love is a member of a tribe that has been driven from its home by the Dusky Men. Face-of-god is instrumental in arranging for his people to join with the Sunbeam's kindred in an attack on the Huns. By the end of the book he has become the elected War-leader of the host. He has also been 'brought face to face with the Sorrow of the Earth, whereof he had known nought heretofore, save it might be as a tale in a minstrel's song' (xv. 201). When the war is over, the Sunbeam's brother Folk-might pays tribute to the change in Face-of-god:

though but few days have gone over thine head, yet many deeds have abided in thine hand, and thou art much aged. Anger hath left thee, and wisdom hath waxed in thee. (xv. 387)

Now ready to take a fully adult place in the life of his people, Face-of-god marries the Sunbeam. The Bride, after fighting in the battle and being gravely wounded, marries Folk-might.

Romance often focuses on the growing-up of the hero. Sir Perceval, whose story Morris used in the prose 'Golden Wings', is a wild young man who has to learn the meaning of true knighthood. Malory's 'The Tale of Sir Gareth' is another

medieval *Bildungsroman*. In both these stories the maturity of
the hero is shown by his acceptance into the courtly society
from which he has at first been excluded, despite having a right
by birth to a place in the community. Similarly, in *The Roots of
the Mountains* Face-of-god goes through a period of alienation
from his society before he reaches adulthood. At the beginning
of the book it appears that his position as the Alderman's son
and the Bride's fiancé is secure. In an early scene we see him at a
feast in his father's House, which places him firmly in the
context of his community. Yet he is subject to a vague discon-
tent, which is expressed by his desire to explore the wood on the
edge of the Dale. It symbolizes for him a place where he is
separated from his people and forced to rely solely on his
individual capacities:

So it was that I fared as if I were seeking something, I know not what,
that should fill up something lacking to me, I know not what. Thus I
felt in myself even so long as I was underneath the black boughs, and
there was none beside me and before me, and none to turn aback to.
(xv. 19)

At first Face-of-god tries to convince himself that everything he
longs for may be found in the Dale, in the traditions of his
community and his love for the Bride. Yet the call of individuality is too strong. Like Thiodolf, he decides to go the 'way of my
will' (xv. 27). In the wood he finds a new love, and his rejection of
the woman whom he ought by custom to marry demonstrates
his willingness to break out of the fellowship. In his anger at his
son's refusal to carry out his obligation to marry the Bride, the
Alderman draws his sword on him at the folk-moot, breaking
one of the most sacred laws of the tribe, which decrees that the
peace of the moot must not be violated. Face-of-god appears to
be prepared selfishly to destroy the unity of his family and
society for the sake of his personal happiness.

From his first meeting with the Sunbeam, however, Face-of-
god's individualism is curbed and channelled into a new sense of
community. The Sunbeam's ruling passion is her love for her
tribe, and her desire to help restore it to prosperity in its ancient
home. She has a broader conception than Face-of-god of the
importance of kinship. This is demonstrated when they first
declare their love for one another. The Sunbeam admits that she
would sleep with Face-of-god if he asked her to, but begs him not

to bring sorrow on her people by dishonouring her. This time Face-of-god is able to control his personal desire, the suggestion that he says is 'egging me on to do my will and die' (xv. 123), because he is beginning to understand that he can be truly happy only in the context of his acceptance by the community. He is learning to wish for the place of a chieftain, and to do deeds which will benefit the fellowship. When he says this, the Sunbeam rejoices in his growing maturity:

full glad am I that I have not plighted my troth to a mere goodly lad, but rather to a chieftain and a warrior. (xv. 126)

She reminds Face-of-god also that in his love for her he must reverence not only the kindred to which she belongs, but the ancestors who made her what she is. Thus Face-of-god moves gradually from a position of revolt against the requirements of his society, through an assertion of his individual will, to a new acceptance of the importance of fellowship. By the end of the book he knows that he has no right to disturb the harmony of the community for the sake of his personal wishes:

he knew it might not be, that he, the chosen War-leader, should trouble the peace of the kindred. (xv. 378)

He tells his father that when he first went to the wood, he was 'one against the world' (xv. 379). Now he has attained his rightful position as a leader of his people. His integration is symbolized when the Sunbeam is made a member of the House of the Steer, so that in marrying her he is after all taking a bride from the due House.

The Alderman attempts to draw a distinction between his son's rejection of the Bride for an alien woman and his prowess as War-leader:

Erewhile, when thou wanderedst out into the Wild-wood, seeking thou knewest not what from out of the Land of Dreams, thou didst but bring aback to us grief and shame; but now that thou hast gone forth with the neighbours seeking thy foemen, thou hast come aback to us with thine hands full of honour and joy for us. (xv. 218)

This is to oversimplify. Face-of-god only learns the importance of a sense of kindred through loving a woman who is outside his community. Had he fulfilled his commitment to the Bride, he would not have been able to unite his people with the

Sunbeam's tribe in the glorious defeat of the Dusky Men. Even from the beginning, we learn later, he loved the Bride much less than she loved him. Face-of-god needed to escape from his community and defy its customs before he was able to accept the position within it to which he had been called. Morris is taking his concept of fellowship a stage further than he did in *The House of the Wolfings*. He is suggesting that true fellowship can only exist if the individual members have stepped outside the community and learnt the precise degree of their self-sufficiency, before returning with a new understanding of their need for the support of their fellows. The process is a difficult and dangerous one; the discovery of self-hood and the growth of self-knowledge do not come easily. Face-of-god enters the wood aware that his experiences there may change him. An old man of the House of the Face warns him against the forest, with the tale of his own meeting with a fairy woman who deserted him, and left him with an eternally empty and unsatisfied life. When Face-of-god meets the Sunbeam, he takes her for just such a fairy, and for many pages neither the hero nor the reader is certain that her influence on him is good. And as well as danger to himself, the hero must also risk the destruction of other people's happiness as he seeks his own. Although the Bride ends the book a wife and mother, taking a central role in the creation of harmonious unity between two tribes and two families, she has suffered both mental anguish and physical hurt for the sake of Face-of-god – it is hard not to see her (like the Wood-Sun) as a sacrifice. The joy of the final chapters is continually shadowed by the Alderman's grief at the loss of the Bride for his daughter-in-law. The wood, then, is a place of both good and evil, containing 'desire and peril and beguiling and death, and love unto Death itself' (xv. 118). Morris is using the wood in the same way as Shakespeare used it in *A Midsummer Night's Dream* or Barrie in *Dear Brutus*; it is the place where if we have the courage we may discover our real personalities. There is always the danger that we may lose ourselves completely and never recover our identities.

For Morris an individual may only truly be fulfilled within a fellowship. In *The Roots of the Mountains* he emphasizes this by making Face-of-god's happiness conditional on the success-ful outcome of the war. The happy ending embraces hero and society alike. Once again Morris also suggests a wider context, making the victory of good over evil an expression of the ascendancy of light over darkness in the world as a whole. The Dalesmen are aware of their Aryan origins; they declare that:

> of older time we abided 'neath the mountains of the Earth,
> O'er which the Sun ariseth to waken woe and mirth.   (xv. 288)

The relevance of the Sunbeam's name is clear, and Face-of-god is described throughout the book in terms of a solar hero. He has plenteous golden hair, and as a result has been given the nickname Gold-mane. The symbol of his House, similar to that of the Wolfings, is a warrior whose head is surrounded by rays like the sun, and who is portrayed killing a dragon. The conflict between the Dalesmen and the Dusky Men is a battle between light and darkness. The Dalesmen wear gold ornaments; the Dusky Men, who are dark-skinned as their name implies, use silver, symbolizing the moon. When the Sunbeam's people take their place once more in the Hall of their fathers, they sing of the return of the day and describe the war as the driving out of darkness by light:

> O'er the Dale then was litten the Candle of Day,
> Night-sorrow was smitten, and gloom fled away.   (xv. 359)

Face-of-god's marriage to the Sunbeam takes place at Midsummer. In his romances Morris never forgets the lesson he learned while writing *Sigurd the Volsung*, that men must get into harmony with nature and with the processes of time if they are to fulfil their potential for good. If they do this, they may be able to create a real Earthly Paradise. The Dale, with its river and fruitful trees, is a kind of Paradise; the people are described in this way:

> so glad were they, and so friendly, that you might rather have deemed that this was the land whereof tales tell, wherein people die not, but live for ever . . . In sooth, both the land and the folk were fair enough to be that land and the folk thereof. (xv. 232)

The Dale is not in fact Paradise; Morris is careful to assure us that its people will not stagnate through unending happiness. Face-of-god will often have to lead his men to war to protect their valley, and is glad of this since to face troubles is part of the life of a man. Yet the Dalesmen, and especially Face-of-god,

The political romances

have attained a degree of joyful unity with nature and with the past which makes their land an approximation to Paradise. No doubt Morris hoped that his romance would inspire his contemporaries to find the way to their own ideal society.

IV

In a paper read to the twelfth Annual Meeting of the SPAB, in July 1889, Morris said:

> As for romance, what does romance mean? I have heard people miscalled for being romantic, but what romance means is the capacity for a true conception of history, a power of making the past part of the present.[34]

At this time he had written two stories which attempted to do exactly that. His next prose fiction was *News from Nowhere*, in which he moved completely into the Paradise he hoped the world would one day gain. During the publication of his Utopia, however, he issued another romance which seems to contain a warning against a premature withdrawal into the vision of delight. *The Story of the Glittering Plain, which has also been called the Land of Living Men or the Acre of the Undying* was serialized in the *English Illustrated Magazine* from June to September 1890, and appeared in book form from the Kelmscott Press in 1891. This work employs the form and conventions of romance in order to criticize an unquestioning acceptance of the romance ethos. It is as if Morris were warning himself not to place too much reliance on the coming of his Utopia.

The Glittering Plain is the shortest of the romances, pared down to its essential components. The book does not begin with a description of the land and the people of the story, but launches straight into a brief picture of the hero: his name (Hallblithe), his appearance and strength, which are such as befit a hero, and his House (the Raven). Like Face-of-god, Hallblithe is betrothed to a maiden of a House from which it is right that he should choose a bride; her name is the Hostage, of the House of the Rose. The setting of the story is vaguely Icelandic, but on this occasion Morris is less concerned with historical parallels than with the timeless problem with which Hallblithe is faced. The story opens when Hallblithe is visited

151

by three travel-worn men who ask the way to the Land of Living Men. Hallblithe is 'not yet a yokefellow of sorrow' (xiv. 212) and has never heard of the Land. Thus the Land is established as a place of escape from the troubles of the world. Immediately after the pilgrims have departed, Hallblithe is overtaken by sorrow when he learns that the Hostage has been abducted by pirates. He sets off to seek her, and in a dream is told by her that she will be found on the Glittering Plain. He reaches the Land, which is an Earthly Paradise of eternal youth and springtime, but the woman who awaits him there is not the Hostage but the King's Daughter, who has seen his picture in a book and fallen in love with him. The abduction of the Hostage, and the dream, were ruses to bring Hallblithe to the woman who desires him. Despite the allurements of the Glittering Plain, he rejects the happiness it seems to offer. He escapes in a boat, finds the Hostage at last, and returns to the Hall of his people. The book ends with his wedding to the Hostage.

A pattern is clearly emerging in Morris's romances. The hero is taken (either spiritually, as in Thiodolf's case, or physically) outside the community in which he lives, and is made to reconsider his place in the society of his fathers. So far all the romances have ended with the hero's decision to return home. The journey up the Thames to Kelmscott Manor in *News from Nowhere* is a variant on this motif, implying that the new Socialist society offers a kind of collective home-coming, a return to one's roots, for the lost souls of the nineteenth century. In Hallblithe's case his journey is into a land of fantasy where dreams come true. The Glittering Plain conforms to the traditional description of the Earthly Paradise. The sun is always shining, there are fruitful trees and rivers and men are rejuvenated when they step onto the soil of the Land. Hallblithe naturally expects to find there his heart's desire, the Hostage. Yet in *The Earthly Paradise* Morris questioned the wisdom of an exclusive search for one's heart's desire. Like the heroes of that poem, Hallblithe fails to find what he wants. The Land turns out to be one of lies and evasions. The people are beautiful and happy, but they cannot face the idea of sorrow and death; it is unlawful to refer to the Land as 'the Acre of the Undying', and when Hallblithe exhibits his misery the women of the Land recoil from him instead of offering comfort. When Hallblithe is shown the woman he ought to marry, she turns out to be not the Hostage but the Princess. He discovers that during the whole of his quest he has been duped by false dreams and promises:

I am accursed and beguiled; and I wander round and round in a tangle that I may not escape from. I am not far from deeming that this is a land of dreams made for my beguiling. Or has the earth become so full of lies, that there is no room amidst them for a true man to stand upon his feet and go his ways? (XIV. 264–5)

The King of the Land accuses Hallblithe of seeking an unattainable dream. He replies:

I seek no dream ... but rather the end of dreams. (XIV. 273)

It is the Princess who desires a dream, for she has fallen in love not with a living man but with a picture in a book. The Glittering Plain is a false Paradise for Hallblithe, who discovers that eternal youth and a beautiful land are no substitutes for what he really wants – the woman to whom he has promised his love.

The Glittering Plain is a place of retreat from real life. This is linked with the idea of a denial of one's kindred, by the story of the Sea-eagle. Hallblithe meets him as a bed-ridden old man while on his way to the Glittering Plain, and they travel together. When they reach the Plain, the Sea-eagle recovers his youth and strength. Hallblithe asks him how he can bear to be forever separated from his people:

Who shall heed thee or tell the tale of thy glory, which thou hast covered over with the hand of a light woman, whom thy kindred knoweth not, and who was not born in a house wherefrom it hath been appointed thee from of old to take the pleasure of woman? (XIV. 256)

Here the achievement of the Sea-eagle's desire for renewed youth is shown to involve a rejection of the customs of his tribe and a refusal to accept his place within it. The Sea-eagle, however, denies that he should venerate the past of his ancestors; he has chosen personal immortality instead of death within the community. Hallblithe fears that one day his friend will regret his choice, as he grows weary of the static, unending bliss of the Glittering Plain. For Hallblithe himself, true happiness is to follow in the steps of his ancestors and till the ground which they tilled before him. It is a poem which he remembers from the days of his youth at home in Cleveland by the Sea which prompts him to build a boat and escape from the perfect, unsatisfying life in the Glittering Plain.

When he leaves the Plain, Hallblithe at last finds the Hostage. Before he may take her back to Cleveland, however, he has to pass a final test. The Glittering Plain was a land of illusion, in which appearances counted for everything and a woman could fall in love with a picture. It was based on deception, and involved a renunciation of the values and traditions of the community in which each inhabitant of the Land had been brought up. Hallblithe seeks the real living body of the woman whom he ought by tradition to marry, and believes that he will find truth at home if he rejects 'the falseness of this unchanging land' (XIV. 272). He has first to prove the strength of his allegiance to truth. On his way home he reaches the Isle of Ransom, where he originally met the Sea-eagle. He is in danger of being killed by the pirates who live on the island, but a wizard, the Puny Fox, offers to help him. Together Hallblithe and the wizard, whose trade is in illusion, devise a charade which will enable Hallblithe to avoid the malice of his hosts. At the vital moment Hallblithe throws off his disguise and refuses to save his life by means of a lie. The Puny Fox is furious, accusing Hallblithe of ensuring that:

I, who have lied so long and well, must now pay for all, and die for a barren truth. (XIV. 309)

Yet it is only when Hallblithe has taken this stand for the truth that he is reunited with the Hostage. His enemies admire his courage and allow him to go free. They also bring into the Hall a woman who appears to be the Hostage. At first Hallblithe, remembering all the deceptions to which he has been subjected, doubts whether the woman is really his beloved. Then she asks him a question which relates to their childhood in Cleveland, and he is able to give the correct answer. The truth has been established at last; Hallblithe takes the Hostage home and marries her, reassuming his place in the Hall of his fathers. The Puny Fox goes with the lovers to Cleveland, where he loses his powers of wizardry and becomes a truthful man.

Morris has written a warning, on the same lines as *The Earthly Paradise*, against trusting in illusion and dream. The

Glittering Plain seems to offer happiness, but it is a retreat from real life into the static death-in-life which Morris so much feared. The King of the Land is correct when he says that outside his realm exist the evils of war and famine, unsatisfied desire, unrest and fear. Yet there also exists, as Hallblithe asserts, the hope that things may change for the better. A life without the possibility of change is anathema to Morris. In *The Glittering Plain* he once more makes a plea for the facing and acceptance of evil and sorrow, for a reliance on the truth however unpleasant it may be, so that life may be full of hope for the future. It seems that this romance may relate directly to *News from Nowhere*, as a caution against trusting too deeply in the Utopia Morris was creating. One of the unsolved problems of Morris's Nowhere is that the people have nothing left to hope for, and must fear change because it could only be change for the worse. They have attained Paradise, but have they any guarantee that it will endure for ever? Morris was aware that his vision of a Utopian paradise was subject to the same criticisms as he had once levelled at escapist fantasies. In his lecture on 'The Society of the Future' he tried to counter the assertion that his dream of the new society was too static:

some may say such a condition of things might lead indeed to happiness but also to stagnation. Well, to my mind that would be a contradiction in terms, if indeed we agree that happiness is caused by the pleasurable exercise of our faculties. And yet suppose the worst, and that the world did rest after so many troubles – where would be the harm?[35]

News from Nowhere is subtitled 'An Epoch of Rest'. Yet for Morris rest always implied elsewhere a renewal of energy rather than final relaxation. In *News from Nowhere* there is tension between the idea that the world has finally become an ideal place and the fear of the inhabitants lest their Paradise turn out to be only temporary – a fear expressed by the repeated dread of the day when work becomes scarce and men find themselves in enforced idleness. A reading of *The Glittering Plain* suggests that in the 1880s Morris had to control his longing for escape into a dream of the future as he had once had to stop himself from retreating into an idealized vision of the past.

v

May Morris viewed her father's romances in the light of escapism, as a refuge from political realities:

These stories ... have come to fill his leisure writing-hours and are avowedly his principal solace: a pathetic withdrawal, at moments, from the anxieties of the outer world where he so unflinchingly took his stand.[36]

But it seems to me more true to say that romance provided a form and focus for Morris's political convictions. In the past he had written about lost or unattainable Paradises for which mankind longed in vain. Now he had espoused a faith in the inevitable existence of a real and very earthly Paradise, a post-revolutionary Golden Age. Yet for him and his contemporaries this Paradise was as lost as those of the past. As Morris became more and more certain that the revolution would not occur in his lifetime, he had increasing reason to seek to define and experience through art the transformation which he believed was approaching for later generations. Such transformation could take place for him only through the mythopoeic power of romance which makes it possible to grasp in fantasy what is evasive in reality.

Morris knew he needed the romances in a way he had not needed his earlier writing. After finishing *The Roots of the Mountains* he wrote to Janey:

I have begun another story, but do not intend to hurry it – I must have a story to write now as long as I live. (xv. xij)

He fulfilled this ambition, dictating from his death-bed to his secretary Sydney Cockerell the final pages of *The Sundering Flood*. Romance had become for Morris in his last years a sustaining force, a necessary adjunct to his political commitment, because only romance could adequately capture the quality of hope.

CHAPTER 5

'The very Garden of God': the last romances

One of Morris's late romances, *Child Christopher and Goldilind the Fair* (1895), is a retelling of the medieval *Lay of Havelok the Dane*. This thirteenth-century poem is notable, among other things, for the extreme precision with which events are located. Each Lincolnshire town involved in the story is carefully named, and the extent of the kingdom of England is defined beyond any possible doubt as stretching 'fro Rokesburw al into Douere'.[1] This may be romance, but it takes place in a highly specific world. Morris's version begins with an unmistakable indication that we are moving into a world of pure fantasy:

Of old there was a land which was so much a woodland, that a minstrel thereof said it that a squirrel might go from end to end, and all about, from tree to tree, and never touch the earth: therefore was that land called Oakenrealm. (XVII. 133)

The historical verisimilitude of *The House of the Wolfings*, which so impressed Morris's German correspondent, has given way to fairy-tale imprecision about time and place.

All Morris's later romances develop the trend first shown in *The Glittering Plain* towards a less historical and more purely imaginative approach. Not that Morris discards his considerable knowledge of medieval habits and customs; but he is content now to draw eclectically upon it, choosing whichever aspect of his learning or experience will provide him with the image he needs irrespective of chronological or geographical coherence. Thus highly developed late medieval guild systems may operate in a town only days' journey from people living in conditions of primitive barbarism. Moving from one to the other the hero will leave medieval Christianity for paganism, and probably also turn from a landscape reminiscent of Kelmscott to a scene of wild desolation drawn from Morris's

memories of Iceland. Yet no one will have any difficulty understanding his language. In Morris's early romances, historical
fact was a guiding force; but in the later ones it merely colours
the inventions of a freely roving imagination.

Perhaps related to this decrease in historical accuracy is the
fact that in Morris's later romances Socialist propaganda
becomes generally harder to detect. Again, this is a trend begun
in The Glittering Plain, which had little or none of the Socialist
reference implied by the societies of The House of the Wolfings
and The Roots of the Mountains. Naturally many things happen
in the romances which bear a political interpretation, but only
rarely – mainly in the final romance, The Sundering Flood
(1898) – can Morris's political convictions be seen to provide the
organizing force of the tales. This fact is so marked, indeed, that
some critics have taken the later romances as evidence for
Morris's so-called loss of interest in Socialism during the last
years of his life.

Recent criticism has defended Morris against the charge of
having 'gone soft in the head',[2] as one critic put it, during the
period of his final romances. Biographers such as E. P.
Thompson and Jack Lindsay[3] have shown that his Socialist faith
did not wane in the 1890s. Although he became less convinced
that the revolution would occur in his lifetime, he was no less
certain of its inevitability. Does the alteration in style detectable in his prose writing, however, mark a return to escapism?
Superficially, the later romances do seem to operate at a distance from Morris's political concerns and to present a world
unconnected with practical reality. Yet since the period of the
early romances Morris had been experiencing a gradual eman-
cipation from literary, as well as political, escapism. The last
romances may be seen as the culmination of his attempts to
master the romance form and as expressions of his conviction
that it provided a powerful and valuable vehicle for serious
ideas.

I

Morris did not cease to be a Socialist when he sat down to write
fiction. A clear piece of propaganda occurs, for example, in The
Sundering Flood, the story on which Morris was working when

he died. In this tale Morris employs again the technique of *The House of the Wolfings* and *The Roots of the Mountains*, in which a battle between a free people and an oppressive race imaged the struggle between Socialism and capitalism. The last romance's hero, Osberne, is brought up in a society similar to that of the Icelandic sagas. The people, rural inhabitants of a rugged land, have no hereditary rulers; they are governed by a Mote of the whole community and relish their freedom and individuality. When in his travels Osberne comes to a city in which such political freedom does not exist he is naturally eager to help the oppressed escape from tyranny. The city's economy is based on trade and commerce; but the ordinary workers and craftsmen are controlled by a king and by an association of the greater merchants known as the Porte. Eventually Osberne is able to assist the guilds of the lesser crafts to take up arms against the aristocratic and bourgeois sections of the city. Victorious, the workers abolish the office of king, and we are not surprised by the result: 'most men felt the lighter-hearted therefor [*sic*]. And the City throve as well as ever it had done' (XXI. 182). Here Morris unequivocally requires us to see our own situation mirrored by the romance fiction, and to take to heart the lesson which is offered.

Other romances contain less overt propaganda,[4] but several show a concern with the organization of society which relates very closely to Morris's Socialist ideas. In his longest and greatest romance *The Well at the World's End* (1896) the hero visits and examines a series of societies where he is required to make judgements about the quality of life and government. Ralph is the son of the king of Upmeads, a tiny kingdom which is in theory a monarchy but in practice more like a democracy. Very early in the book this is made clear:

the men of that country were stubborn and sturdy vavassors, and might not away with masterful doings, but were like to pay back a blow with a blow, and a foul word with a buffet. (XVIII. 1)

Ralph naturally tends to take his country for granted. On his quest, however, he discovers that the form of government at Upmeads is a privilege worth dying to defend. He comes first to a town called Higham-on-the-Way, where the ruler is the abbot of the monastery. This does not imply a peaceable government; on the contrary, Higham is a militaristic society dominated by the abbot's men-at-arms. They ensure the continuance of law and order, but at the expense of humane attitudes towards the people. They control the crowds as if they were animals:

There were rows of men-at-arms in bright armour also to keep the folk in their places, like as hurdles pen the sheep up. (XVIII. 26)

Ralph is strongly pressed to join the men-at-arms, but does not feel that he would be happy under army discipline:

I wot not that I am come forth to seek a master. (XVIII. 29)

It is well that he begins his stand for freedom at Higham, for in the next town, the Burg of the Four Friths, he finds apparent prosperity built on the foundation of oppression and slave-labour. He soon begins to feel 'unfree therein' (XVIII. 76) and in fact he has eventually to flee for his life from the town. As he journeys east towards the Well at the World's End he finds that freedom is increasingly overwhelmed by savagery and slavery. He discovers places where the rule of law does not operate, where the reciprocal rights and duties which should bind together the various component groups of society are abrogated. Instead, force and cruelty are employed by one class to control another. In Goldburg Ralph finds something even worse than slavery. The poor there have no master, no one whose duty it is at least to feed them:

so that they toiled and swinked and died with none heeding them, save that they had the work of their hands good cheap ... these poor wretches were slaves without a price. (XVIII. 262)

Morris, taking his cue once again from Carlyle, wrote several non-fictional tirades against nineteenth-century capitalism couched in very similar language.[5] In a society where one class recognizes no responsibility towards another, the ideal of community has been almost completely destroyed. Yet there is one step further down. In Utterbol, Ralph comes to the nadir of social organization. A brutal and depraved tyrant rules by terror a demoralized, degraded population. The people who live there describe it as little better than Hell. And in an effective symbolic moment, the tendency of this regime to dehumanize its people is indicated when Ralph is threatened with castration.

The last romances

Naturally enough, after escaping from Utterbol Ralph and his lover Ursula need a period of recuperation and time to reassess their potential relation to society. They spend the winter alone in a mountain cave, as if retreating far back in time to a period before civilization. On re-emerging, they encounter first an idyllic pastoral community known as the Innocent Folk. Here Ralph and Ursula are formally married. Morris does not suggest that the answer to the horrors of civilization is to retreat into isolation, into an individualistic Paradise. Ralph and Ursula cannot stay in the cave, beyond law and custom. They must begin again man's journey from isolation to community. Their first step along this road is their acceptance of the need for a rite of marriage, so that their love may be ratified by the social group. Nor do they stay with the Innocent Folk, despite Morris's affection for pastoral societies. The Folk remain uncorrupted by hiding behind the mountain wall which protects them from the rest of the world. Ralph and Ursula must return to the world beyond the mountains, and eventually to Upmeads. Ralph, fortified by the power of the Well at the World's End, comes to understand the nature and value of his country's democracy and is successful in defending it against its enemies. One of his tests on the road to the Well is a question about what he will do with the power the Well confers. He passes the test by dedicating himself to the welfare of his community:

When I have accomplished this quest, I would get me home again to the little land of Upmeads, to see my father and my mother, and to guard its meadows from waste and its houses from fire-raising: to hold war aloof and walk in the free fields, and see my children growing up about me, and lie at last beside my fathers in the choir of St. Laurence. (xix. 37)

Like Face-of-god and Thiodolf, he has experienced a period of separation from his community in order to return to it with a new commitment.

In a similar pattern are the adventures of Golden Walter in *The Wood Beyond the World* (1894). With his newly won bride he emerges from a land of mythic wonders and magic into the mountains, where the two find peace. But again they cannot remain alone even in happiness. Walter's beloved, the Maid, knows that they need a social group for protection:

For I feel afraid in the wilderness, and as if I needed help and protection against my Mistress, though she be dead; and I need the comfort of many people, and the throngs of the cities. (XVII. 114)

The Mistress is a witch, whose passion for Walter almost destroys both him and the Maid. Here the Maid indicates that although the Mistress herself is dead, the destructive forces associated with her must be controlled by social organization. Walter and the Maid arrive first at the stronghold of a primitive people, the Bears, who are still living in a state of barbarism. This is a stage towards civilization, though not a very satisfactory one. The next society, however, is a Christian town. Despite its strangely cruel and archaic method of choosing a king (which Walter abolishes) it is a place in which the reciprocal affection between Walter and the Maid finds an appropriate setting. They become the town's king and queen; and the love of the people for them and theirs for the people creates a mutually protective structure:

the Maid spake softly to King Walter and said: 'Here then is the wilderness left behind a long way, and here is warding and protection against the foes of our life and soul.' (XVII. 124)

The ideal community both supports and is supported by good men and women. There is no sense of the individual being submerged by the community; on the contrary, individualism flourishes when nurtured by a suitably strong communal organization. It is tyranny which dehumanizes.

The question of the relationship of an individual to a community is examined also in *The Water of the Wondrous Isles* (1897). Here the central character is a woman named Birdalone, who as her name implies is at first isolated from human contact. As a baby she is stolen by a witch from her family and the town where she was born. She is brought up in a remote cottage cut off from the rest of the world by a forest and a vast lake. When she reaches adolescence she escapes across the lake in search of a community to provide her with support and companionship. Her journey takes her to the rescue of three women (Aurea, Viridis and Atra) who have also fallen under the spell of a witch; Birdalone is instrumental in reuniting them with their lovers, and her restoration of a broken fellowship enables her to be received into it as the dear friend of all six companions. Birdalone is not yet able, however, to subdue her individualism for the sake of the group. By her wilful refusal to conform to the taboos of her new society she causes the death of Baudoin, Aurea's lover. Furthermore, she and Atra's lover Arthur have fallen in love. So she leaves the community lest she should finally destroy it. As in previous romances, Morris is here examining the nature of fellowship, questioning the extent to which the individual may find fulfilment if altruism conflicts with strong personal desire. Like Face-of-god, Birdalone finds herself causing irrevocable damage to her community.

Like Face-of-god also, Birdalone is able to act as the preserver of her community when her personal desire has been satisfied. At the end of the romance she has returned to the witch's cottage, which becomes a place of love instead of torment when she there consummates her passion for Arthur. After the first few days of delight the lovers find that, like Walter and the Maid, they do not wish to live in isolation. Birdalone says to Arthur:

whereas I have sought thee and thou me, and we have found each other ... now I would that we should seek our fellows and have joy in them, and thole sorrow with them as in days gone by. (xx. 355)

Arthur agrees that they should try to 'knit up the links of the fellowship once more' (xx. 356). It turns out that the other members of the broken fellowship are also seeking their lost companions. Birdalone and Arthur are able to rescue their friends from thieves in the forest and the newly united group settles in the town from which Birdalone was stolen as a baby. The romance is thus insistently circular in form. Unlike Walter, whose experience of a magic world leads him to a new home and a new role, Birdalone recalls Hallblithe in that her adventures replace her in her original community. She returns there conscious of the need for fellowship and able to form part of a tolerant, therapeutic social group. Once again Morris has employed the quest-form of romance to indicate that what we search for is often to be found not in some far-away place or in fantasy but in the ordinary world of home and everyday realities.

It will have been noticed that, apart from *The Sundering Flood*, the romances do not assert the value only of societies organized precisely on Socialist principles. Upmeads and Golden Walter's final home are monarchies; for Birdalone the unit of community is a group of friends, not a political system. Morris no longer uses his fiction to present specific patterns of behaviour to be copied by Socialists. Through the events of a romance narrative he is content to suggest relationships between the individual and the community which may have a Socialist application. In a sense the later romances are increasingly self-referential, without overtly requiring us to draw parallels with the world beyond the fiction. They function as concentrations, distillations, of Morris's thought – his final assertion of his belief that art becomes relevant to life not by a naturalistic reflection of reality but by achieving a delicate metaphorical equivalence with it. We do not find in Morris a blueprint for Socialist systems of government. We do discover an image of the essence of Socialism, presented through the highly formalized patterning of romance.

II

The metaphorical relationship between the romances and the everyday experience of their readers is achieved not only by strangeness of setting and event within the story but also by idiosyncrasies of language. Morris had always sought a style related to medieval rather than contemporary models, in language as in everything else. In the romances he achieves a highly formalized and predominantly archaic diction. Critical response to the stories has to confront the question of their linguistic success.

The prose aims specifically to reproduce a language as far as possible undamaged by the intrusion of Latin and French influences, closer to the pre-Conquest English which Morris admired. Building on the stylistic foundations laid down in his previous work, especially in *Sigurd*, he employed two main techniques to give his writing a medieval flavour: the choice of archaic vocabulary and the use of a very simple, not to say simplistic, syntax. The combination of these two characteristics gives rise to the special quality of Morris's prose. Here is a passage from *The Well at the World's End*:

On the morrow early they all fared on together, and thereafter they went for two days more till they came into a valley amidst of the mountains, which was fair and lovely, and therein was the dwelling or town of this Folk of the Fells. It was indeed no stronghold, save that it was not easy to find, and that the way thither was well defensible were foemen to try it. The houses thereof were artless, the chiefest of them like to the great barn of an abbey in our land, the others low and small; but the people, both men and women, haunted mostly the big house. As for the folk, they were for the more part like those whom they had met afore: strong men, but not high of stature, black-haired, with blue or grey eyes, cheerful of countenance, and of many words. Their women were mostly somewhat more than comely, smiling, kind of speech, but not suffering the caresses of aliens. They saw no thralls amongst them; and when Ralph asked hereof, how that might be, since they were men-catchers, they told him that when they took men and women, as oft they did, they always sold them for what they would bring to the plain-dwellers; or else slew them, or held them to ransom, but never brought them home to their stead. Howbeit, when they took children, as whiles befell, they sometimes brought them home, and made them very children of their Folk with many uncouth prayers and worship of their Gods, who were indeed, as they deemed, but forefathers of the Folk. (XIX. 128–9)

Many of Morris's favourite devices may be seen in this extract. He habitually uses 'deemed' for 'thought', 'thrall' for 'slave', 'stead' for 'dwelling-place'. Common also in Morris's writing are the archaic conjunctions ('howbeit'), adverbs ('oft','whiles') and adverbial compounds ('therein', 'thereof'); the deployment of words in their old or literal meaning ('very' for 'true', 'artless' indicating lack of architectural decoration); and the coining of hyphenated synonyms in imitation of Icelandic and Old English diction, so that the folk become 'men-catchers' instead of the more likely (and more perjorative) Latinate 'bandits'.[6] With this goes a tendency to alter the order of words from what would have been expected in modern English; for example, the reversing of adverb and verb ('haunted mostly') and the biblical cadence of 'Ralph asked hereof, how that might be'. And it is all too common for Morris to use circumlocutionary phrases such as 'high of stature' in place of the simple adjective 'tall'. Yet this persistent wrenching of language into an unexpected form in terms of vocabulary and structure does not disguise the unsophisticated, even banal, basic pattern of the sentences. Morris writes a very shapeless prose. Neither within individual sentences nor in paragraphs as a whole is there any sense of movement to and from a specific telling phrase; instead the sentences characteristically fall away into a series of statements each less arresting than the preceding one. This occurs in the two sentences describing the men and women of the Folk and in the final sentence – the major impression given by this kind of writing is one of lingering anti-climax.

These infelicitous qualities of language are repeated more or less precisely through all the romances. At its worst the writing is overwhelmingly bland and repetitive. The rambling, sequential sentences lack incisiveness or tension, reducing every event or description to monotony. Although the romances, as befits the genre, are full of potentially stirring incident, there is little heightening of language to convey excitement. Here is Ralph, the hero of *The Well at the World's End*, in deadly combat:

There and then had the tale ended, but Ralph, who was wary, though he were young, and had Falcon well in hand, turned his wrist and made the horse swerve, so that the man-at-arms missed his attaint, but could not draw rein speedily enough to stay his horse ... the sword caught the foeman on the neck betwixt sallet and jack, and nought held before it, neither leather nor ring-mail, so that the man's head was nigh smitten off. (xviii. 49–50)

Morris is more concerned with the technical details of the encounter than with evoking its violent, swift and bloody nature. Similarly, when Ralph is suffering extreme grief the language remains undistorted:

his breast arose and his face was wryed, and he wept loud and long, and as if he should never make an end of it. (xviii. 202)

The measured progression of the prose precludes involvement on the part of the reader. We are observers of the events and emotions portrayed, always distanced from them by the cool sameness of the language. There is also a lack of distinctiveness in the characters' speech. All the people in Morris's romances, whether queens or slaves, civilized or barbarian, talk in almost exactly the same way. Again this fact ensures detachment in the reader, a consciousness of the artificial nature of the world he is entering which is a typical requirement of romance – but it can make for less than enthralling writing.

Morris, moreover, was always subject to the temptations of prolixity. Perhaps it was a wish to transfer to fiction something of the quality of pattern designing, which satisfies by repetition, that led him to construct stories in which, for instance, outward journeys must be reversed almost step by step at the end of the book. This occurs in both *The Well at the World's End* and *The Water of the Wondrous Isles*; and while the changes in the various places along the route may be instructive, the moral design of the romance does not justify the lengthy recapitulations that such a construction inevitably entails. When aligned with the flatness already identified as one of the problematic aspects of Morris's prose, this expansiveness contributes to the failure of the romances always to hold the attention even of a committed reader. It is revealing to compare the longest romances with Morris's early short stories; the vivid imagery and startling oddities of syntax in the earlier works point clearly the degree to which the romances are vague in description and over-extended in plot.

To look at the romances in this way may, however, be to fail in response. Some moments of grief, anger or excitement are compelling – when Ralph and Ursula complete their quest for the Well the language achieves a moving simplicity and control. And the irritating qualities of diction and construction may, if only slightly differently perceived, become bearable, even positively valuable, as the requisite style for romance. Repetition in romance is natural, particularly in medieval romance where events evolve in apparently endless series. And a lack of distinctiveness in character or description may occur because in romance individuals and specific actions must be subordinate to the accretions of the plot as a whole. If we compare Morris's language to that of Malory, for example, some of the same 'problems' may be identified. Here is an extract from 'The Tale of King Arthur':

Now turne we unto Accalon of Gaule, that whan he awoke he founde hymself by a depe welles syde within half a foote, in grete perell of deth. And there com oute of that fountayne a pype of sylver, and oute of that pype ran water all on hyghe in a stone of marbil. Whan sir Accolon sawe this he blyssed hym and seyde, 'Jesu, save my lorde kynge Arthure and kynge Uryence, for thes damysels in this shippe hath betrayed us. They were fendis and no women. And if I may ascape this mysadventure I shall distroye them, all that I may fynde of thes false damysels that faryth thus with theire inchauntementes.'
And ryght with that there com a dwarf with a grete mowthe and a flatte nose, and salewed sir Accalon and tolde hym how he cam fromme quene Morgan le Fay.[7]

Accalon's deadly peril is mentioned with the same matter-of-fact flatness with which, in the next sentence, the dangerous well is described. The arrival of the deformed dwarf causes no detectable surprise in Accalon and therefore raises none in the reader; it is simply the next event in a sequence, neither more nor less disturbing than the danger to Accalon or the appearance of the fountain. This prose lacks climaxes just as Morris's does. Even in Accalon's denunciation of the treacherous damsels no attempt is made to represent the anguished state of mind of the speaker. In true romance fashion, Malory depicts but does not imitate the strong emotions of his characters.

Of course Malory also writes in a more modern style, when, for example, he seeks to express the pathos of Launcelot and Guinevere's farewell. At such moments he attains a rhythmic power that is beyond Morris's capacity. Yet Malory's example suggests that by seeking in Morris's stories for language that is in itself exciting or stimulating we are searching in the wrong place for the tales' centre of interest. The power of Morris's writing is not in the diction. It is to be found in the symbols and thematic patterns which structure each romance. Here the metaphorical relationship between the literary work and reality exists in its most potent form. Each story is organized around a number of symbolic phenomena: places, people, events. Often the central symbol is indicated in the title: the Wood beyond the world, the Well at the World's End. Within the romance the symbols do not have their meaning blurred by emotive or even particularly descriptive language. They are presented with as much clarity of outline as Morris can achieve. We 'read' the romances by setting one symbol against another, looking always for pattern, for repetition and diversity, for subtle variation and unexpected similarity. We must follow the line of the adventure through space and time, finding in the forward moves and setbacks of the quest the significance of the story. Morris does not wish us to pause over the elegance of a sentence but to retain clearly the organization of the whole lengthy narrative. In the subsequent analysis of some of the romances' symbols, we shall not linger to regret flatness of character or imprecision of statement. We shall focus on the images which are at the heart of the romances and to which we are required to pay scrupulous attention. Sometimes they are familiar and powerful because we recognize them and respond to them with knowledge of their force in other fiction or in mythology: solar imagery will operate in this way. Sometimes we must discover their force by careful examination of the patterns in which they occur.

This symbolic technique stresses static representation, the series of pictures or motifs. There is indeed a consequent loss of tension as compared with Morris's early prose. But it may be that this newly reassuring style reflects Morris's emphasis on integration and confidence, without which he could not write romance at all. The most profound moments in romance are those of recognition, when we respond to an expected but delayed reaffirmation that all is ultimately well. In *Pericles* the divine harmony, the music of the spheres, is Shakespeare's image for the clarity and control which may be perceived beneath the apparent disorder of things. We have seen Morris approach a conviction that harmony was, or would be, attainable. His political propaganda basically involved a projection of the coming 'epoch of rest', the Nowhere of all men's dreams where all discords are resolved. His romances have this quality of rest as their major structural imperative. Battles, sorrow and death certainly occur, but their disruptive effect is mitigated by the reassurance of the prose, which is not dislocated by the disturbing events it describes. And the slow but inexorable progression of the plot towards the successful end of the quest images the process of benevolent time in which Morris had come to trust.

III

Integration between the present and the past, hardly attainable in Morris's early prose works, is a secure achievement in the last romances. In *The House of the Wolfings* and *The Roots of the Mountains* this integration was suggested by the implied relationship between the historical setting and the reader's present experience. In the later works the unity is achieved on a more personal level. Indeed, in some cases Morris seems to be conducting a psychological enquiry, using the symbols and motifs of romance, into his hero's personality.

An example of the romance protagonists' need to come to terms with their own past occurs in *The Water of the Wondrous*

Isles. Birdalone, snatched from her home and her mother, is brought up by the witch whose control over the child parodies the care of a natural parent. From this tyranny Birdalone escapes with the aid of a second substitute mother, the wood-spirit Habundia, whose benevolence opposes the witch's cruelty. The plot of the romance moves the heroine continually away from her past. Eventually, however, she meets her real mother and experiences a period of calm, contented life with her. When her mother dies Birdalone is drawn to retrace her steps. She returns to the castle where she last saw her friends and from there repeats in reverse the journey by boat across the lake. At length she arrives, naked as she left, at the house of her witch-mistress – to find that powerful figure of her childhood dead at the door of the cottage:

here was that which once was so great a thing unto her for the shaping of her life-days ... and now it was nought but a carven log unto her. (xx. 318)

Having buried the witch's body Birdalone enters into free possession of the house:

a soft content came over her, that all this was free unto her to hold in peace, and to take her pleasure in. (xx. 319)

The cottage now becomes a place of love for Birdalone and Arthur. And there too Birdalone's new ascendancy over Habundia is demonstrated: when the spirit enters the cottage she immediately diminishes in size.

As in fairy-tales of the wicked stepmother, the several mother figures in this romance seem to embody ambivalent feelings in the child towards its parent. Feelings of frustration at the exercising of adult control are projected onto the witch; the need to trust a loving adult is related to Habundia. When Birdalone has set childhood behind her (and faced adult problems connected with her own sexuality) she meets her mother as an equal and friend, without the mediation of fantasy figures. Yet she does not fully escape from the emotional force of her own past until her mother dies, leaving Birdalone an autonomous human being. Then she is able to face her past and to discover that the witch-mother has no further power – while the spirit-mother, still benevolent, is less powerful than Birdalone herself. In her new adult selfhood, then, Birdalone can become a mature woman through sexual experience. Her feelings of contented security in the cottage express her integration with her past, which is no longer a source of remembered pain and fear.

The pattern of a girl brought up by a witch, and sometimes also tutored by a wise woman, is a recurrent one in Morris's late romances. In *The Wood Beyond the World* the Maid has learned magic from an old woman which enables her to defeat the Mistress. Elfhild, heroine of *The Sundering Flood*, is helped and protected by an old woman who has knowledge of magic. The teaching by a benevolent witch and captivity in the power of an evil one both occur in *The Well at the World's End* and a similar concept operates in Morris's unpublished fragment of a romance, 'The Widow's House by the Great Water'. In turning so regularly to this particular story-pattern, Morris may have been recalling a tale he read as a young man in Carlyle's *German Romance* (1827). One of the stories translated by Carlyle is Tieck's 'The Fair-haired Eckbert'. In this tale the heroine, Bertha, narrates the story of her childhood. The daughter of an unhappy home, she runs away, and is taken in by an old woman who lives alone in a cottage far from human contact. In the cottage is a bird who lays jewelled eggs. At first Bertha is very happy in her solitude, but after some years she becomes restless and yearns to go out into the world. She describes in the following terms her conflicting feelings about her home:

I felt pressed and hampered in my heart; I wished to stay where I was, and yet the thought of that afflicted me; there was a strange contention in my soul, as if between two discordant spirits. One moment my peaceful solitude would seem to me so beautiful; the next the image of a new world, with its many wonders, would again enchant me.[8]

At last the desire for freedom becomes paramount. She takes the magic bird, and leaves the cottage secretly. The world does not prove as glorious as she imagined; and one day, maddened by the bird's song which reminds her of the cottage, she strangles it. This double crime, theft and murder, haunts her for the rest of her life.

In this picture of a young girl both dreading and desiring to leave the protective environment in which she has been brought up, and her eventual escape which involves committing a crime, Tieck is describing the movement from childhood to adolescence. The child is tired of her enclosed world and impatient of its restraints, but fears the life outside, to which she is also irresistibly attracted. Her rejection of her childhood carries with it an acceptance of a burden of guilt, as she encounters the moral responsibilities of adult society. As Bertha says, 'it is the misery of man that he arrives at understanding through the loss of innocence'.[9] While she does not regret her progression from childhood to maturity, she continues to look back on her childish purity with a sense of loss. Tieck is here using the patterns of his story to yield psychological insight into the problems both of Bertha herself and of all young people facing adulthood.

Morris takes over Tieck's images for a similar purpose. The girl held captive in a remote cottage represents a child unable to take a place in adult society, entirely subject to the whims and moods of the adult in whose charge it is placed. The magic powers of the guardian remind us that to the child the adult is omnipotent. In Morris's stories the controlling adult is not the child's mother,[10] so that the child's feelings of anger and frustration in the face of adult constraints may be safely projected onto an authority figure who is seen as evil and cruel. Moreover, the witch usually has distinctly questionable motives for raising her protégée. In the case of Birdalone, these are hinted at when the witch foretells the child's future:

the time is coming when thou shalt see here a many of the fairest of men ... and all those shall love and worship thee, and thou mayst gladden whom thou wilt, and whom thou wilt mayst sadden. (xx. 31)

This suggestion of Birdalone's forthcoming power over many lovers may be compared with a plot for a romance which Morris noted down but never used. A Dwarf-king, informed that a baby boy has been born who will destroy the dwarf kingdom, sleeps with a mortal woman:

so that he might get a daughter on her to be a temptation to the manchild when she grew up & gave her to a woodwitch when she was old enough who brought her up in evil & wiles ... In due time the youth is tempted into the woods and comes to the wodwifes [sic] house.[11]

Here the fragment breaks off, and we shall never know whether the Dwarf-king's plan was to be successful. Did Morris see the nineteenth-century education of children, especially of girls, as a potentially warping and destructive process? We may compare the strictures in *News from Nowhere* against formal schooling, and any except the lightest controls over the child's physical and mental development.

Birdalone's progression to maturity involves her rejection of the power of the witch over her actions. As an adolescent (she is seventeen when she first meets Habundia) she begins to learn about the world, and with knowledge inevitably comes loss of innocence. When she goes back to her mistress after her first talk with Habundia, she discovers that 'in her heart now was some guile born to meet the witch's guile' (xx. 22). She finds a new courage, which enables her to stand up to her mistress's scoldings and threats, and the witch herself seems to realize that Birdalone has attained a degree of maturity. It is not enough, however, for the child to begin to assert itself against the controlling powers. It must at length take responsibility for its actions, and escape altogether from parental rule. Against Habundia's wishes, Birdalone eventually refuses to continue her life of deception in the witch's cottage. She tells her wood-mother:

thy wisdom which thou hast set in my heart hath learned me that for these last months I have been meeting guile with guile and lies with lies. And now will I do so no more, lest I become a guileful woman. (xx. 46)

She flees, naked, from the witch, and enters the world. Yet she is not free from the effects of her upbringing; ironically, her beauty and goodness do cause some of the misery and havoc which her mistress intended to provoke. She cannot find rest and fulfilled love, as we have seen, until she has returned to the cottage to face the wrath of her mistress. In other words, she must confront the power which ruled and tried to warp her childhood to prove that she has broken free from it.

It will be clear that the focus of *The Water of the Wondrous Isles* is the personality of the heroine as expressed through the story and characters of the tale. This psychological interest is very obvious in an episode in which Morris makes one of his most telling uses of the conventions of romance. When the three knights set off to rescue their ladies from the witch, Birdalone is left behind at the Castle of the Quest. She is anxious and lonely, but her physical and mental restlessness seems out of all proportion to her actual situation. She has only to wait until the knights return, and control her fears for their safety; yet on several occasions she appears almost deranged by her grief. The reason is that she is suffering not merely from anxiety but also from sexual deprivation. She has not admitted to herself that she loves Arthur, but her anguish of mind and body stems from her separation from him. In this mood, she is greatly struck by a legend which she hears, referring to a valley in the mountain range beyond the castle. It is said that the great grey stones in the valley are really giants, which if certain conditions are fulfilled may come alive and grant a wish to anyone who has the courage to awaken them. Wilfully ignoring all warnings of danger, Birdalone determines to try the adventure. She goes alone to the valley, waits until she thinks that one of the stones is stirring, and makes her wish:

O Earth, thou and thy first children, I crave of you that he may come back now at once and loving me. (xx. 159)

Immediately a knight in black appears from behind the stone. He takes Birdalone away into the mountains, and only with difficulty does she prevent him from raping her. Her honour is preserved, but it is in rescuing Birdalone from the knight's evil lord, the Red Baron, that Baudoin is killed. The granting of Birdalone's wish seems to lead directly to a savage and permanently damaging attack upon the fellowship.

In the first draft of *The Water of the Wondrous Isles* this adventure is just another episode in the picaresque wanderings of the heroine. It was apparently while making the fair copy for the printer that Morris realized how the story could be used to express the disastrous effect on the fellowship of Birdalone's love for Arthur. In the first draft Birdalone's wish is much less insistent:

O Earth thou and thy first children, I crave of you that one day I may be happy with him and he with me.[12]

There is no indication, as there is in the printed text, that she immediately regrets what she has said. In the printer's copy Morris writes first:

I crave of you that he may come back now at once and make me happy.[13]

He then alters this sentence to read as it does in the printed text. The words which were finally printed are, then, Morris's third thoughts about the degree of selfishness and uncontrolled desire which he wished to attribute to Birdalone. At the same late stage (if one may judge from the colour of the ink in the manuscript) he made the crucial innovation which links together the knight who captures Birdalone, and her lover. Arthur is always known as the Black Squire. In the first draft of the romance, the knight is unnamed; in the fair copy, Morris adds the words 'may we call him the Black Knight'.[14] Now the relationship of the tale to the whole romance may fall into place. Birdalone, desiring Arthur too strongly, is driven to wish that their love may be swiftly consummated, whatever might be the effect on the rest of the fellowship. Although she at once attempts to take back her words, it is too late. The Black Knight, raised as if by the power of Birdalone's request, immediately appears to fulfil her desire. He represents Arthur as he might be, the lover of Birdalone's fantasy; his power over her, and the probability that he will rape her, is created by her own sexual passion not for him, but for Arthur. Characters in romance may always stand for ideas and emotions in the mind of the protagonist, as well as being people in the story. Morris makes use of this freedom to tell us, by a series of events rather than by psychological description, exactly how dangerous is Birdalone's feeling and how far she is controlled by it. Then he shows us its terrible effect. When the three knights ride to save Birdalone, we feel confident of their success. We are only half-way through the book; heroes of romance always survive until the end and win their battles. The shock of Baudoin's death is therefore extreme. Birdalone has not only broken the fellowship, but has caused the romance (which is itself an image of harmony) to fail of its happy ending, because one of the heroes has been lost. Secure in the control of his medium, Morris has cleverly played on the expectations of the experienced romance reader in order to bring home the enormity of Birdalone's crime.

The last romances

Morris never finished the fair copy of *The Water of the Wondrous Isles*; it breaks off half-way through Birdalone's adventure with the Black Knight, and the rest of the romance was printed from the first draft. We do not know whether he would have developed further the concept of the Black Knight as a representation of the Black Squire, or how he might have linked Arthur's seduction by the witch on the Isle of Increase Unsought with the attempted rape of Birdalone in the mountains. Enough of Morris's second and third thoughts remain, however, to show clearly how the romance is to be seen as occurring within the personality of the heroine as well as externally. Birdalone is in the process of coming to understand herself, and among other things has to come to terms with the depths of her selfish passions. Her period of exile from the fellowship may thus be seen as a penance for the harm she did, both in reality and desire, to the unity of the group. When Birdalone visits the Isle of the Young and the Old, an ancient man tells her that 'love rendeth apart that which was joined together' (xx. 86). Birdalone, intent on her mission of reuniting the separated lovers, is incredulous of his words. She has to learn, through her fatal mistake and the sorrow it brings, that in some circumstances love may be a destructive and divisive force. Not until she has thoroughly learned this lesson can she find the happiness she craves.

The Wood Beyond the World is a romance which is even more exclusively concerned with the inner development of the hero. Golden Walter (whose name is one of the last traces of solar imagery in Morris's work) is the son of a merchant, and after an unhappy marriage he goes on a trading voyage to try to forget his troubles. While he does regain his spirits, he is haunted by a recurring vision of a beautiful woman, a young slave-girl and a hideous dwarf, which seems somehow to hold an important meaning for him. On his way home he finds his way into a land beyond the mountains, which is said to offer mysterious adventures to the traveller. There he meets first the dwarf, then the Maid, with whom he falls in love, and lastly the Mistress, who has drawn him to her by magic and who succeeds in seducing him. After many days of conflict between the fascination exerted on him by the Mistress and his genuine love for the Maid, Walter is able to escape from the Wood. The Maid contrives the death of the Mistress, and she and Walter flee together. Before they can escape completely, however, Walter has to kill the dwarf. The Maid's magic enables the lovers to pass safely through the land of the Bears, a primitive people who practise human sacrifice, and they come at last to a medieval city called Stark-wall, of which Walter becomes king.

This romance is written with an intensity which sets it apart from Morris's more diffuse compositions. After a brief introduction, the action takes place almost exclusively in the mysterious Wood beyond the World, where there are only five characters: Walter, the three figures of his vision, and the Mistress's former lover, known as the King's Son, who desires the Maid. A dream-like atmosphere surrounds Walter's sojourn with the Mistress. Not surprisingly, early critics felt that the story meant more than it appeared to say. One reviewer analysed it as an allegory of Capital and Labour, which flagrant misrepresentation drew a dignified refutation from Morris, in one of the few public comments he made on his work.[15] If we attempt to discover the true significance of the action of the romance, we may begin by noting a verbal echo which reminds us of phrases used elsewhere by Morris. The Maid tells Walter that the Mistress has 'cast her net and caught thee' (xvii. 35). The image of being caught in a net was used frequently in *Sigurd the Volsung* and in *The Glittering Plain* to describe the plight of the heroes when their power was curtailed by treachery or sorcery. At the beginning of *The Wood Beyond the World* the image is used again, this time with reference to Walter's marriage. He is said to have 'fallen into the toils of love of a woman exceeding fair' (xvii. 1). If, prompted by the similarity of these expressions, we ask what might be the relationship between the Mistress and Walter's unfaithful wife, we may begin to see the pattern which underlies the mysterious happenings in the Wood. Walter was driven away from home and into his adventure because he had made a disastrous choice of marriage partner; instead of choosing freely, the image suggests, he allowed his judgement to be overridden by the passionate desire he felt for his wife. In the Wood he is offered another choice between two women, two different kinds of love. This time his life depends on his making the right choice.

The relationship of Walter and the Mistress is one based

purely on lust, in which Walter's position is that of a servant, a squire adapting himself to each whim of his lady. The presence of the King's Son reminds Walter that the Mistress has had many other lovers, and will tire of him too. He knows that he is deceived and tormented by her, and that her land is one of guile and lies. Yet he is not proof against her voluptuous beauty, any more than he was against that of his wife. In sharp contrast to the Mistress, the Maid is kind and simple; instead of displaying her physical charms, she covers up her bare legs and arms when Walter first sees her. Far from seducing him, she will not let him touch her. One of her reasons for this shows us that Walter is undergoing a test of his good intentions:

Whether this thy love shall outlast the first time that thou holdest my body in thine arms, I wot not, nor dost thou. (XVII. 33)

While he is in the magic Wood, Walter must discover which kind of love he really desires. Only when he genuinely rejects the dominating, fickle passion represented by the Mistress, and which he chose in reality when he married, will the Maid give herself to him.

Walter very nearly fails the test. He does sleep with the Mistress, and he is twice unable to distinguish between the Mistress and the Maid, mistaking one for the other when he sees them at a distance. Eventually, however, he comes fully to understand that the relationship between him and the Mistress can never be a satisfying one. Its basis in lies is made clear by the working-out of the Maid's plot to effect Walter's escape. She first lures the King's Son to her bed by a false promise to sleep with him. Then she drugs him with a strong narcotic, and throws over him by magic the appearance of Walter. She has already seen to it that the Mistress believes that the Maid and Walter will be sleeping together that same night. This chain of deception works as the Maid had planned. The Mistress comes to the Maid's room, finds, as she expects, the figure of Walter, and kills him in her jealousy. Then, overcome by frustrated passion, she kills herself. When the false semblance of himself has been killed by his Mistress, Walter can give his undivided love to the Maid. His first independent action is to kill the dwarf; this creature, as his language about the Maid indicates, embodies the violent passions of lust and hatred which Walter has now definitively rejected.

On one occasion Morris describes the country beyond the confines of the enchanted Wood as 'the outward world' (XVII. 105). By contrast we may see the Wood as an 'inward world'; it is the world inside Walter's head, the landscape in which his fantasies are played out and in which he learns to discriminate between a slavish sexual passion and a free, reciprocal love. When he emerges from the Wood, he has attained so much self-knowledge and self-control that he easily passes the test imposed by the men of Stark-wall and shows himself worthy to be their king. In *The Wood Beyond the World* Morris makes effective use of the isolation of romance from the real world. He turns the story into a representation of the inner development of a personality, in the guise of an adventure undertaken by the outward semblance of the hero. The figures of the Mistress, the Maid, the dwarf and the King's Son may seem merely two-dimensional if judged by the criteria of realism. Their function in the romance, however, is to incarnate certain aspects of Walter's character (the dwarf and the King's Son) or the objects of his desires (the Mistress and the Maid). Eventually Walter commits himself to the beneficent and productive type of love, becomes once again integrated into society and puts right the grave mistake he made when first falling in love.

Morris professed to despise novels, which dealt with what he called 'dreary introspective nonsense' (XVI. 151) about the characters' psychological problems. Yet he shows impressive skill in his handling of the externalizing power of romance, using the events of the story to reveal psychological truths. This analysis is placed at the service of an assertion of the need for, and possibility of, integration – between man and nature, past and present, man's own warring propensities and desires. This last is a preoccupation almost unique to the romances within Morris's work. Yet it may come as no surprise that, following his increased ability to endorse the romance impetus towards eventual calmness and fulfilment, he should add an examination of psychological wholeness to his discussion about other kinds of unity. In *News from Nowhere* the 'epoch of rest' was presented as a homecoming for mankind and a return to the clarity and peace of childhood. In the romances too the progress is towards the poise that comes from a man's peace with himself, his environment, his past. Perhaps only romance, with its structural demand for harmony, can adequately and unsentimentally suggest the possibility of attaining that peace.

IV

The inability of man to attain harmony with the natural world was a common theme in Morris's earlier work. The individual, aware of his own mortality, was mocked by the 'changeless change' (VI. 175) of nature; but attempts to halt the process of growth, ageing and death led only to sterility and death-in-life. In the political romances, achieved social harmony tended to involve increased unity between man and nature, as when Thiodolf's commitment to his people replaced him securely within the natural cycle. In the last romances Morris concentrates increasingly on the possibility of man's acquiring a productive relationship with nature.

In *Child Christopher*, as has already been noted, Morris removes the story from an historical England and sets it in a fairy-tale forest. The result is not merely a picturesque background for the tale; more importantly, the huge forest comes to signify the power which enfolds and protects the central characters, an encompassing and regenerative nature. Christopher and Goldilind are both displaced and orphaned. He is rightful king of Oakenrealm, she is true queen of the adjacent land of Meadham, but each has been supplanted by a usurper. Both flee into the wood, and both find it a place of refuge. For Christopher, especially, the forest provides healing, in a literal as well as a psychological sense. When he has been badly wounded he feels a new identification with the beauties of nature, as if all were 'one great show done for the behoof and pleasure of him, the man come from the peril of death and the sick-bed' (XVII. 167). It is within the forest that Christopher and Goldilind meet and fall in love. Their passion is nearly destroyed, however, when for a short time they leave the wood and are caught up again in the complex evil of the world beyond. The usurper of Goldilind's throne, wishing to be rid of her without actually harming her, insists that she marry Christopher, whom all think to be only a forester. Goldilind would be happy to take Christopher as a lover but is horrified at the idea of marrying a commoner. Thus social patterns, the characters' conditioned acceptance of a class system, come between two people who in a natural state were able simply to accept their mutual sexual attraction. This is neatly expressed by clothing imagery. When they first meet in the wood, Christopher and Goldilind are both wearing green, the colour of the forest. For their forced marriage they are dressed up in rich robes, and while wearing them they remain estranged from one another. It is not until they are back in the forest and have exchanged the robes for their old country garments that the constraints are lifted and their love can be consummated. While they live in the forest Goldilind gradually comes to feel the same sense of communion with nature as Christopher:

it seemed to her ... as if all this bright beauty of tree and flower, and beast and bird, was but made for her alone. (xvii. 211)

The house where they live is decorated with tapestries depicting Adam and Eve in Paradise.

Natural relationships, then, flourish in the forest but are distorted outside it. Beyond the wood, also, 'natural' social positions are reversed in that both countries have lost their true rulers. Christopher and Goldilind use the power of the wood to help them to regain their rightful places as king and queen. Typically, Morris does not allow the lovers to remain in their isolated and individualistic Paradise. Like Walter and the Maid, or Birdalone and Arthur, they have social duties as well as duties to themselves. Two figures who aid them in their return to their kingdoms both reflect the power of the forest, ensuring that Christopher and Goldilind will carry with them into their civilized lives the natural strength and joy which they dis-covered in the wood. One is a living man: an outlaw in the style of Robin Hood, called Jack of the Tofts, who is Christopher's companion and champion. Dressed in green to indicate his unity with nature, he provides the physical force necessary for Christopher to regain his throne. Spiritual power comes from a wood-spirit who appears in a dream to the usurper Rolf the Marshal, warning him that he cannot hope unlawfully to retain control of the kingdom. As a woman dressed only in oak leaves, she is also portrayed on the banner of Oakenrealm under which

Christopher fights. In this romance those who are in harmony with nature are helped by it to attain their 'natural' and rightful positions. The usurpers are awkward and frightened in the face of nature and Rolf is put to flight by the forces under the banner of the wood-woman.

This wood-spirit, helper of the romance heroes and heroines, appears in several of Morris's romances. In 'The Widow's House by the Great Water' the heroine Katherine meets a fairy woman in the wood who is able to assume Katherine's appearance and can see into the inmost heart of the mortal she resembles. In another unfinished story, *Kilian of the Closes*, a woodland spirit in a green gown enables Kilian to see a fountain magically hidden from mortal eyes and to experience a vision of Paradise. Most importantly, in *The Water of the Wondrous Isles*, Bird-alone is given vital support by the wood-woman Habundia. She first appears when Birdalone is sitting in the wood where, like Christopher, she finds solace for her troubles; naked, she is embroidering a green gown with flowers and animals, creating a robe to symbolize her affinity with the natural world. Habundia is also naked and as like to Birdalone as if she were her mirror-image. Like the spirit in *Child Christopher* she wears a garland of oak leaves round her loins. It is from Habundia that Birdalone learns the wisdom and courage to face up to the evil of her witch-mistress and to escape across the lake. Habundia also saves Birdalone's life when called upon for aid, and restores Arthur to sanity when he has been driven mad by desire for Birdalone. A projection of the natural goodness in Birdalone that cannot be warped by the witch, Habundia indicates the need to rely on the power of nature when human wisdom is insufficient.

Habundia's name leads us to the source for this recurrent wood-spirit. Once again it was Grimm's *Teutonic Mythology* which provided the stimulus to Morris's imagination. Grimm examines the transmutation of ancient Teutonic earth-goddesses into post-Christian legendary figures such as dryads. One spirit he specifically mentions is called 'domina Abundia' or 'dame Habonde';[16] she is said to give prosperity to houses in which she is seen and to be visible in the woods in the shape of a woman or a girl. In the later romances Morris gives to the nature-spirit a centrality which he previously accorded to the solar deity. Was he aware that in 1890 Frazer had replaced the sun at the heart of Aryan mythological systems by the sacred tree? It is impossible to say with certainty that Morris read *The Golden Bough*, but he seems to have been familiar with the title: he designed a silk and linen textile pattern containing an oak leaf which he called 'Golden Bough'. Morris's friend and SPAB colleague W. R. Lethaby refers to Frazer's book in *Architecture Mysticism and Myth* (1891); and if, as his daughter suggested, Morris read many contemporary works on mythology and anthropology, he may have studied a translation of Goblet d'Alviella's *The Migration of Symbols* (1894). For all these scholars, the tree was a central focus of veneration in the worship of early man. *The Migration of Symbols* traces the image of the sacred tree back to Mesopotamia and links it with the concept of a life-force. Semitic peoples, d'Alviella believes:

> frequently represented by a tree the female personification of Nature, who, under various names, and even with different attributes, seems above all to have embodied in their opinion the conceptions of life, of fecundity, and of universal renovation.[17]

There was also 'an allied class of myths which we find fully developed amongst the Aryans'.[18] Most importantly for Morris, Grimm stressed that for the forest-dwelling Teutons the tree was divine. Even their word for 'temple' also meant 'wood': 'the grand general worship of the people has its seat in the *grove*'.[19] As the solar mythology theory dominated mythological studies during the 1870s when Morris was writing *Sigurd*, by the 1890s the pre-eminent idea was of tree-worship.[20]

By turning to this nature motif Morris was of course developing images that had been present in his work long before. He was aware in the 1870s that the most potent symbol of Paradise was the fruitful tree surrounded by water; in *The Earthly Paradise* this image, and perversions of it, are crucial. The flowers and fruit on the Pope's staff indicate the positive antithesis of the false and barren Paradises like Sthenoboea's artificial garden. In *Sigurd* the blossoming tree relates to the power of the hero. In the last romances Morris returns most insistently to the conjunction between tree and water, showing how the life-forces implied by this symbol must be properly and reverently employed by the hero. Walter has to go to a wood beyond the world to achieve a new integration of his personality, and the two women whom he loves are associated with true and false representations of nature. The Mistress's palace is reminiscent of Sthenoboea's garden:

a hall many-pillared, and vaulted over, the walls painted with gold and ultramarine, the floor dark, and spangled with many colours, and the windows glazed with knots and pictures. Midmost thereof was a fountain of gold, whence the water ran two ways in gold-lined runnels, spanned twice with little bridges of silver. (XVII. 38–9)

The most glittering jewel in this gorgeous setting is the gold-clad Mistress herself. When she and Walter sleep together it is in an enclosed garden crossed by a stream and apparently containing all the attributes of Paradise; but the next day Walter can find no trace of it. The Mistress, then, can ape nature with jewelled art-work and can create a false Paradise, but the Maid in contrast is in close contact with nature itself. In the Wood, Walter first sees her in a setting which is pointedly different from the Mistress's palace:

he saw a little way ahead a grey rock rising up from amidst of a ring of oak-trees ... and as he went he saw that there was a fountain gushing out from under the rock, which ran thence in a fair little stream. And when he had the rock and the fountain and the stream clear before him, lo! a child of Adam sitting beside the fountain under the shadow of the rock. (XVII. 30)

The Maid is dressed in green 'like the sward whereon she lay' (XVII. 30). That her power is in some sense a 'natural' magic is indicated by its connection with her virginity. When the Maid and Walter meet with the Bears they escape because the Maid turns herself into a vision of the nature-goddess whom the Bears worship. Like the people described by Frazer and Grimm, this tribe trusts in a goddess who is protected by a male consort. The Maid is able to convince them that she is an incarnation of their goddess when by her magic she is clad in living flowers:

Lo then! as she spake, the faded flowers that hung about her gathered life and grew fresh again; the woodbine round her neck and her sleek shoulders knit itself together and embraced her freshly, and cast its scent about her face. (XVII. 107)

Walter was summoned to the Wood by the Mistress to take the place of the King's Son in her affections – that is, to perform the role, analysed by Frazer, of killer and supplanter of the nature-goddess's old consort. In fact he becomes the champion of the nature-goddess in her benevolent instead of her destructive phase; and after uniting himself with the Maid and moving from barbarism to civilization he informs his new social group with the natural strength which the Maid represents. Even when her magic has disappeared she remains 'the land's increase' (XVII. 128).

Walter, then, achieves something which was often attempted in vain by heroes of *The Earthly Paradise*. Instead of remaining in the changeless land which only seems natural, and participating in a cyclical, repetitive pattern, he moves out into a world where heroism and natural growth can be related. In *The Water of the Wondrous Isles*, similarly, there is a warning against perversions of nature and an endorsement of the power of undistorted natural development. When Birdalone crosses the great lake, the islands which she visits present images of various aberrations of natural order. The Isle of the Young and the Old is inhabited only by an ancient man and two children who will never grow up. On the Isle of Queens Birdalone finds a hall in which are many ladies who seem at first to be alive, but who neither move nor speak; they surround a bier on which lies a dead king. On the next island, the Isle of Kings, the situation is reversed, so that petrified knights gaze at a dead queen. These images of sterility and stasis, so familiar from Morris's early poetry and prose, culminate when Birdalone reaches the Isle of Nothing. This is a wasteland: perfectly flat, completely empty of plant or living creature, and shrouded in a thick mist. Birdalone loses her way there and is saved from death only when she calls on Habundia's aid. The ultimate perversion of nature is deadly. Equally deplorable, however, is a distortion of nature which produces the opposite effect from that on the Isle of Nothing. The first island Birdalone visits is the Isle of Increase Unsought, ruled by another witch (sister of her mistress) who holds three maidens in captivity. This island is luxuriously fertile. The women do nothing to cultivate the plants or to provide themselves with food and clothing. The witch's magic ensures an abundant supply of everything they need. Yet this hypernatural fruitfulness is a transgression of the natural limits on growth – it is a false Paradise, like the Venusberg. Birdalone helps to destroy it by ensuring that the captive women's lovers are able to find the island and free the prisoners. When the sexes are united and the witch is dead all the islands change. The Isle of Increase Unsought becomes barren. When Birdalone revisits the Isle of the Young and the Old she finds many children but no old man; living women now inhabit the Isle of Kings and men the Isle of Queens. These partial restorations of natural order are overshadowed by the triumphant renewal of life on the Isle of Nothing. Here fertility has returned and on the island lives a group of simple, pastoral people. They delight in the processes of growth and in the children who are being born to them. Their hopeful joy in the future fruitfulness of their land and in their descendants reminds us of the need to treat nature as our friend.

In *Sigurd the Volsung* and *The House of the Wolfings* Morris suggested that man need not feel himself at odds with nature despite the reminders it constantly offered of his own mortality. Through perceiving the relationship of an individual hero to the cosmic patterns of Aryan mythology, we may come to understand personal dissolution as a necessary and acceptable part of a process in which each act of heroism contributes to the ultimate good. This is how the death of Thiodolf is received in *The House of the Wolfings*. Thus there is no longer any necessity for a vain struggle against time and change. In the romances even the last traces of stoicism are expunged. The romance heroes and heroines joyfully identify themselves with nature and learn from it all they can – not abrogating their humanity but integrating it with the natural cycles of growth, death and rebirth.[21] This is particularly clear in *The Well at the World's End*, where the quest for natural vitality and power is at the heart of the adventure.

The romance concentrates on that staple character of fairy-tale, the youngest son who turns out to be stronger and wiser than his elder brothers. I have already described how Ralph leaves his father's kingdom and travels through cities and wildernesses in search of the Well at the World's End. He does so against his parents' will. When his elder brothers are allowed to seek their fortunes in the world beyond Upmeads, Ralph is considered too young to risk the dangers of such an adventure. He runs away, therefore; and the story shows how, unlike his more experienced brothers, he matures into a mighty hero, able to return and save Upmeads from its enemies. At the end of the story he has taken over the throne from his abdicating father and is about to establish Upmeads in prosperity and safety.

The romance is on one level a study of growing up. Like Birdalone, Ralph must learn what it is to be an autonomous human being. His development, like hers, is imaged by his movement away from home and its restrictions, and his return with new power. (The pattern is also like that of Face-of-god in *The Roots of the Mountains*.) Ralph makes two major discoveries on his journey, both of which find parallels in *The Water of the Wondrous Isles*. He learns, as I have already indicated, something about societal organization and the value of true democracy. Like Birdalone, he adds to his increased understanding of the nature of community an experience of sexual passion and a recognition of its potential for destruction. In this he is also reminiscent of Golden Walter, for Ralph too falls in love with two women. His first love, who relates to Walter's Mistress, is variously described as a fairy, a witch and a benevolent nature-goddess: her name is the Lady of Abundance. Ralph saves her life in the Wood Perilous and becomes obsessed with her beauty and power. She eventually allows him to consummate his passion and we infer that it is his first sexual experience. The Lady foreshadows Habundia in her name, her connection with fruitful nature and her role as teacher of the romance protagonist. Yet the benevolence which we might expect from such a figure in Morris's work sits uneasily with her position as older, sexually dominant and seductive woman, for this is the doubtfully valuable relationship of the Mistress towards Walter. Indeed, to many people in the romance, the Lady of Abundance is an evil force. She is another of the girls brought up to be a snare to men, and her beauty does bring with it anguish and death – a tendency which culminates when she is herself murdered by her jealous husband after she has slept with Ralph. Ralph kills the husband in retaliation, thus becoming involved in the pattern of hatred and bloodshed that goes with the Lady and the passion she inspires. As in *Sigurd*, the hero is threatened by a cyclical and repetitive evil. Also reminiscent of *Sigurd*, however, is the sense of the hero as solar deity. The Lady's husband is the Knight of the Sun; Ralph kills him as 'the last rays of the setting sun' (XVIII. 201) shine on his armour. Two mythological motifs are here juxtaposed. Had Ralph killed the Knight of the Sun before he became the Lady's lover, he would have been performing the role of new consort to the nature-goddess which is marked out for Walter in *The Wood Beyond the World*. This condition is linked in the romances with sterile and false Paradises and with recurrent evil. But Ralph is closer to the solar hero who is involved in a cycle that brings life and hope. Like Walter he finds an alternative beloved. Ursula has little of the obvious sexual attractiveness flaunted by the Lady. Instead of meeting her in danger, from which he must heroically rescue her, Ralph first sees Ursula in the ordinary situation of an inn at which he buys food; later she escapes from the castle of the Lord of Utterbol without assistance from Ralph. She has no magic powers. Above all, her relationship with Ralph is one of equal and friend, not of mistress to servant. The Lady has already drunk from the Well and planned before her death to lead Ralph there. Ursula is a fellow-seeker with Ralph. By choosing Ursula, Ralph becomes part of a sustaining union between partners, not a slave to the overwhelming force of sexuality, as he was with the Lady.

Ralph sleeps with the Lady in secret, adulterously. Ursula insists on a formal marriage ceremony before sleeping with Ralph. Thus Ralph's second love is associated with his growing understanding about the need for community; and his change from one kind of love to the other is linked with his move from adolescent self-absorption to socially committed recognition of the role he must perform in the wider world. The first love is not forgotten, nor is Ralph ashamed of it. It appears as a valuable, even necessary experience, part of a process of growing to maturity. Ralph, it seems, has to fall in love with the Lady before the greater rewards of the kind of love Ursula offers are clear to him. Until he has discovered the potentially destructive power of sensuality he cannot accept a less irrational affection. His old servant, however, is relieved when Ralph's emotional allegiance alters:

now hast thou wedded into the World of living men, and not to a dream of the Land of Fairy. (XIX. 137)

Even Ralph, using an image prevalent in *The Wood Beyond the World*, describes his infatuation with the Lady as having been 'taken in the toils of love' (XVIII. 266). Thus, like Walter and Birdalone, he progresses through a period of sexual obsession to form a fully adult relationship in which lust has given way to fruitful affection and commitment.

Ralph gains, then, both political and sexual wisdom during his adventure. Yet this increased knowledge is only part of the wider development which changes him from a youth to a man and a hero. Ursula thus describes what has happened to him:

> thou art changed since yester-year, and since we met on the want-way of the Wood Perilous ... for then thou wert but a lad, high-born and beautiful, but simple maybe, and untried; whereas now thou art meet to sit in the Kaiser's throne and rule the world from the Holy City. (XIX. 130–1)

Ralph assumes his kingship because he has completed a quest: he has discovered the Well at the World's End. In order to understand some of the implications of this, the romance's central symbol, we must relate it to similar phenomena in Morris's other work. Like the Wanderers in *The Earthly Paradise*, Ralph leaves home to search for an ideal. He has, even less than they, scant knowledge of where to look or even what it is he seeks. Yet, like them, he has as the object of his quest a life-giving force. The water of the Well is for those who drink it a source of longevity, power, youthful strength and energy and protection from evil – Ralph and Ursula will be immune from danger in the final battle because they have completed the quest:

> the hands and the eyes that be behind the bows have other hands and eyes behind them which shall not suffer that a Friend of the Well shall be hurt. (XIX. 207)

Clearly the Well is related to the spring which is one of the legendary attributes of Paradise. Medieval descriptions of the Earthly Paradise, drawing on the account in Genesis of the four rivers which went out from Eden to water the earth, almost invariably include a well or spring. In Mandeville's *Travels* the author claims to have seen a magic well which originates from Paradise:

> And whoso drynketh iii. tymes fasting of that water of that welle, he is hool of alle maner sykeness that he hath. And thei that duellen there

and drynken often of that welle, thei neuere han sekeness and thei semen alleweys yonge ... Sum men clepen it the Welle of Youthe.[22]

We have already seen that Morris was aware of this tradition when he wrote *The Earthly Paradise*. In *The Well at the World's End* Ralph has to pass by a deadly parody of the life-giving spring he seeks. He has heard that the Well may only be reached by way of the Dry Tree, and he finds it in the middle of an arid, stony desert. The tree stands with its roots in a stagnant pool and is surrounded by what at first seem living people:

all down the sides of the valley sat or lay children of men; some women, but most men-folk, of whom the more part were weaponed, and some with their drawn swords in their hands. Whatever semblance of moving was in them was when the eddying wind of the valley stirred the rags of their raiment, or the long hair of the women. But a very midmost of this dreary theatre rose up a huge and monstrous tree. (XIX. 73)

Again Morris powerfully returns to the picture of death-in-life. Ralph is nearly deceived by this savage mirror-image of the Well he is seeking. Fascinated, he comes close to drinking the poisoned water and joining his predecessors in immobility. He is saved by Ursula, who recognizes the evil; and by the provision of a substitute victim in the shape of a crow which flies down to the water, drinks and dies. Morris is here reworking images which were central to *The Earthly Paradise*. Ralph is on a quest for a life-force that will enable him to defeat evil and death. Like some of the searchers in the poem, he discovers a source of power which appears to cheat the process of change and decay but which in reality only offers the unfruitful stasis of arrested growth. The difference between Ralph and many of the *Earthly Paradise* characters is that he is able to pass through the deathly experience and discover a true Paradise beyond. The crow seems to act as a kind of proxy for Ralph and to die in his place. Death must be faced, not evaded, if one is to attain the Paradise. Unlike most of the heroes in *The Earthly Paradise*, Ralph passes this test and is rewarded with a draught from the waters of life.

The World's End is described in terms which relate it closely to Eden. Animals are tame there; Ralph and Ursula feel that they have 'come into the very Garden of God' (XIX. 87). Bathing in the sea, the source of life, they discover that old scars have been washed away in a process of healing and revitalizing. Eventually they seem to have returned to a primal strength and beauty, so that Ursula looks to Ralph like a reincarnation of Eve:

here is no mark nor blemish, but the best handiwork of God, as when he first made a woman from the side of the Ancient Father. (xix. 85)

All the imagery reminds us that the true Paradise, in contrast to the false one, involves a return to a harmony between man and nature. One of Ralph's qualifications for becoming a seeker after the Well is his belief in the primacy of nature. When the monks at Higham ask him to join their retreat from the world, Ralph is adamant that the world is the creation of a benevolent God and not, therefore, to be escaped from:

'Wilt thou tell me, father, whose work was the world's fashion?'
The monk reddened, but answered nought, and Ralph spake again: 'Forsooth, did the craftsman of it fumble over his work?' (xviii. 36)

Part of his vow, when asked what he would do with the power conferred by the Well, is a promise never to deny his relationship with nature:

The dead would I love and remember; the living would I love and cherish; and Earth shall be the well-beloved house of my Fathers, and Heaven the highest hall thereof. (xix. 37)

As he drinks the water he calls a health over the cup which similarly unites man and the natural world: 'To the Earth, and the World of Manfolk!' (xix. 83). Morris claims, as he does in *Child Christopher* and *The Water of the Wondrous Isles*, that the power of the hero is not a transcendence of natural laws but their greatest fulfilment; the true hero becomes so only when he is fully in harmony with nature. To remind us of this, the sign carved on the rock to guide the seekers to the Well combines an image of heroic strength, a sword, with the natural symbol so important to Frazer: a 'three-leaved bough' (xix. 39).

The Well at the World's End synthesizes the images that have been crucial to Morris's literary imagination throughout his career. Ralph, vestigially a solar hero, seeks a true Earthly Paradise where he can find regeneration. He is offered two false Paradises: one in terms of the love of a dominant woman, who like Morgan le Fay in *The Earthly Paradise* provides endless but unproductive bliss, the other more clearly evil since it is an obvious parody of the well and the tree of life that he seeks. These two, however, are really one and the same – for the Lady of Abundance, whose name promises fertility, is also the queen of the Champions of the Dry Tree. Though the Tree itself is widely separated in the story from the events concerning the Lady, its eventual appearance fully demonstrates the danger she represented to Ralph. In escaping it, he becomes qualified to discover the Tree of Life. But where is this final symbol? Not at the World's End; though it contains so many images that relate it to Eden, it does not contain a tree. Has Morris omitted it through an oversight? That he has not becomes clear when we realize that as well as a parody of the complete Paradise symbol, there is after all in the romance a combination of fruitful tree and water. This does not exist, however, in a place through which Ralph travels. In fact he bears it with him throughout his quest – for it is the badge of Upmeads:

his surcoat ... was of fine green cloth, and the coat-armour of Upmeads was beaten on it, to wit, on a gold ground an apple-tree fruited, standing by a river-side. (XVIII. 101)

The story, then, is of a hero who finds a true but incomplete Earthly Paradise. The quest for Ralph is not linear but circular; he must leave home to discover the source of life and heroic power, but for a full expression of his new heroism he must return home. Only there, the tree imagery suggests, is the complete Paradise.

By employing the Aryan image of the tree Morris combines nature and history – the two pivots of his imagination – into a single, potent focus for his romance. And he also attempts to claim universal significance for his story. With the tree and the well, another image also drawn from the remote past provides him with a second motif around which the romance's meaning may be organized. In several of Morris's designs, especially those dating from the 1880s,[23] can be found the pattern of a tree, pillar or flame flanked by animals or monsters. In his lecture 'The History of Pattern Designing' he discusses its significance. The Holy Tree or Holy Fire, he says, originated in Chaldea, and 'both the fire and the tree are symbols of life and creation' (XXII. 228). As for the supporting beasts, he admits that they may be guardian spirits, but adds another suggestion:

I have, however, seen a different guess at their meaning; to wit, that they represent the opposing powers of good and evil that form the leading idea of the dualism that fixed itself to the ancient Zoroastrian creed. (xxii. 228)

The image of the life-force fought over by opposing good and evil spirits appears in *The Well at the World's End* when Ralph leaves Upmeads and crosses the downs which lie south of his home. He sees a shape cut out from the turf above him:

A tree with leaves was done on that hill-side, and on either hand of it a beast like a bear ramping up against the tree. (xviii. 19)

The tree, as we have seen, appears again many times in the romance. The bears also recur. Sometimes they seem to be threatening forces. The second, wicked queen of the Champions of the Dry Tree is described by Ursula as 'like a grey she-bear' (xix. 175) and the Lord of Utterbol carries the bear as his badge. Ursula is almost killed by a bear in the mountains. Yet bears may also be on the side of good, as are the shepherds of the downs who help Ralph in the final battle and who believe themselves descended from a 'Bear-father' (xix. 203). Ursula's name means 'little bear'. Thus bears can be associated both with life and death. The duality reflects the image of opposed forces struggling for control of the life-giving tree which Ralph sees as he begins his quest. His task is to recognize, and align himself with, the side of right. Only when he has done so can he achieve his apotheosis – a description in which he is revealed as the solar hero:

there, standing by himself, was Ralph, holding the ancient lettered war-staff; his head was bare, for now he had done off his sallet, and the sun and the wind played in his bright hair; glorious was his face, and his grey eyes gleamed with wrath and mastery as he spake in a clear voice. (xix. 231)

Once more, triumphantly, Morris reminds us that all heroes are one hero. Ralph's search for life, his enrolment in the band of those who are on the side of good in the long struggle against evil, follows the pattern established for Aryan heroes in the dawn of history – a pattern which must inspire us to emulation.

Medieval writers used the Dry Tree as a symbol of the death which entered the world at the Fall but which is overcome by Christ's sacrifice. In Malory, Sir Bors sees a Dry Tree with a pelican in its branches, feeding its young with its own blood. This is an icon of Christ:

by the bare tre betokenyth the worlde, whych ys naked and nedy, withoute fruyte, but if hit com of oure Lorde.[24]

No such interpretation may be attached to Morris's Dry Tree. Ralph is not saved by any divine intervention; he has himself to enter the lost Eden and take a drink from the Well of Life. And when he has found Paradise he does not reach a place of retreat from the dangers of a fallen world. On the wall of the guest house at the Abbey of Higham he sees a tapestry depicting the pilgrimage of the soul of man. He too is a pilgrim; but his quest will not take him out of the world into a spiritual realm. He travels to the World's End but no further. He must return the way he came and put what he has achieved into practical use in order to preserve his own home, which is the true Paradise. In this romance Morris provided the final answer to the escapist seekers after Earthly Paradises. By all means, he seems to say, seek an ideal and make it your motivating force. But remember that ideals must be tested and applied in the real world if they are to be life-giving rather than attenuating or destructive. When this practical setting of the ideal at the service of reality is achieved, the Earthly Paradise is attainable not in fantasy but in actuality. By this means man may join with the unfettered powers of nature to make time and change benevolent, for each moment brings us nearer to the ultimate romance happy ending – the Socialist society. Morris believed in its inevitability and his romances are deeply imbued with this conviction. In symbol and structure they reflect his hope.

v

In the introduction were identified three basic qualities of romance: the distancing in time and place, the use of 'flat' characters and the happy ending. We have seen how in Morris's early work all these aspects of the form were questioned by the ambiguities with which he surrounded them. Though so many of the stories had as a major theme the power of the past, the use of the past as a setting was criticized as escapist. Art based on the past could be falsificatory and restrictive, offering an illu-

sion of permanence that killed or ossified the life it was supposed to capture. The heroic characters seemed inadequate
when the values they endorsed were so doubtfully practical.
Above all, the happy ending was a consolatory sham, reflecting
wish-fulfilment rather than reality. In Morris's later literature
these doubts were gradually eroded. Largely through reading the
sagas, he began to see the possibility of a genuine heroism. His
researches into Aryan imagery allowed him to envisage man as
organically linked with the past, a view reinforced by Marxist
historical analysis. So to study and write about the past became
necessary, not escapist. Finally, the Socialist hope made
romance happy endings the required formal expression of
Morris's political conviction that the true Earthly Paradise
would eventually be attained.

Morris's own word for the kind of art he created in the
romances was 'typical'. He used it of the woes of Sigurd in the
Nibelungenlied, while he was still searching for a style in which
he could hope to convey, as he believed Wagner had not, the true
quality of the medieval story.[25] By the time of the romances he
had become confident in his use of the heroic quest as a type for
all actions which try to change the world. And thus for Morris
romance provided not only a fictional satisfaction of his aesthetic and emotional desires, but a radically effective expression
of his social and political views. He had always known that his
literary and artistic bent was towards the transmission of
fantasy or dream-experience. As a young man his description of
himself as one whose work was 'the embodiment of dreams'
was in the specific context of a rejection of political commitment. In *The Earthly Paradise* he identified himself again as
'dreamer of dreams' and seemed, to a large extent, to despair of
ever setting 'the crooked straight' (III. 1). In *News from
Nowhere*, however, Morris drew a distinction between two
kinds of fantasy when he hoped that his story of life after the
revolution might be 'a vision rather than a dream' (XVI. 211). In
other words, he hoped that it might be the kind of imaginative
construct that had practical results. In the lecture 'The Society
of the Future' he clarified the difference between 'vision' and
'dream'. Here visionaries are defined not, as we might expect, as
escapists, but as the truly *'practical people'*;[26] their perception
of the ideal for which they are struggling is a more powerful

motivating force than the arid speculations of economists. The embodiment, not certainly of self-protective dreams but of practically operative visions, became for Morris the most creatively political act of which he was capable.

When in *The Earthly Paradise* Morris wrote of himself as the poor dreamer, he was deeply troubled by the paradox that the imaginative freedom from the torment of time and change he imaged in the Earthly Paradise was itself destructive: because it was eternal it denied the possibility of hope and therefore of life. In 'The Hill of Venus' his hero is appalled by the 'never-ending, hopeless day' (VI. 302) of the Venusberg. The June lyric contains a Paradise-style secluded haven where in a 'rare happy dream' the poet and his mistress can escape from the world and from states of emotional intensity:

> See, we have left our hopes and fears behind. (IV. 87)

Yet here as in other Paradises to give up fear means to give up hope also. In contrast, when he was writing the romances Morris had come to see time as benevolent, leading the 'pilgrims of hope' forward to a true Earthly Paradise. With this insight went an ability to combine past and future in a fruitful way: so the tree imagery in *The Well at the World's End* develops the organic imagery of *The Earthly Paradise* into positive symbols of hope. As we have seen, Morris knew that this could only be done by romance, that 'capacity for a true conception of history'.[27] Much later an outstanding literary critic had a similar perception:

> the recreation of romance brings us into a present where past and future are gathered.[28]

Northrop Frye has comprehensively demonstrated the need to take romance seriously. In analysing the structure of the genre, he has defended it against charges of escapism, irrelevance and naïvety. For Frye, romance is a revolutionary mode, since it operates in freedom from particular social constraints. Thus it is entirely appropriate that Morris the Socialist should have been also a writer of romance – indeed, one of the 'three major centers [*sic*] of romance' (the others are Spenser and Scott) in its 'continuous tradition'.[29] Frye also stresses the essentially circular nature of romance form:

most romances exhibit a cyclical movement of descent into a night world and a return to the idyllic world, or to some symbol of it like a marriage.[30]

This insight relates precisely to the central quality of Morris's romances. They are attempts to gain access to the 'idyllic world', the point of rest where stasis is achieved not through stagnation but by creative tension between past and future. Morris knew he would not see the Earthly Paradise; but he achieved artistic projection of it in his last romances.

Notes

The following abbreviations are used throughout these notes:

Artist Writer Socialist: May Morris, *William Morris Artist Writer Socialist*, 2 vols. (Oxford, 1936)

Critical Heritage: *William Morris: the Critical Heritage*, edited by Peter Faulkner (London, 1973)

Henderson: Philip Henderson, *William Morris: his Life, Work and Friends*, second edition (Harmondsworth, 1967)

LeMire: *The Unpublished Lectures of William Morris*, edited by Eugene D. LeMire (Detroit, 1969)

Letters: *The Letters of William Morris to his Family and Friends*, edited by Philip Henderson (London, 1950)

Mackail: J. W. Mackail, *The Life of William Morris*, 2 vols. (London, 1899)

OCM: *Oxford and Cambridge Magazine*, 1, 1856

Introduction: 'The embodiment of dreams'

1 George Moore, *Esther Waters* (London, 1894), p. 1.
2 William Morris, *The Wood Beyond the World*, facsimile of the Kelmscott Press edition (1894) (New York, 1972), p. 1.
3 Quoted in Richard Stang, *The Theory of the Novel in England 1850–1870* (London, 1959), p. 147. The article appeared in the *Westminster Review*, 60 (1853), 343–5; according to Stang, it was attributed to George Eliot by Gordon S. Haight. With reference to this section, see also Kenneth Graham, *English Criticism of the Novel 1865–1900* (Oxford, 1965).
4 Edmund Gosse, 'The Tyranny of the Novel', *National Review*, 19 (1892), 163–75 (p. 175).
5 D. F. Hannigan, 'The Decline of Romance', *Westminster Review*, 141 (1894), 33–6 (p. 35).
6 Ben Jonson, 'Ode to Himself', in *Ben Jonson: the Complete Poems*, edited by George Parfitt (Harmondsworth, 1975), p. 283.
7 Ian Maclaren, 'Ugliness in Fiction', *Literature*, 1 (1897), 80–1; quoted in Graham, *English Criticism of the Novel*, p. 30.
8 Robert Louis Stevenson, 'A Gossip on Romance', *Longman's Magazine*, 1 (1882–3), 69–79 (p. 77).
9 Robert Louis Stevenson, 'A Humble Remonstrance', *Longman's Magazine*, 5 (1884–5), 139–47 (p. 147).
10 Ibid.

11 H. Rider Haggard, 'About Fiction', *Contemporary Review*, 51 (1887), 172–80 (p. 174).

12 Ibid., p. 180.

13 Andrew Lang, 'Realism and Romance', *Contemporary Review*, 52 (1887), 683–93 (p. 693).

14 In, for example, 'The Decay of Lying: a Dialogue', *Nineteenth Century*, 25 (1889), 35–56.

15 Hall Caine, 'The New Watchwords of Fiction', *Contemporary Review*, 57 (1890), 479–88 (p. 484). The quotation is from a letter written by James Russell Lowell to Harriet Beecher Stowe; the 'watchwords' are Romanticism and Idealism.

16 Ibid., p. 488.

17 Gillian Beer, *The Romance* (London, 1970), p. 10.

18 *The Collected Works of William Morris*, edited by May Morris, 24 vols. (London, 1910–15), XXIII, p. 279. Subsequent references to this edition will appear in the text.

19 Alice Chandler, *A Dream of Order* (London, 1971), p. 1.

20 *The Poems of Tennyson*, edited by Christopher Ricks (London, 1969), pp. 610, 613.

21 *Letters*, p. 17. Written July 1856.

22 Mackail, I, p. 45.

23 The *Oxford and Cambridge Magazine* ran for twelve monthly issues during 1856. Morris provided the financial backing and edited the first issue; William Fulford then took over as editor. Articles in *OCM* are, with two exceptions, unsigned. I have based my attributions on a MS list in the copy of *OCM* in the library of the University of Nottingham. It appears that this list is a version of another compiled by Vernon Lushington (a contributor) and W. Bell Scott. I have compared its attributions with those in *Wellesley Index to Victorian Periodicals 1824–1900*, edited by Walter E. Houghton, 2 vols. (Toronto, 1966–72). See also Henderson, pp. 50–3; and Robert Stahr Hosmon, 'The Germ (1850) and The Oxford and Cambridge Magazine (1856)', *Victorian Periodicals Newsletter*, 4 (1969), 36–47.

24 'The Work of Young Men in the Present Age' appeared in the September issue (558–64); in the *Wellesley Index* it is attributed to either Fulford or Cormell Price. 'On Popular Lectures' appeared in May and August (316–19, 453–62); the *Wellesley Index* suggests it may have been by Bernard Cracroft or Fulford. 'Cavalay' was printed in three parts from September to November (535–48, 620–32, 664–76).

25 'Carlyle', *OCM*, 193–211, 292–310, 336–52, 697–712, 743–71 (p. 301). The influence of Carlyle is strikingly apparent throughout the magazine; compare for example Carlyle's remarks on heroes with the story of Cavalay.

26 'The Druid and the Maiden', *OCM*, 676–97 (p. 676).

27 'Oxford', *OCM*, 234–57 (p. 234).

28 'Shakespeare's Troilus and Cressida', *OCM*, 280–92 (p. 284).

29 'Sir Philip Sidney', *OCM*, 1–7, 129–36 (p. 2).

30 *OCM*, p. 744.

31 *OCM*, p. 746.
32 *OCM*, p. 2.
33 Ibid.
34 'Mr. Macaulay', *OCM*, 173–84 (p. 173).
35 'Rogers's Table Talk', *OCM*, 641–4 (p. 641).
36 'A Story of the North', *OCM*, 81–99 (p. 82). The *Wellesley Index* attributes this story to Burne-Jones.
37 *OCM*, p. 99.
38 'Froude's History of England', *OCM*, 362–88 (p. 364).
39 *Letters*, p. 17. The sentence quoted here follows the passage quoted above, p. 000.

1 'That old beautiful land': the early romances

1 There is some dispute over which contributions to *OCM* may be attributed to Morris. Most scholars agree on the following list:

January: 'The Story of the Unknown Church'; 'Winter Weather' (poem).
February: 'The Churches of North France 1. Shadows of Amiens'.
March: 'A Dream'; 'Men and Women'.
April: 'Frank's Sealed Letter'.
May: 'Riding Together' (poem).
June: 'Ruskin and the Quarterly'.
July: 'Gertha's Lovers', Part 1; 'Hands' (poem).
August: ' "Death the Avenger" and "Death the Friend" ' (descriptions of woodcuts by Alfred Rethel); 'Svend and his Brethren'; 'Gertha's Lovers', Part 2.
September: 'Lindenborg Pool'; 'The Hollow Land', Part 1; 'The Chapel in Lyonesse' (poem).
October: 'The Hollow Land', Part 2; 'Pray but One Prayer for Me' (poem).
December: 'Golden Wings'.

A story in the May issue entitled 'A Night in a Cathedral' is also assigned to Morris by some critics, notably by Helen Timo in 'A Church Without God: a Study of the Prose Romances and Unfinished Novel of William Morris' (unpublished Ph.D. thesis, University of Nottingham, 1980). H. Buxton Forman claimed that Morris also wrote a tale called 'The Two Partings' which appeared in the February issue of *OCM*; this attribution is defended by Robert Stahr Hosmon, *'The Germ'*, and by J.-M. Baïssus, 'Morris and the *Oxford and Cambridge Magazine*', *Journal of the William Morris Society*, 5 (1982), 2–13.
   Although neither 'A Night in a Cathedral' nor 'The Two Partings' has a medieval setting, they do not therefore invalidate my argument. The former story takes place within a medieval building and in fact moves quickly into a nightmare world in which external objects are chiefly important in so far as they focus the emotional state of the narrator. The latter does take place in recognizably nineteenth-century surroundings;

yet even more than in 'Frank's Sealed Letter' it exhibits a colourless insipidity highly uncharacteristic of Morris, which reinforces my contention that he was temperamentally incapable of writing successfully unless his imagination was fired by medievalism.

2 According to Philip Henderson (Henderson, p. 38) it was begun in 1854.

3 The final sentence of the story, 'Lord, keep my memory green!' (I. 325), reproduces the last words of Dickens's 1848 Christmas Book *The Haunted Man*. Throughout his life Morris had a great admiration for Dickens.

4 See Benjamin Thorpe, *Northern Mythology*, 3 vols. (London, 1851–2), II, pp. 214–15.

5 See *The Thornton Romances*, edited by James Orchard Halliwell (London (Camden Society), 1844), p. 1. Morris slightly misquotes the lines as given by Halliwell.

6 Other versions include the story of 'Peredur Son of Efrawg' in *The Mabinogion* and Chrétien de Troyes's *Conte du Graal*.

7 I am aware that in the carol quoted above Morris links the colours red and gold with Joseph and Mary, which seems to contradict their use elsewhere as symbols for violence and evil. The answer may be that Morris is employing them in the carol to suggest human fallibility; Christ's crown of invulnerable diamond indicates his transcendence of earthly imperfection.

8 In later years, when questioned about religious topics, Morris called himself an atheist or a pagan. After *The Defence of Guenevere* religious images are used in his writing increasingly to evoke atmosphere, rather than with any belief in the images as symbols of truth. On the idea of a link between Christianity and the formal structure of romance, see J. R. R. Tolkien, *Tree and Leaf* (London, 1964), pp. 61–3.

9 John M. Patrick, 'Morris and Froissart Again: "Sir Peter Harpdon's End"', *Notes and Queries*, 204 (1959), 331–3 (p. 331).

10 Laurence Perrine, 'Morris's Guenevere: an Interpretation', *Philological Quarterly*, 39 (1960), 234–41 (p. 241).

2 'The dread eternity': *The Earthly Paradise*

1 *Athenaeum*, no. 1588 (1858), 427–8 (p. 427). The unsigned review is attributed to H. F. Chorley by Peter Faulkner in *Critical Heritage*.

2 See *Critical Heritage*, pp. 32–7.

3 *Letters*, p. 46. Written 22 June 1872.

4 *Love is Enough* was published in 1872, with the imprint of 1873.

5 See Howard Rollin Patch, *The Other World According to Descriptions in Medieval Literature* (Cambridge, Mass., 1950); and A. Bartlett Giamatti, *The Earthly Paradise and the Renaissance Epic* (Princeton, 1966).

6 The stories of *The Earthly Paradise* are as follows:

March: 'Atalanta's Race'; 'The Man Born to be King'.
April: 'The Doom of King Acrisius'; 'The Proud King'.

May: 'The Story of Cupid and Psyche'; 'The Writing on the Image'.

June: 'The Love of Alcestis'; 'The Lady of the Land'.

July: 'The Son of Croesus'; 'The Watching of the Falcon'.

August: 'Pygmalion and the Image'; 'Ogier the Dane'.

September: 'The Death of Paris'; 'The Land East of the Sun and West of the Moon'.

October: 'The Story of Acontius and Cydippe'; 'The Man who Never Laughed Again'.

November: 'The Story of Rhodope'; 'The Lovers of Gudrun'.

December: 'The Golden Apples'; 'The Fostering of Aslaug'.

January: 'Bellerophon at Argos'; 'The Ring Given to Venus'.

February: 'Bellerophon in Lycia'; 'The Hill of Venus'.

7 Percy Bysshe Shelley, *Poetical Works*, edited by Thomas Hutchinson (London, 1943), p. 603.

8 See *Collected Works*, III, pp. xj–xiij, for a discussion of the projected and/or uncompleted *Earthly Paradise* tales. On the MS 'Story of Dorothea', see K. L. Goodwin, 'An Unpublished Tale from *The Earthly Paradise*', *Victorian Poetry*, 3, nos. 3 and 4 (1975), 91–102.

9 Unlike Chaucer, Morris does not link his tales with the characters of their narrators, except in two cases. Laurence, the Swabian priest, tells the stories in which magic and evil spirits make the most prominent appearance; Rolf, the leader of the Wanderers and the narrator of the Prologue, tells the important stories of other worlds: 'Ogier the Dane' and 'The Man who Never Laughed Again'.

10 Eugène Vinaver, *Form and Meaning in Medieval Romance* ([Cambridge], 1966), p. 11.

11 *Ibid.*, pp. 11–12.

12 *Letters*, p. 9. Written in April 1855.

13 *Ibid.*, pp. 17–18. Written in July 1856.

14 BM Add. MS 45328, f.26v. All spelling and punctuation *sic*.

15 *Letters*, p. 47.

16 Unsigned review, *Spectator*, 43 (1870), 332–4. Quoted from *Critical Heritage*, p. 112.

17 *Ibid.*

18 [Alfred Austin], *Temple Bar*, 27 (1869), 45–51. Quoted from *Critical Heritage*, pp. 94–5. Austin's series of articles was published in book form as *The Poetry of the Period* in 1870.

3 'The dawn that waketh the dead': *Sigurd the Volsung*

1 Carlyle's review of a translation of the *Nibelungenlied* appeared in *Westminster Review*, 29 (1831). See *The Works of Thomas Carlyle*, edited by H. D. Traill, 30 vols. (London, 1896–9), XXVII, pp. 216–73.

2 For information about the availability of Icelandic literature to Victorian readers, see Frank Edgar Farley, *Scandinavian Influences in the English Romantic Movement*, Studies and Notes in Philology and

Literature, 9 (Boston, 1903); Karl Litzenberg, *The Victorians and the Vikings: a Bibliographical Essay on Anglo-Norse Literary Relations*, The University of Michigan Contributions in Modern Philology, 3 ([Ann Arbor], 1947); and Conrad Hjalmar Nordby, *The Influences of Old Norse Literature upon English Literature*, second edition (New York, 1966).

3 Contains, beside the stories of Gunnlaug and Frithiof, 'The Story of Viglund the Fair', 'The Tale of Hogni and Hedinn', 'The Tale of Roi the Fool' and 'The Tale of Thorstein Staff-Smitten'.

4 The contents are as follows:

Vol. 1 (1891):	'The Story of Howard the Halt'.
	'The Story of the Banded Men'.
	'The Story of Hen Thorir'.
Vol. 2 (1892):	'The Story of the Ere-dwellers'.
Vol. 3 (1893):	'The Stories of the Kings of Norway called the Round World (Heimskringla) by Snorri Sturluson', Part 1.
Vol. 4 (1894):	'Heimskringla', Part 2.
Vol. 5 (1895):	'Heimskringla', Part 3.

Magnússon alone completed the series with Volume 6, notes and indexes for the *Heimskringla*, in 1905.

5 *Collected Works*, v, pp. xxj–xxij; vii, pp. xxxij–xxxiij. Another early Icelandic-influenced poem is the unfinished 'The Wooing of Swanhild', written during the *Earthly Paradise* period about the tragic death of the daughter of Sigurd and Gudrun.

6 *Northern Mythology*, i, p. 113.

7 Ibid., i, p. 111.

8 Except one concession to Victorian sensibilities, when Kiartan humiliates Bodli and Gudrun by besieging them in their house for three days. Morris omits to mention that the point of the siege is to deny the household access to the outdoor privy. (See *Laxdaela Saga*, translated by Magnus Magnusson and Hermann Pálson (Harmondsworth, 1969), p. 167.)

9 *The Pall Mall Budget*, 4 (1869), 26–7. Quoted from *Critical Heritage*, p. 103.

10 *Critical Heritage*, p. 107.

11 Ibid., p. 116. From *Spectator*, 43 (1870), 332–4.

12 *Letters*, pp. 30–1. Written 21 December 1869.

13 *Laxdaela Saga*, p. 34.

14 Ibid., p. 157.

15 Dorothy M. Hoare, *The Works of Morris and of Yeats in Relation to Early Saga Literature* (Cambridge, 1937), p. 11.

16 *Letters*, p. 84. Written January 1877.

17 Ibid., p. 186. Written 5 September 1883.

18 LeMire, p. 185.

19 *The Works of Thomas Carlyle*, v, p. 197. This quotation is from the lecture on 'The Hero as King'. In the first lecture, on 'The Hero as Divinity', Carlyle's example is Odin, whom he conceives of as the historical leader of his people. He characterizes the Norse religion as

'*Consecration of Valour*' (*The Works of Thomas Carlyle*, v, p. 41); this phrase anticipates Morris's 'the worship of Courage'.

20 Donald J. Gray has discussed the problem of heroism as it appears in Victorian poetry in 'Arthur, Roland, Empedocles, Sigurd, and the Despair of Heroes in Victorian Poetry', *Boston University Studies in English*, 5 (1961), 1–17. He takes a more pessimistic view of *Sigurd the Volsung* than will be found in this chapter.

21 *Letters*, p. 84.

22 [Paul Henri] Mallet, *Northern Antiquities*, translated by Bishop Percy, revised by I. A. Blackwell (London, 1847), pp. 57–8.

23 Grenville Pigott, *A Manual of Scandinavian Mythology* (London, 1839), p. vii.

24 Ibid., p. viii.

25 'Iceland in the Year One Thousand', *Fraser's Magazine*, 46 (1852), 643–52 (p. 644).

26 'The Odin-Religion', *Westminster Review*, NS 6 (1854), 311–44 (p. 317 note 1).

27 'The Legendary Lore of Iceland', *Westminster Review*, NS 30 (1866), 122–47 (p. 130).

28 Ibid., pp. 146–7.

29 Karl Blind, 'Germanic Mythology', *Contemporary Review*, 23 (1873–4), 621–37 (p. 632).

30 Ibid., p. 636.

31 Nirad C. Chaudhuri, *Scholar Extraordinary* (London, 1974), p. 199.

32 Friedrich Max Müller, *Lectures on the Science of Language*, 2 vols. (London, 1861–4), I, p. 11.

33 See for example *The Science of Language*, and the four volumes of essays and lectures called *Chips from a German Workshop* (1867–75). Max Müller lectured on the subject of mythology to the Philosophical Institution, Edinburgh, in 1863 and to the Royal Institution in 1871.

34 Friedrich Max Müller, 'Comparative Mythology', *Oxford Essays* (London, 1856), pp. 1–87 (p. 66).

35 Ibid.

36 Ibid., p. 67.

37 Ibid.

38 George W. Cox, *The Mythology of the Aryan Nations*, 2 vols. (London, 1870), I, p. 274.

39 Ibid., I, p. 281.

40 See F. A. Paley, 'On the Origin of the "Solar Myth", and its Bearing on the History of Ancient Thought', *Dublin Review*, third series 2 (1879), 90–111. Paley is convinced of the truth of the solar mythology theory, and is particularly scathing about an explorer who was pretending not only that the Trojan War was an historical fact, but that he had actually found 'Priam's palace and Agamemnon's skeleton' (p. 97). To Paley (and Cox), though not to Schliemann, the Trojan War was yet another version of the solar myth.

41 Edward A. Freeman, 'Stray Thoughts on Comparative Mythology', *Fortnightly Review*, NS 8 (1870), 536–48 (pp. 536–7).

42 Ibid., p. 548. Among other articles which discuss the theory of Aryan

mythology are A. S. Wilkins, 'The Mythology of the Aryan Nations', *Theological Review*, 7 (1870), 504–25; 'Myths of the Aryans', *London Quarterly Review*, 35 (1870–1), 77–100; [T. S. Baynes], 'Cox's *Aryan Mythology*', *Edinburgh Review*, 132 (1870), 330–63; 'Aryan Mythology', *Christian Observer*, 71 (1871), 122–32; A[ndrew] Lang, 'Mythology and Fairy Tales', *Fortnightly Review*, NS 13 (1873), 618–31.

43 *Oxford Essays*, p. 3.
44 Ibid., p. 4. Max Müller denied that his theory had any racial implications, believing that the existence of a common language did not necessarily imply common blood. See *The Science of Language*, I, p. 314. Yet some Hindu nationalists were much encouraged by Max Müller's ideas, which seemed to give them racial parity with their British rulers.
45 Karl Blind, 'Germanic Mythology', p. 635.
46 *Artist Writer Socialist*, I, p. 126.
47 Ibid.
48 LeMire, p. 55.
49 There is no evidence that the two men ever met. A tenuous connection between them is that Morris's *OCM* colleague Godfrey Lushington was a Fellow of All Souls', Oxford, at the same time as Max Müller.
50 *Letters*, p. 247; in a list of 'the Best Hundred Books' contributed to the *Pall Mall Gazette* in 1886. Since Morris could not read German, he can only have known the work in the translation by James Steven Stallybrass published in 4 volumes in 1882–8. The book was first published in Germany in 1835.
51 See *Catalogue of a Portion of the Valuable Collection of Manuscripts, Early Printed Books etc. of the Late William Morris, of Kelmscott House, Hammersmith* (London, 1898).
52 'Myths of the Aryans', *London Quarterly Review*, 35 (1870–1), 77–100 (p. 97).
53 Ibid., p. 100.
54 See *Collected Works*, XII, p. xxiij.
55 *Letters*, p. 32. Written 21 December [1869].
56 Ibid., pp. 60–1. Written 12 November 1873 to H. Buxton Forman, who had sent Morris a versified translation of Wagner's libretto for *Die Walküre*.
57 On Victorian scientists' emphasis on organic relationships between and within entities, see Tess Cosslett, *The 'Scientific Movement' and Victorian Literature* (Brighton, 1982); and Gillian Beer, *Darwin's Plots* (London, 1983).
58 John 1.10–11.

4 'A true conception of history': the political romances

1 Apart from some poems of Socialist propaganda, the most important of which is the long poem sequence *The Pilgrims of Hope* which appeared in *Commonweal* in 1885–6. Morris was himself doubtful about its literary value and only reprinted three of its thirteen sections when he published a collection of his verse in 1891.

2 Five of Morris's lectures on art were published as *Hopes and Fears for Art* in 1882.

3 It appeared in 1887. Morris also published verse translations of *The Aeneids [sic] of Virgil* (1875) and *Beowulf* (1895; with the help of A.J. Wyatt).

4 *Letters*, p. 132. Written in October 1879.

5 Ibid., p. 158.

6 Ibid.

7 H. Halliday Sparling, *The Kelmscott Press and William Morris Master-Craftsman* (London, 1924), p. 103.

8 LeMire, p. 81. The lecture was given to the Birmingham and Midland Institute in Birmingham, 10 March 1884.

9 Published between May 1886 and May 1888, the articles provided the basis for Morris's and Bax's book *Socialism: its Growth and Outcome* (1893).

10 *Artist Writer Socialist*, I, p. 240.

11 Ibid., II, p. 465. The lecture was printed in three sections in *Commonweal*, 5 (1889), 98–9, 108–9, 114–15.

12 See introduction, p. 5.

13 *Artist Writer Socialist*, I, p. 304.

14 Ibid., I, p. 306.

15 Ibid., I, pp. 287–8.

16 Ibid., II, p. 420.

17 Although *News from Nowhere* is the only work to which Morris himself gave this title; he called it 'Chapters from a Utopian Romance'.

18 H. Halliday Sparling, *Kelmscott Press*, p. 50.

19 [Gilbert Stuart], *An Historical Dissertation Concerning the Antiquity of the English Constitution* (Edinburgh, 1768), p. iv.

20 William Stubbs, *The Constitutional History of England in its Origin and Development*, 3 vols. (London, 1874–8), I, p. iii.

21 Ibid., p. 2. Later he remarks that one could 'work back, through obvious generalisations and comparisons with the early phenomena of society in other nations, to the primitive civilisation of the Aryan or Indo-Germanic family' (p. 32).

22 John Richard Green, *A Short History of the English People*, second edition (London, 1888), p. 4.

23 Edward A. Freeman, *The History of the Norman Conquest of England, its Causes and its Results*, second edition, 6 vols. (Oxford, 1870–9), I, p. 79. It will be recalled that Freeman was to some extent an advocate of the solar mythology theory.

24 Ibid., I, p. 112.

25 'The Revival of Architecture', published in *Fortnightly Review*, May 1888.

26 Lewis H. Morgan, *Ancient Society*, edited by Leslie A. White (Cambridge, Mass., 1964), p. 12.

27 Friedrich Engels, *The Origin of the Family, Private Property and the State*, translation of the fourth edition (London, 1940), p. 177.

28 Ibid., p. 204.

29 In 1864 Charles Kingsley published a series of lectures under the title

The Roman and the Teuton, which also traces English laws to their Teutonic origins, and sees the Gothic sack of Rome as a visitation of God's anger at the debauchery and degradation of Roman society. The reasons to which he assigns the Goths' superiority are, however, rather different from those of Engels: 'the energy which springs from health; the self-respect which comes from self-restraint; and the spirit which shrinks from neither God nor man, and feels it light to die for wife and child, for people, and for Queen' (second edition, with a preface by Max Müller (London, 1877), p. 46).

30 *Letters*, p. 236. Written 13 May 1885.

31 LeMire, p. 146.

32 'The Development of Modern Society 5', *Commonweal*, 6 (1890), 260–1 (p. 261).

33 *Letters*, p. 302. Written 17 November [1888].

34 *Artist Writer Socialist*, I, p. 148.

35 Ibid., II, pp. 467–8.

36 Ibid., I, p. 503. Some modern critics have agreed: Philip Henderson's biography of Morris almost entirely ignores the romances, and claims that 'socialism can scarcely be detected' in the later ones (Henderson, p. 404). In his introduction to *Letters* he remarks that the romances 'provided Morris, as he confessed, with a much-needed escape from reality' (*Letters*, p. lxii). Paul Thompson is even more scathing, castigating the romances as 'pure escape', 'gothic fancies' and 'regrettable eccentricities' (Paul Thompson, *The Work of William Morris* (London, 1967), pp. 158, 159).

5 'The very Garden of God': the last romances

1 *The Lay of Havelok the Dane*, edited by Walter W. Skeat, second edition, revised by K. Sisam (Oxford, 1915), line 139.

2 E. P. Thompson, *William Morris: Romantic to Revolutionary*, second edition (London, 1977), p. 680. Although he defends the romances, Thompson seems not altogether sympathetic towards them, believing them to be dominated by a mood of 'pure self-indulgence in pleasurable reverie in which neither Morris's intellect nor his deeper feelings are seriously engaged' (p. 678).

3 See above; and Jack Lindsay, *William Morris: his Life and Work* (London, 1975). For the opposing view, see Roderick Marshall, *William Morris and his Earthly Paradises* (Tisbury, Wilts., 1979).

4 The unfinished romance called by May Morris *The Story of Desiderius* would probably have been concerned with the themes of freedom and revolution. The hero is a rich Roman who falls in love with one of his mother's slaves. As we would expect, Morris describes the lethargy and decadence of the Roman upper classes, and wishes that the oppressed slaves would rise against their effete masters. However, the story breaks off before any signs of revolution appear.

5 See for example the third chapter of 'Socialism from the Root Up', entitled 'The Break-up of Feudalism', *Commonweal*, 2 (1886), 69.

6 English as it might have been had there been no Norman Conquest is discussed by Richard Chenevix Trench in *English Past and Present* (1855) which was in its seventh edition by 1870. He suggests that instead of taking over French and Latin words, we might have followed the German example and created a language rich in compound words: 'blood-bath' for 'massacre', 'sin-flood' for 'deluge', 'two-fight' for 'duel'. This is advocated in William Barnes's extraordinary book *An Outline of English Speech-Craft* (1878) in which all non-English words are replaced by such coinings – even to renaming the index 'clue to matters handled'.

7 *Malory: Works*, edited by Eugène Vinaver, second edition (London, 1971), p. 84.

8 *The Works of Thomas Carlyle*, XXI, p. 279.

9 Ibid., XXI, p. 278.

10 Except in 'The Widow's House by the Great Water', where Katherine is not treated harshly by her mother but with indulgence.

11 BM Add. MS 45328, f.198.

12 BM Add. MS 45322, f.164.

13 BM Add. MS 45323, f.183.

14 Ibid., f.185.

15 See *Letters*, pp. 370–1. Written to the editor of the *Spectator*, 20 July 1895.

16 Jacob Grimm, *Teutonic Mythology*, translated by James Steven Stallybrass, 4 vols. (London, 1882–8), I, p. 286.

17 The Count Goblet d'Alviella, *The Migration of Symbols* (London, 1894), p. 142. This book was first published in Paris in 1891.

18 Ibid., p. 174. Both Lethaby and d'Alviella refer to the Scandinavian World Tree Yggdrasil, which would of course have been an image familiar to Morris from his Norse studies.

19 Jacob Grimm, *Teutonic Mythology*, I, p. 69.

20 For a survey of Morris's borrowings from mythology, anthropology and history, and an analysis of his romances in Frazerian terms, see Carole Silver, 'Myth and Ritual in the Last Romances of William Morris', in Blue Calhoun et al., *Studies in the Late Romances of William Morris* (New York, 1976), pp. 115–39.

21 Several other authors in the 1880s emphasized the need for a reunification of man and nature. In 1885 Richard Jefferies published his fantasy novel *After London: or, Wild England*, in which he describes England after a return to barbarism. The lake in this book may have influenced *The Water of the Wondrous Isles*. Morris read *After London* in the train while going to visit Edward Carpenter, whose book *Civilisation, its Cause and Cure and Other Essays* (1889) occasionally prefigures Morris's romances in theme and imagery.

22 *Mandeville's Travels*, edited by M. C. Seymour (Oxford, 1967), p. 124.

23 For example, the 'Bird' woven fabric (late 1870s), and the printed fabrics 'Brother Rabbit' (1882) and 'Strawberry Thief' (1883).

24 *Malory: Works*, p. 572. See Rose Jeffries Peebles, 'The Dry Tree: Symbol of Death', in *Vassar Mediaeval Studies*, edited by Christabel Forsyth Fiske (New Haven, 1928), pp. 59–79.

25 See above, p. 105.
26 *Artist Writer Socialist*, ii, p. 455.
27 Ibid., i, p. 148.
28 Northrop Frye, *The Secular Scripture: a Study of the Structure of Romance* (Cambridge, Mass., 1976), p. 179.
29 Ibid., p. 6.
30 Ibid., p. 54.

Select bibliography

Where I have used an edition other than the first, the date of the first edition is given in separate parentheses.

1. Works by Morris

The majority of Morris's writing is to be found in the standard collection: *The Collected Works of William Morris*, edited by May Morris, 24 vols. (London, 1910–15).

See also:

Henderson, Philip (ed.), *The Letters of William Morris to his Family and Friends* (London, 1950).
LeMire, Eugène D. (ed.), *The Unpublished Lectures of William Morris* (Detroit, 1969).
Morris, May, *William Morris Artist Writer Socialist*, 2 vols. (Oxford, 1936).
Morris, William, *The Novel on Blue Paper*, edited by Penelope Fitzgerald (London, 1982).
Oxford and Cambridge Magazine, 1, 1856.

Manuscript material:

Plot of a story, and draft of *The Water of the Wondrous Isles*	BM Add. MS 45322
Fair copy of *The Water of the Wondrous Isles*	BM Add. MS 45323
'The Widow's House by the Great Water'	BM Add. MS 45324
Draft of the poetic version of *The Water of the Wondrous Isles*	BM Add. MS 45325
Draft of *The Sundering Flood*	BM Add. MS 45326
'Giles of the Long Frank'	BM Add. MS 45327
Unfinished novel; *Kilian of the Closes, The Folk of the Mountain Door, The Story of Desiderius*	BM Add. MS 45328

2. Works by Morris's contemporaries

Barnes, William, *An Outline of English Speech-Craft* (London, 1878).
    Tiw; or, A View of the Roots and Stems of the English as a Teutonic Tongue (London, 1862).
Bellamy, Edward, *Looking Backward 2000–1887* (1888) (New York, 1951).
Blind, Karl, 'Germanic Mythology, *Contemporary Review*, 23 (1873–4), 621–37.

Select bibliography

Caine, Hall, 'The New Watchwords of Fiction', *Contemporary Review*, 57 (1890), 479–88.

Carpenter, Edward, *Civilisation, its Cause and Cure and Other Essays* (London, 1889).

Cox, George W., *The Mythology of the Aryan Nations*, 2 vols. (London, 1870).

Engels, Friedrich, *The Origin of the Family, Private Property and the State* (1884) (London, 1940).

Frazer, James George, *The Golden Bough*, 2 vols. (London, 1890).

Totemism (Edinburgh, 1887).

Freeman, Edward A., *The History of the Norman Conquest of England, its Causes and its Results* (1867–79), 6 vols. (Oxford, 1870–9).

'Stray Thoughts on Comparative Mythology', *Fortnightly Review*, NS 8 (1870), 536–48.

Goblet d'Alviella, Count, *The Migration of Symbols* (London, 1894).

Green, John Richard, *A Short History of the English People* (1874) (London, 1888).

Grimm, Jacob, *Teutonic Mythology*, translated by James Steven Stallybrass, 4 vols. (London, 1882–8).

Haggard, H. Rider, 'About Fiction', *Contemporary Review*, 51 (1887), 172–80.

Jefferies, Richard, *After London; or, Wild England* (London, 1885).

Kingsley, Charles, *The Roman and the Teuton* (1864) (London, 1877).

Lang, Andrew, *Custom and Myth* (1884) (London, 1901).

'Mr Max Müller's Philosophy of Mythology', *Fraser's Magazine*, NS 24 (1881), 166–87.

'Mythology and Fairy Tales', *Fortnightly Review*, NS 13 (1873), 618–31.

'Realism and Romance', *Contemporary Review*, 52 (1887), 683–93.

Lethaby, W. R., *Architecture Mysticism and Myth* (1891) (London, 1974).

Maine, Henry Sumner, *Ancient Law* (1861) (London, 1901).

Mallet [Paul Henri], *Northern Antiquities*, translated by Bishop Percy, revised by I. A. Blackwell (London, 1847).

Max Müller, Friedrich, *Chips from a German Workshop* (1867–75), 4 vols. (New York, 1876).

'Comparative Mythology', *Oxford Essays* (London, 1856), 1–87.

Lectures on the Science of Language, 2 vols. (London, 1861–4).

Morgan, Lewis H., *Ancient Society* (1877), edited by Leslie A. White (Cambridge, Mass., 1964).

Rydberg, Viktor, *Teutonic Mythology*, translated by Rasmus B. Anderson (London, 1891).

Stevenson, Robert Louis, 'A Gossip on Romance', *Longman's Magazine*, 1 (1882–3), 69–79.

'A Humble Remonstrance', *Longman's Magazine*, 5 (1884–5), 139–47.

Stubbs, William, *The Constitutional History of England in its Origin and Development*, 3 vols. (London, 1874–8).

Thorpe, Benjamin, *Northern Mythology*, 3 vols. (London, 1851–2).

Trench, Richard Chenevix, *English Past and Present* (1855) (London, 1870).

Select bibliography

3. Later criticism

Beer, Gillian, *The Romance* (London, 1970).

Berry, Ralph, 'A Defense of *Guenevere*', *Victorian Poetry*, 9 (1971), 277–86.

Buckley, Jerome Hamilton, *The Triumph of Time* (London, 1967).

Calhoun, Blue, *The Pastoral Vision of William Morris: The Earthly Paradise* (Athens, Georgia, 1975).

    et al., *Studies in the Late Romances of William Morris* (New York, 1976).

Chandler, Alice, *A Dream of Order* (London, 1971).

Currie, Robert, 'Had Morris Gone Soft in the Head?', *Essays in Criticism*, 29 (1979), 341–56.

Dunlap, Joseph R., *The Book that Never Was* (New York, 1971).

Ellison, R. C., ' "The Undying Glory of Dreams": William Morris and the "Northland of Old" ', *Victorian Poetry*, Stratford-upon-Avon Studies, 15 (London, 1972), 139–75.

Farley, Frank Edgar, *Scandinavian Influences in the English Romantic Movement*, Studies and Notes in Philology and Literature, 9 (Boston, 1903).

Faulkner, Peter, *Against the Age: an Introduction to William Morris* (London, 1980).

    (ed.), *William Morris: the Critical Heritage* (London, 1973).

Fredeman, William E. (ed.), *Victorian Poetry* (special Morris issue), 13 nos. 3 and 4 (1975), *passim*.

Frye, Northrop, *Anatomy of Criticism* (Princeton, 1957).

    The Secular Scripture (Cambridge, Mass., 1976).

Gent, Margaret, ' "To Flinch from Modern Varnish": the Appeal of the Past to the Victorian Imagination', *Victorian Poetry*, Stratford-upon-Avon Studies, 15 (London, 1972), 11–35.

Giamatti, A. Bartlett, *The Earthly Paradise and the Renaissance Epic* (Princeton, 1966).

Goode, John, 'William Morris and the Dream of Revolution', in John Lucas (ed.), *Literature and Politics in the Nineteenth Century* (London, 1971), 221–80.

Graham, Kenneth, *English Criticism of the Novel 1865–1900* (Oxford, 1965).

Gray, Donald J., 'Arthur, Roland, Empedocles, Sigurd, and the Despair of Heroes in Victorian Poetry', *Boston University Studies in English*, 5 (1961), 1–17.

Grennan, Margaret R., *William Morris: Medievalist and Revolutionary* (New York, 1945).

Henderson, Philip, *William Morris: his Life, Work and Friends* (1967) (Harmondsworth, 1973).

Hoare, Dorothy M., *The Works of Morris and of Yeats in Relation to Early Saga Literature* (Cambridge, 1937).

Hollow, John (ed.), *The After-Summer Seed: Reconsiderations of William*

Select bibliography

Morris's 'The Story of Sigurd the Volsung' (New York, 1978).

Houghton, Walter E., *The Victorian Frame of Mind 1830–1870* (London, 1957).

Hunt, John Dixon, *The Pre-Raphaelite Imagination 1848–1900* (London, 1968).

Lindsay, Jack, *William Morris: his Life and Work* (London, 1975).

Litzenberg, Karl, *The Victorians and the Vikings: a Bibliographical Essay on Anglo-Norse Literary Relations*, University of Michigan Contributions in Modern Philology, 3 ([Ann Arbor], 1947).

Mackail, J. W., *The Life of William Morris*, 2 vols. (London, 1899).

Marshall, Roderick, *William Morris and his Earthly Paradises* (Tisbury, Wilts., 1979).

Mathews, Richard, *Worlds Beyond the World: the Fantastic Vision of William Morris* (San Bernardino, California, 1978).

Meier, Paul, *William Morris: the Marxist Dreamer*, translated by Frank Grubb, 2 vols. (Hassocks, Sussex, 1978).

Nordby, Conrad Hjalmar, *The Influence of Old Norse Literature upon English Literature* (1901) (New York, 1966).

Oberg, Charlotte H., *A Pagan Prophet: William Morris* (Charlottesville, Virginia, 1978).

Patch, Howard Rollin, *The Other World According to Descriptions in Medieval Literature* (Cambridge, Mass., 1950).

Patrick, John M., 'Morris and Froissart: "Geffray Teste Noir" and "The Haystack in the Floods"', *Notes and Queries*, 203 (1958), 425–7.

'Morris and Froissart Again: "Sir Peter Harpdon's End"', *Notes and Queries*, 204 (1959), 331–3.

Peebles, Rose Jeffries, 'The Dry Tree: Symbol of Death', in Christabel Forsyth Fiske (ed.), *Vassar Mediaeval Studies* (New Haven, 1923), 59–79.

Perrine, Laurence, 'Morris's Guenevere: an Interpretation', *Philological Quarterly*, 39 (1960), 234–41.

Silver, Carole, 'Eden and Apocalypse: William Morris' Marxist Vision in the 1880s', *University of Hartford Studies in Literature*, 13 (1981), 62–77.

(ed.), *The Golden Chain: Essays on William Morris and Pre-Raphaelitism* (New York, 1982).

The Romance of William Morris (Athens, Ohio, 1982).

Sparling, H. Halliday, *The Kelmscott Press and William Morris Master-Craftsman* (London, 1924).

Stanford, Derek (ed.), *Pre-Raphaelite Writing* (London, 1973).

Stang, Richard, *The Theory of the Novel in England 1850–1870* (London, 1959).

Talbot, Norman, 'Women and Goddesses in the Romances of William Morris', *Southern Review*, 3 (1968–9), 339–57.

Thompson, E. P., *William Morris: Romantic to Revolutionary* (1955) (London, 1977).

Thompson, Paul, *The Work of William Morris* (London, 1967).

Timo, Helen Ann, 'A Church Without God: a Study of the Prose Romances

Select bibliography

and Unfinished Novel of William Morris', unpublished Ph.D. thesis, University of Nottingham, 1980.

Tolkien, J. R. R., *Tree and Leaf* (London, 1970).

Vinaver, Eugène, *Form and Meaning in Medieval Romance* ([Cambridge], 1966).

Index

Index

Index

and *The Roots of the Mountains*, 145–6, 149
and *The Sundering Flood*, 159
and *The Well at the World's End*, 161

Iceland, 84, 90, 157–8
'In Prison', 49

James, Henry, 3, 4

Kelmscott House, 128
Kelmscott Manor, 90, 128, 152
Kelmscott Press, 1, 151
Kilian of the Closes, 182
Kingsley, Charles, 73, 93, 206 n29

'Lady of the Land, The', 55–6, 57, 67–8
'Land East of the Sun, The', 58, 76–7, 118
Lang, Andrew, 6
Lethaby, W. R., 183
Life and Death of Jason, The, 51, 67
'Lindenborg Pool', 26–9, 30, 32, 83
Love is Enough, 50, 69
'Love of Alcestis, The', 55, 57, 67–8
'Lovers of Gudrun, The', 84, 85, 86–8, 92
Lushington, Godfrey, 15
Lushington, Vernon, 14, 15–16

Maclaren, Ian, 4
Magnússon, Eiríkr, 83–4, 103, 105
Mallet, Paul, 83, 95
Malory, Thomas, 11, 146, 167–8, 193–4
'Man Who Never Laughed Again, The', 58–9
Mandeville, John, 53, 189–90
Marie de France, 54
Marx, Karl, 123, 126, 136, 142

Max Müller, Friedrich, 98–102, 103, 104, 115–16, 139
medievalism, 11–13
Moore, George, 1–2, 3, 4
Morgan, Lewis, 136–7, 145
Morris, William
    and art, 13, 30–1, 36, 44–6, 69, 72–4, 89–90, 118–19, 121–2, 129–33
    against escapism, 13, 32–4, 53–4, 59, 70, 75–6, 80, 91–2, 154–5
    fear of mutability, 51, 63–6
    hope for the future, 80, 110–12, 122, 140, 144, 169, 177
    and Icelandic sagas, 82–94, 105–6
    and medievalism, 10–13, 36, 44, 157
    and mythology, 102–5
    and romance, 17–18, 45–6, 74–5, 132–3, 151, 156, 157–8, 164–9, 179–89, 194–7
    and Socialism, 83, 119, 121–33, 158–64
    use of medieval forms, 19, 44–5, 51–2, 67–9
Müller, Karl, 97
mythology, 51, 83, 96–105
    solar, 99–105, 115–18, 139, 150, 187–8, 193

naturalism, *see* realism
nature
    and art, 35
    man's relationship with, 64–6, 78–80, 112–14, 143–4, 150–1, 180–6, 190–2
nature goddess, 170, 173, 181–2, 184–5, 187
News from Nowhere, 121–2, 127–33, 140, 151, 152, 155, 173, 179, 195
Nibelungenlied, 83, 195
Novel on Blue Paper, The, *see* unfinished novel

Odyssey, 120

217

Index

Index